D0916841

The Pleasures of the Torture Chamber

Representation of the Tortures used in the Inquisition, particularly racking with the head downwards, tormenting in the trough, drawing up by means of pullies, with the hands tied behind till the joints are all dislocated, burning the soles of the feet, etc.

The
Pleasures
of the
Torture
Chamber

by
John Swain

Dorset Press
New York

Originally published in 1931.

This edition published by Dorset Press,
a division of Barnes & Noble, Inc.

1995 Dorset Press

ISBN 1-56619-772-4

Printed and bound in the United States of America

M 9 8 7 6 5 4 3 2 1

CONTENTS

ILLUSTRATIONS

The illustrations and their captions are taken from old books and are not necessarily referred to in the text, the intention being to give an idea of some of the tortures described.

Representation of the Tortures used in the Inquisition, particularly racking with the head downwards, tormenting in the trough, drawing up by means of pulleys, with the hands tied behind till the joints are all dislocated, burning the soles of the feet, etc.   *Frontispiece*

THE PLEASURES OF THE TORTURE CHAMBER

PREFACE

Cruelty is no more the cure of crimes than it is the cure of sufferings.—LANDOR

WHEN I set out to write this book I intended it to be an encyclopædia of the various instruments and methods of torture used either as a means of punishment, or for the purpose of forcing a confession, but I soon found that the amount of material I had collected would fill several volumes with not very interesting matter. I therefore changed my design to a short description of the more common tortures used by our ancestors. To bring the book up to date I have added a chapter on tortures practised in this century.

It is first very important to understand the actual meaning of the word "torture", and, to ascertain this clearly, I have set out below the definitions given by Dr. Murray in his *New English Dictionary* and the *Encyclopædia Britannica*.

Dr. Murray gives the definition as follows:—

Torture.—The infliction of excruciating pain, as practised by cruel tyrants, savages, brigands, etc., from a delight in watching the agony of a victim, in hatred or revenge, or as a means of extortion; *spec.* judicial torture, inflicted by a judicial or quasi-judicial authority, for the purpose of forcing an accused or suspected person to confess, or an unwilling witness to give evidence or information.

Let us consider this definition carefully. The first part is fairly simple and excludes individual acts. Thus if "A" dislikes "B" and meeting him alone flogs him, this is not torture; but if "A" orders others to flog "B" while he looks on, it falls within the definition.

The second part of the definition is puzzling. It would appear that punishment for a crime ordered by a judicial or quasi-judicial authority is not torture. This is of the greatest importance and considerably limits the scope of our inquiry. Burning to death as a legal punishment for

9

heretics—Boiling to death as a legal punishment for poisoners—Flogging under the present law, etc., do not come within the definition and, according to Dr. Murray, are not tortures.

To make this point perfectly clear let us consider the case of Francis Ravaillac who murdered King Henry IV of France in 1610.

The Torture and Death of Francis Ravaillac for the Murder of King Henry the Great.

Extracted and translated from the registers of the Parliament of Paris, 1610.

·　　·　　·　　·　　·　　·

May 27, 1610, the Court sat in the afternoon in the Chamber de La-Beuvette.

·　　·　　·　　·　　·　　·

We the presidents, and several of the counsellors being present, the prisoner, Francis Ravaillac, was brought into court, who having been accused and convicted of parricide committed on the person of the late king, he was ordered to kneel, and the clerk of the court pronounced the sentence of death given against him; as likewise that he should be put to the torture to force him to declare his accomplices.

His oath being taken, he was exhorted to redeem himself from the torments preparing for him, by acknowledging the truth, and declaring who those persons were that had persuaded, prompted, and abetted him, in that most wicked action, and to whom he had disclosed his intention of committing it.

He said, by the salvation I hope for, no one but myself was concerned in this action.

He was then ordered to be put to the torture of the brodequin[1] and the first wedge being drove, he cried out, "God have mercy upon my soul, and pardon the crime I have committed: I never disclosed my intention to anyone." This he repeated as he had done in his interrogation.

[1] The brodequin is a strong wooden box, made in the form of a boot, just big enough to contain both the legs of the criminal, which being put therein, a wooden wedge is then driven with a mallet between his knees, and after that is forced quite through, a second wedge is applied in the same manner.

When the second wedge was drove, he said with loud cries and shrieks, "I am a sinner, I know no more than I have declared, by the oath I have taken, and by the truth I owe to God and the court: all I have said was to the little Franciscan, which I have already declared: I never mentioned my design in confession or in any other way: I never spoke of it to the visitor of Angoulême, nor revealed it in confession in this city. I beseech the court not to drive my soul to despair."

The executioner continuing to drive the second wedge, he cried out, "My God, receive this penance as an expiation for the greater crimes I have committed in this world: Oh God! accept these torments in satisfaction for my sins. By the faith I owe to God, I know no more than what I have declared. Oh! do not drive my soul to despair."

The third wedge was then drove lower, near his feet, at which a universal sweat covered his body, and he fainted away. The executioner forced some wine into his mouth, but he could not swallow it, and, being quite speechless, he was released from the torture, and water thrown upon his face and hands. Some wine being forced down his throat, his speech returned, and he was laid upon a mattress in the same place, where he continued till noon. . . .[1]

Up to now we have been dealing with "torture" pure and simple. Ravaillac was being tortured to reveal his accomplices. As Dr. Murray has it, torture was being "inflicted by a judicial authority for the purpose of forcing an accused person to confess". The word "confess" can, I think, be taken to include the revelation of the names of his accomplices.

From now onwards the description is, again, according to Dr. Murray, not of "torture" but of "punishment", and, therefore, outside the scope of this book.

At three o'clock he came from the chapel; and as he was carrying out of the Concièrgerie, the prisoners in great numbers thronged about him, with loud cries and exclamations, calling him traitor, wicked wretch, detestable monster, damned villain, and the like; they would have struck him had they not been hindered by the

[1] Edmund Goldsmid.

archers and the other officers of justice, who kept them off by force.

When he was put into the tumbril, the crowd was so great that it was with the uttermost difficulty the archers and officers of justice could force themselves a passage; and as soon as the prisoner appeared, that vast multitude began to cry out, as above, wicked wretch, traitor, etc.

The enraged populace continued their cries and exclamations till he arrived at the Grève; where, before he was taken out of the tumbril to mount the scaffold, he was again exhorted to reveal his accomplices; but he persisted in his former declaration that he had none; again imploring pardon of the young king, the queen, and the whole kingdom, for the crime he had committed.

When he ascended the scaffold, the two doctors comforted him, and exhorted him to acknowledge the truth; and after performing the duties of their function, the clerk approached him, and urged him to think of his salvation now at the close of his life, and to confess all he knew; to which he only answered as he had done before.

The fire being put to his right hand, holding the knife with which he had stabbed the king, he cried out, "Oh, God!" and often repeated, "Jesu Maria!" while his breast, etc., were tearing with red-hot pincers, he renewed his cries and prayers; during which, being often admonished to acknowledge the truth, he persisted in denying that he had any accomplices. The furious crowd continued to load him with execrations, crying, that he ought not to have a moment's respite. Afterwards, by intervals, melted lead and scalding oil were poured upon his wounds; during which he shrieked aloud and continued his cries and exclamations.

The doctors again admonished him, as likewise the clerk, to confess, and were preparing to offer up publicly the usual prayers for the condemned; but immediately the people, with great tumult and disorder, cried out against it, saying that no prayers ought to be made for that wicked wretch, that damned monster. So that the doctors were obliged to give over. Then the clerk remonstrating to him that the indignation of the people was a judgment upon him which ought to induce him to declare the truth, he persisted to answer as formerly, saying, I only was concerned in the murder.

He was then drawn by four horses, for half an hour, by intervals. Being again questioned and admonished, he persisted in denying that he had any accomplices; while the people of all ranks and degrees, both near and at a distance, continued their exclamations, in token of their great grief for the loss of their king. Several persons set themselves to pull the ropes with the utmost eagerness; and one of the noblesse, who was near the criminal, alighted off his horse, that it might be put in the place of one which was tired with drawing him. At length, when he had been drawn for a full hour by the horses, without being dismembered, the people, rushing on in crowds, threw themselves upon him, and with swords, knives, sticks, and other weapons, they struck, tore, and mangled his limbs; and, violently forcing them from the executioner, they dragged them through the streets with the utmost eagerness and rage, and burnt them in different parts of the city.[1]

With all due respect I cannot bring myself to agree with Dr. Murray. The "punishments" of Ravaillac seem to be very like my idea of "torture".

Let us look at the *Encyclopædia Britannica* (13th edition).

Torture (from Lat. *torquere*, to twist), the general name for innumerable modes of inflicting pain which have been from time to time devised by the perverted ingenuity of man, and especially for those employed in a legal aspect by the civilised nations of antiquity and of modern Europe. From this point of view torture was always inflicted for one of two purposes: (1) as a means of eliciting evidence from a witness or from an accused person either before or after condemnation; (2) as a part of the punishment. The second was the earlier use, its functions as a means of evidence arising when rules were gradually formulated by the experience of legal experts.

Torture as a part of the punishment may be regarded as including every kind of bodily or mental pain beyond what is necessary for the safe custody of the offender (with or without enforced labour) or the destruction of his life—in the language of Bentham an "afflictive" as opposed to a "simple" punishment. Thus the unnecessary sufferings endured in English prisons before

[1] Edmund Goldsmid.

the reforms of John Howard, the *peine forte et dure*, and the drawing and quartering in executions for treason, fall without any straining of terms under the category of torture.

Taking this definition as correct it brings Ravaillac's "punishments" under the heading of torture, as well as those other "punishments" I have mentioned above. This is important, as it shows that torture is still inflicted by English law (the whipping of prisoners), and refutes the statements by such legal authorities as Fortescue, Smith and Coke,[1] who tell us that torture was never legally permitted in England.[2]

If we utilise these two definitions I think we will arrive at the general conception of the word "torture" as follows:—

"The infliction of pain, mental or physical, applied under authority, for any purpose other than the bodily or mental pain necessary for the safe custody of the offender (with or without enforced labour) or the humane destruction of his life."

This definition would, in my opinion, cover not only definite acts of cruelty carried out under the direct order of authority, but also orders under authority inciting acts of cruelty without specifying the manner in which they are to be executed.

Taking this definition, the German and Turkish atrocities in the late war cannot be considered tortures as they were acts of brutality committed by the officers and/or men, without orders from a superior authority. On the other hand, the Austro-Hungarian atrocities inflicted on the Serbians fall within the definition, as the Austro-Hungarian troops were incited by definite orders from their Army Headquarters to punish the non-combatant inhabitants, contrary to International law.

[1] Sir John Fortescue (*De Laudibus Legum Anglicæ*), Sir Thomas Smith (*Commonwealth of England*), Sir Edward Coke (3. *Institute*, 35).
[2] At the time of the trial of Fenton, the assassin of the Duke of Buckingham, it was proposed to put the accused to the torture. The judges, however, pronounced torture to be illegal in England.

So far as England is concerned, legally, torture has never been permitted to exhort a confession, though it has been applied extensively either as a means of punishment, or for the purpose of forcing a prisoner to plead. Apart from the purely legal aspect, torture has been applied in England by order of the Crown to obtain confessions for acts committed against the State. These tortures were chiefly applied during the Tudor and early Stuart periods, and under the authority of the notorious Star Chamber Commission.

In preparing this book, I have drawn freely from various sources and my gratitude is especially due to the *Encyclopædia Britannica*, *The Percy Anecdotes*, various books by W. Andrews on ancient punishments, and to an old copy of Madame Tussaud's catalogue detailing various exhibits in the "Chamber of Horrors". I have also used various editions of Foxe's *Book of Martyrs*, to which I am indebted.

If this book may be found to contain little of historical interest I trust, at any rate, it may effect a diminution in the periodic flow of letters to the Press praying for a return of "The Good Old Days!"

JOHN SWAIN

INTRODUCTION

*Many times death passeth with less pain than the torture of a limb;
for the most vital parts are not the quickest of sense.*—BACON

THE practice of torture may be traced to the remotest antiquity, and evidence of its existence appears everywhere in the history of man. There is no country free from the stigma of having practised torture, and few countries do not practise it to-day. Religion, especially, has played its part in keeping torture in the foreground, and there are few creeds that can escape the accusation.[1]

So far as torture to induce a confession is concerned, it seems to have been first employed in England in 1310 at the instigation of Pope Clement V, in the reign of King Edward II (1307–1327),[2] when the Templars were tortured by Royal Warrant addressed to the Mayor and Sheriffs of London.[3] In this case it was recorded that torture was unknown in England and that no torturer was to be found in the realm.[4] The last case in English history is that of a man named Archer, who was suspected of having taken part in an attack upon the palace of Archbishop Laud, at Lambeth, in 1640.[5]

In Scotland torture continued till the reign of Queen Anne,[6] the last warrant being issued in 1690. Ireland seems to have enjoyed comparative immunity. Torture was not recognised either by the Irish Statute or Common Law.

[1] Mr. Spurgeon once drew the loud applause of his audience by asserting that the Baptists had never persecuted those that differed from them. When the cheers had died down, he dryly added that they never had the chance.
[2] Though a licence to torture is found as early as the Pipe Roll of 34 Hen. II. L. O. Pike's *History of Crime in England*.
[3] Rymer, *Fœdera*.   [4] Walter of Hemingford.
[5] But see Thurloe, iii. 298, who speaks of three Portuguese tortured at Plymouth during the Commonwealth.
[6] "That in future no person accused of any crime in Scotland shall be subjected or liable to any torture." Act for Improving the Union of the Two Kingdoms, 7 Anne, c. 21. s. 5.

In the British Colonies and Dependencies torture was usually regarded as being contrary to the law. In Ceylon torture, which had been allowed by the Dutch Government, was abolished by royal proclamation in 1799. Torture was freely used in the Channel Islands to obtain confessions in seventeenth-century cases of witchcraft.[1] In India torture was not permitted, and the second charge against Warren Hastings was extortion by means of torture. In the present Indian Civil Code and Evidence Acts,[2] there are provisions to prevent the practice of torture.

The case of Sir Thomas Picton is interesting in showing the British feeling with regard to torture. The island of Trinidad surrendered to Sir Ralph Abercrombie in 1797, and he entered into a stipulation by which he conceded to the inhabitants a continuance of their laws until His Majesty's pleasure should be known. Sir Thomas Picton was appointed governor, and in December 1801 he ordered the torture to be applied to a girl of some ten or eleven years of age named Luisa Calderon to obtain her confession to a theft. The girl was informed that if she did not confess, she would be subjected to torture, and her fears were aggravated by the introduction of some negresses into her prison who were to suffer the torture, as a means of extorting a confession to witchcraft. She persisted in maintaining her innocence, and a punishment was inflicted improperly called "picketing".[3] The punishment inflicted on Luisa Calderon was that her great toe was lodged on a sharp piece of wood, her opposite wrist being suspended from the roof by a rope running over a pulley, while the other hand and foot were lashed together. She remained on the spike for three-quarters of an hour on the first day, and the next day for twenty-two minutes; on the second

[1] J. L. Pitts, *Witchcraft in the Channel Islands.*
[2] Secs. 327–331 of Code, Secs. 25–27 of Act.
[3] The military punishment of "picketing" was suspending a prisoner by one arm, the sole of his foot supported by a "picket", or a piece of wood. He was allowed to rest with his free arm.

occasion her feet were changed. She swooned away each time before being taken down, and was then put in the *grillos*, which were long pieces of iron fastened to the wall with two rings for her feet. She remained in this position for eight months. The effect produced by the torture was excruciating pain, and her wrists and ankles were much swollen. Despite the fact that the torture was applied under the existing laws and was known as the "picquet", Sir Thomas was found "Guilty", but a final decree of the King's Bench in 1812 respited the defendant's recognisances till further order.

In France torture does not seem to have existed as a recognised practice before the thirteenth century, and the *question préparatoire* was abolished by royal decree in 1780, and nine years later in the French Dominions.

In Italy the earliest legislation dealing with torture after the Roman law appears to be the constitutions of the Emperor Fredrick II of Sicily, in 1231. Torture was abolished in Tuscany as early as 1786, largely owing to the influence of Beccaria, and the other States followed. However the punishment of the *puntale*[1] seems to have existed in practice at Naples as late as 1857.

Spain, like Italy, adopted the Roman law, and torture, apart from this, did not appear till 1256.[2] The latest legislation on torture was in 1678, but it had become obsolete in 1790. While Aragon was an independent State,[3] torture was very rare, though the nobility had the power of putting a criminal to death by cold, hunger and thirst. Torture was abolished in 1283 except in the case of vagabonds charged with coining, and a Statute in 1335 made it unlawful to put a freeman to the torture.

Torture has existed in Central Europe from time immemorial, partly under Imperial legislation, and partly

[1] Similar to the "picquet" described above.
[2] *Siete partidos*, compiled by Alphonso the Wise, written about 1243.
[3] It was a separate kingdom till 1479.

under the laws of the respective States. Imperial legislation abolished torture in 1776. In Prussia it was practically abolished by Frederick the Great in 1740, and formally in 1805. Torture ceased in Austria and Saxony towards the middle of the eighteenth century, and in Hanover and most of the smaller States towards the end of that century. In Baden it was not abolished till 1831.

In the Netherlands the existing law was codified by Philip II in 1570,[1] but certain cities, e.g. Brabant, claimed the privilege of torturing in cases not permitted by the Ordinance. In the United Provinces torture was abolished in 1798.

There is a notice of torture in the Icelandic Code known as the *Grágás* (about 1119).

Judicial torture is said to have been introduced into Denmark by Valdemar I, in 1157, but in 1683, it was limited to cases of treason by Charles V, and was abolished by the influence of Struenese in 1771.

In Sweden torture never existed as a system, and the Code of 1734[2] expressly forbade it.

In the Slav countries the earliest mention of torture seems to be that of mutilation, provided by the Code of Stephen Dushan in 1349. In Russia torture does not occur in the recensions of the earlier law. It was possibly of Tartar origin, and the earliest mention of it in an official document is probably in the Sudebnik of Ivan the Terrible in 1497. The abolition of torture was recommended in Russia by the Empress Catherine in 1763, but it was not effected till 1801, and it was practised in exceptional cases as late as 1847.

In China torture has always existed in historic times, and exists to-day, though flogging was the only form of torture allowed under the Manchus. Flogging in China is carried out in a very brutal way. The victim (generally an obdurate witness) is laid on his face and the executioner delivers his blows on the upper part of the thighs with the concave

[1] "Ordonnance sur le Style."   [2] Cod. Leg. Svecicarum.

side of a split bamboo, the sharp edges of which mutilate the sufferer terribly. The punishment is continued, in the case of a witness, until he supplies the necessary information or becomes insensible.

It will be seen that torture in its worst forms had a legal recognition by civilised nations practically from the dawn of civilisation up to the nineteenth century.[1]

The reader will recollect that we have excluded from the scope of this work "the humane destruction" of life, but it is interesting to consider, before we start, the methods now in practice for affecting this.

Hanging is the most usual sentence of death, and is in use throughout the British Isles, the British Dominions, Colonies and dependencies, and (with the exception of the States in which capital punishment is abolished,[2] and the States of New York, Massachusetts, New Jersey, North Carolina, Mississippi, Virginia and Ohio) in the United States, Japan, Austria and Hungary.

The British method of hanging is to attach a halter, properly adjusted to the drop, to the criminal's neck, his face being covered with a white cap, while he is placed under the gallows on trap-doors. The trap-doors are released by a mechanical contrivance worked by a lever. The prisoner falls into a pit, the length of the fall being regulated by his height and weight, and death results from a fracture of the cervical vertebræ.[3]

[1] So far as the legal application of torture is concerned, England, Aragon and Sweden form honourable exceptions in comparison with the other countries.

[2] Capital punishment was abolished in Michigan (except for treason) 1846, Wisconsin 1853, Maine 1876, re-enacted 1883, again abolished 1887, and in Rhode Island 1852 and re-enacted in 1882 in cases of murder committed by a person imprisoned for life.

[3] "The hour fixed for execution is 8 a.m. in all the prisons except Wandsworth and Lincoln, where it is 9 a.m. Of course the scaffold and ropes are arranged and the drop decided beforehand. I calculate for three minutes to be occupied from the time of entering the condemned cell to the finish of life's great tragedy for the doomed man, so I enter the cell punctually at three minutes to eight. In order that my action for hanging a man may be legal, it is necessary that I should have what is known as an 'Authority to Hang', which is drawn up and signed by the Sheriff, and handed to me a few minutes before the time for

In some of the American States the criminal is attached to a rope running over a pulley at the other end of which is a weight. The weight being released, he is jerked upwards with a similar result. In the State of Utah the criminal is put on his election whether he will be hanged or shot.

Military law in England and the United States empowers the court-martial to direct the mode of execution, which is usually by shooting or hanging.

Beheading follows closely on hanging as the most popular method of dispatching a victim humanely. Among

execution. Its form varies a good deal. In some cases it is a long, wordy document, full of the 'wherefores' and 'whatsoevers' in which the law delights; but usually it is a simple, official-looking form, engrossed by the gaol clerk. When we enter the condemned cell, the chaplain is already there, and has been for some time. The attendants who have watched through the convict's last nights on earth are also present. At my appearance the convict takes leave of his attendants, to whom he generally gives some small token or keepsake, and I at once proceed to pinion his arms. As soon as the pinioning is done, a procession is formed, generally in the following order:—

Chief Warder

Warder.   Warder.

Chaplain.

Warder.   Warder.

Convict.

Executioner.

Principal Warder.   Principal Warder.

Warder.   Warder.

Governor and Sheriff.

Wand Bearer.   Wand Bearer.

Gaol Surgeon and Attendant.

"On the way from the cell to the scaffold, the chaplain reads the service for the burial of the dead, and as the procession moves, I place the white cap upon the head of the convict. Just as we reach the scaffold, I pull the cap over his eyes. Then I place the convict under the beam, pinion the legs just below the knees with a strap similar to the one used for the elbows, adjust the rope, pull the bolt, and the trap falls. Death is instantaneous, but the body is left hanging for an hour, and is then lowered into a coffin made in the prison and carried to the mortuary to await the inquest. The inquest usually takes place at ten o'clock, but in some few places it is held at noon. After the inquest, the body is surrounded by quicklime and buried in the prison grounds."—*My Experiences as an Executioner*, by James Berry.

22

the Greeks and Romans it was considered the most honourable death. It was introduced into England by William the Conqueror in 1076, the first execution being that of Waltheof, Earl of Huntingdon, Northampton and Northumberland; and was reserved for offenders of high rank until 1747.[1] In England the victim was beheaded by a blow from an axe severing his neck, which was placed on a block hollowed at the top.[2] In Scotland and France the criminal knelt and his head was taken off with a sweep of the sword.

Beheading was the death punishment under the Roman law, and the countries which adopted the Roman Code also adopted this method of inflicting the death penalty.

The sword was used in Holland, France[3] and Belgium, until capital punishment was abolished in Holland in 1870, and until France and Belgium[4] introduced the guillotine towards the end of the eighteenth century.

To discover the origin of the guillotine we must come to England and consider the Halifax gibbet, which was set up by some of the Norman barons and was described by Holinshed as follows[5]:—

There is, and has been, of ancient time, a law, or rather custom, at Halifax, that whosoever doth commit a felony, and is taken with the same, or confess the fact upon examination, if it be valued by four constables to amount to the sum of thirteenpence-halfpenny, he is forthwith beheaded upon one of the next market-days (which fall usually upon the Tuesdays, Thursdays and Saturdays), or else upon the same day that he is convicted, if market be holden. The engine wherewith the execution is done is a square block of wood, of the length of four feet and a half, which doth ride up and down in a slot, rabet, or regall, between two

[1] Simon Lord Lovat was the last person beheaded in England, 9th April, 1747. Lord Farrars' petition to be beheaded in 1760 was refused, and he was hanged. Beheading did not cease to be a legal punishment till 1814.
[2] Anne Boleyn, however, was decapitated in the French way with a sword.
[3] Before the French Revolution beheading was reserved for aristocratic offenders. The common people were hanged.
[4] No execution has taken place since 1863.   [5] *Chronicle*, edition 1587.

pieces of timber that are framed and set up right, of five yards in height. In the nether end of a sliding block is an axe, keyed or fastened with an iron into the wood, which, being drawn up to the top of the frame, is there fastened by a wooden pin (with a notch made in the same, after the manner of a Samson's post) unto the middest of which pin also there is a long rope fastened, that cometh down among the people; so that when the offender hath made his confession, and hath laid his neck over the nethermost block, every man there present doth either take hold of the rope (or putteth forth his arm so near to the same as he can get, in token that he is willing to see justice executed), and pulling out the pin in this manner, the lead-block wherein the axe is fastened doth fall down with such a violence, that if the neck of the transgressor were so big as that of a bull, it should be cut in sunder at a stroke, and roll from the body by a huge distance. If it be so that the offender be apprehended for an ox, sheep, kine, horse, or any such cattle, the self beast or other of its kind shall have the end of the rope tied somewhere unto them, so that they being driven, do draw out the pin whereby the offender is executed.

Towards the middle of the sixteenth century, the Earl of Morton, Regent of Scotland, witnessed an execution at the Halifax gibbet, and on his return home in 1565 he had a similar engine erected in Edinburgh which was named "The Maiden".[1] Its use was discontinued in 1710.[2] It was an instrument similar, in principle, to this that Dr. Joseph Ignatius Guillotin introduced into France during the time of the Revolution, and which is in use in France at the present day.

In Germany beheading [3] has been abolished in many States, but it is still on the Statute books of Denmark (by the axe) and Sweden.

[1] According to Rogers, its appellation is from the Celtic *Mod-dun*, originally signifying the place where justice was administered, but it is more probable that it was named after a similar mode of execution used in Italy from the thirteenth century, and known as *Mannaia*. A similar instrument was used in some of the German States in the sixteenth century.
[2] The last person executed was the Earl of Argyll in 1685.
[3] Methods vary according to the States.

24

Decapitation by the sword is the usual method in China. The executioner's assistant seizes the victim's head and stretches the neck whilst the executioner does his work.

In Spain the death sentence is very seldom imposed, except under military law, and the method used is the *garrote*.[1] The criminal is conducted to the place of execution in a cart, wearing a black tunic and attended by a procession of priests. He is seated on a scaffold, fastened to an upright post by an iron collar, and a nob worked by a screw or lever dislocates his spinal column, or a small blade severs the spinal column at the base of the brain. Executions in Spain are still held in public.

Electrocution took the place of hanging in the State of New York in January 1889,[2] and was introduced into Ohio (1896), Massachusetts (1898), New Jersey (1906), Virginia (1908), and North Carolina (1910). The prisoner is placed in the "Death Chair", his head, chest, arms and legs are secured by broad straps; one electrode thoroughly moistened with salt-solution is affixed to the head and another to the calf of one leg. The current is then switched on (1,700–1,800 volts) for 5 to 7 seconds which is afterwards reduced in strength. Two or three applications of the current are usually given.

Capital punishment has been abolished in Finland (1824), Italy (1888),[3] Norway (1905),[4] Portugal (1867), Russia prior to Bolshevik regime (1864), and Switzerland (1874).[5]

[1] The word means "cudgel", and the punishment gets its name from the original form of execution, which was to tie a rope or band round the neck of a criminal who was seated against a post. A stick was then inserted between the cord and the neck and twisted till strangulation ensued. A not dissimilar method was used in Turkey but without the post.

[2] The first criminal executed by electricity was William Kemmler on the 6th August, 1890, at Auburn Prison.

[3] So far as Tuscany is concerned, 1786.

[4] There has been no execution in Norway since 1876. Prior to that the method was beheading.

[5] In 1879 power was given to each Canton to restore the death penalty for offences in its territory should it desire to do so.

THE PLEASURES OF
THE TORTURE CHAMBER

CHAPTER I

MISCELLANEOUS MERRIMENTS OF THE OLDEN TIME

BEING THE TORTURES IN VOGUE BEFORE THE CHRISTIAN ERA, WITH SOME MENTION OF THE MARTYRDOMS OF THE EARLY CHRISTIANS

Solomon said in accents mild,
"Spare the rod and spoil the child;
Be they man or be they maid,
Whip and wallop 'em," Solomon said.

Christians bound to Axelltrees pitched in y^e Ground in Rowes and so burned.

IN all ancient kingdoms torture was practised as a matter of course, but it was nearly always used as a punishment and not as a means to extorting a confession. Torture for the purpose of a confession appears only to have come into force under the Roman law, which gives the question of torture very careful consideration.

In all primitive countries whipping was the method of punishing milder offences, but the modes of executing the criminal varied according to different peoples. The most common form of dispatching the accused was by crucifixion, and this was the punishment used by the Assyrians, Persians, Egyptians, Carthaginians, Greeks and Romans.

There were three crimes which seem to have been considered the most heinous by the early races: parricide, adultery and being taken a prisoner of war. The former two were always punished by death, the latter by the victim being sold as a slave.

Most of the early civilisations used the same methods of torture, and it will be sufficient for our purpose to consider the tortures common to the most famous of the old empires and to notice any unusual methods of punishment executed by the others. In fact, if one considers carefully the modes of punishment known to the Romans one finds, except in a few outstanding cases, nearly every previous method of torment brought to a higher state of perfection.

In Egypt[1] the customary mode of punishment was, hanging for capital offences, and, for lesser crimes, whipping was common. Whipping was inflicted on women whilst kneeling and on men whilst prostrated on the ground. The victims were stripped and the blows given on their backs. These whippings were very severe, a man receiving as many as a thousand blows for adultery with a bond-woman. Adultery with a free woman was punished by mutilation, and in any case the woman who committed the crime lost her nose.

A false accuser received the same sentence that the accused would have done had the offence been proved against him. British legislators please note.

In all ancient countries the most severe penalties were reserved for parricide, and included cruel chastisements with the bastinado, laceration of the flesh with sharp reeds, being thrown and rolled in thorns, followed by burning to death. The parent, on the other hand, who slew his offspring was compelled to pass three days and nights with the corpse fastened to his neck.

The ancient Egyptians showed great ingenuity in their binding of captives of war. They understood more thoroughly than any other people the pain that could be extracted from a piece of cord. The prisoners were led,

[1] Wilkinson's *Ancient Egyptians.*

tied neck to neck, in a long column, the cord being bound round their throats as tightly as possible without danger of strangulation; the prisoners staggered along under the whips of their conquerors choking and coughing with either their elbows tied tightly together behind their backs, their arms tied in a strained and unnatural position above their heads, their arms twisted behind them and their wrists bound to a cord fastened tightly round their necks,[1] or their wrists bound to their waists and their elbows tied together in front of them. The prisoners who survived and reached their destination were sold as slaves. The male prisoners usually had their eyes put out or their tongues excised before sale.

The Assyrians were also guilty of numerous barbarities; again, chiefly with respect to prisoners of war whose usual fate was to be flayed alive. The sculptures of Nineveh show, with the greatest fidelity, this atrocious process. According to Professor Sayce: "The barbarities which followed the capture of a town would be almost incredible were they not a subject of boast in the inscriptions which record them. Assurnatsir-pals' cruelties were especially revolting. Pyramids of human heads marked the paths of the conqueror. Boys and girls were burned alive or reserved for a worse fate; men were impaled, flayed alive, blinded, deprived of their hands and feet, or of their ears and noses. During the second Assyrian Empire, warfare was a little more human, but the most horrible tortures were exercised upon the vanquished."

The following description, taken from Foxe, the martyrologist,[2] quoting Josephus as his authority,[3] shows very

---

[1] The ingenuity of this is that if the victim struggled to relieve the unnatural position of his arms he increased the pressure on his throat.

[2] I am using three editions of Foxe, two published at London, 1641 and 1811, and the other at Leeds, 1813. The present quotation is taken from the 1813 edition.

[3] "I have already said that whenever Foxe prints documents instead of relating hearsays, I have found him uniformly trustworthy; so far, that is to say, as there are means of testing him" (J. A. Froude).

clearly the forms of torture in use in Syria before the Christian era.

When the tyrant Antiochus has seated himself on a tribunal, surrounded by his counsellors, and a strong body of armed men, he commanded many of the Hebrews to be brought by force before him, and compelled them to eat of swine's flesh, and meats offered to idols, upon pain of the torture in case of a refusal.

In compliance with this order, there were brought before the tyrant seven sons, and their mother, who was very old. The men, from the symmetry of their form and elegance of their deportment, attracted his notice: and therefore, after beholding them with a sort of approbation, he thus accosted them:

"I invite you to comply with me, under an assurance of my particular friendship, for I have it in my power to oblige and advance them that obey me, in as eminent a manner as I have to punish those who withstand my commands. Be assured, then, you shall not fail of preferments, but have places of honour and profit under me, provided you will renounce your country's customs, and be content to live after the Greek manner; but I assure you, that in case of disobedience you have nothing to expect but racks, torture, fire and death."

The tyrant had no sooner thus spoken than he commanded the instruments of torture to be produced, in order to work the more strongly on their fears. When the guards had set before the brethren the wheels, racks, manacles, combustible matter and other implements of horror, and execution, Antiochus, taking the advantage of the impression he supposed this spectacle would make, once more applied to them to this effect:

"Young men, consider the consequences; your compliance is no longer a wilful offence; you may rest assured that the Deity you worship will consider your case, in being compelled to violate your law."

But they were so far from being terrified at the consequences of a refusal, that their resolutions became stronger, and through the power of reason, aided by religion, they secretly triumphed over his barbarity.

These intrepid youths, exulting in the magnanimity of their conduct, made Antiochus the following reply:

"To what purpose, O king, is this delay? If with design to

30

know our final resolution, be assured we are ready to encounter death in its most frightful forms, rather than transgress the laws of our forefathers; for, besides the reverence due to their example on other accounts, this is what our obedience to the law and the precepts of Moses particularly requires from us. Do not any more then attempt to persuade us to apostacy; do not put on a counter-feit pity for those who know you hate them; even death itself is more supportable than such an insulting, dissembling compassion, as would save our lives with the loss of our innocence. Try us, therefore, and see if it be in your power to destroy our souls, when we suffer in the cause of God and religion. Your cruelty cannot hurt us; for all the effect your pains can have, will be to secure us the glorious rewards due to unshaken patience and injured virtue."

The tyrant, enraged at their contumacy, gave the word of command, and the guards immediately brought forth the eldest of the seven brethren; and having torn off his garment, and tied his hands behind, cruelly scourged him; and continued their lashes till they were tired; but it availed nothing. They put him on the wheel, where his body being extended, he underwent the severest tortures of the rack. They then put fire under him, and exposed his body as much extended as possible to the devouring flames, insomuch that he exhibited a spectacle horrible beyond descrip-tion; and thus continued till nothing was left of the human form but a skeleton of broken bones.

This brave youth was not heard to utter a single groan; he bore his torments with such invincible fortitude, as if he had been translated to immutability in the midst of the flames.

The guards now advanced with the second brother, and fixed his hands in manacles of iron, but before they put him to rack, they demanded if he would accept the conditions. Finding by his reply he possessed the same resolution as his brother, they tore off his flesh with pincers, and flayed the skin off his face and head. He bore this torture with singular magnaminity, saying, "How welcome is death in any form, when we suffer for our religion and laws!"

The third brother was next produced, and pressed with argu-ments and entreaties to preserve his life. But he nobly replied, with some vehemence, "Are you ignorant that I am the son of the same father and the same mother with those that went before me?

Shall I then at this awful period renounce the honour of that alliance? The same institutions were taught us all; and I will abide by them while I breathe." The freedom of this speech enraged the executioners, who, to express their malice and resentment, stretched his hands and feet on the engine, and broke them to pieces; but when they found it did not deprive him of life, they drew off his skin at the end of his fingers, and flayed him from the very crown of the head. Not content with mangling his body in this merciless manner, they dragged him to the wheel; where, being yet more distended, his flesh was torn from him, and streams of blood gushed from his body, till at last he expired.

The guards now produced the fourth brother, whom they persuaded to bethink himself, and be wiser than those who had gone before him. But his answer was, "Your fire has not heat enough in it to make me renounce my opinion. I solemnly vow I will not renounce the truth." Antiochus, on hearing these words, was so excessively enraged, that he gave immediate orders to have his tongue cut out: whereupon the intrepid youth thus proceeded: "You may deprive me of the instrument of utterance; but that God who seeth the heart knows the inward sensations of the silent. Here is the member; you cannot by this act deprive me of reason. O that I could lose my life by inches to support the cause of religion. Though you take away the tongue which chaunts the praises of God, remember that His high hand will very soon let its vengeance fall down on your guilty head.'

When this brother, exhausted with pain and miserably mangled, had resigned his breath, the fifth instantly sprang forward of his own accord, exclaiming: "Prepare your torments! I am here ready to suffer the worst you can inflict. I come voluntarily to die in the cause of virtue; what have I done, wherein have I transgressed, to deserve this merciless treatment? Do we not worship the universal Parent of nature according to His own decrees? Do we not act in conformity to the institution of His most holy law? These are truths, that ought to meet with reward instead of punishment."

While these words were in his mouth the tormentors bound and dragged him to the wheel; to which fastening his knees with iron rings, they stretched him round the engine and then broke his joints. Thus after undergoing similar torments with his heroic brothers, he expired.

ADRIAN CHALINSKY, a Protestant Clergyman, roasted alive
by a slow fire, in the Great Duchy of Lithuania.

The sixth youth was then brought before Antiochus; and being asked by the tyrant whether he would accept deliverance on the terms aforementioned, resolutely answered:

"It is true indeed, I am younger than my brothers; but my mind is as firm as theirs was. We had all of us the same parents, and the same instructions; and it is but necessary that we should all die alike for them: therefore if you are determined to put me to the torment on my refusal to eat, torment me at once!"

Hereupon they fastened him to the wheel; and having broken his bones, put fire under him: the guards then heated their spears, and thrust them into his back and sides, till his very entrails were burnt up. In the midst of these torments he exclaimed, "O glorious conflict, in which so many brethren have engaged so victoriously for the sake of their religion. I will accompany my brothers: and relying on my God as my defence, cheerfully submit to death."

The sixth brother was at length dispatched by being thrown into a boiling cauldron; when the seventh and youngest appeared whom when the tyrant saw fettered and pinioned, his heart began to relent. Calling upon him therefore to approach the tribunal, he endeavoured to sooth him.

"You see what horrid kinds of deaths your brothers have undergone; but their disobedience and contumacy have been the sole cause of all the torments and cruelties they have sustained. Yet you, if you obey not my commands, shall be exposed to the same, nay, worse torments, and so suffer a premature death; but if you comply with my desires, I will take you into the number of my friends." Not content with these persuasions, he addressed himself to the mother with a seeming compassion for her loss, entreating her to prevail upon her child, in pity to her at least, to save this small remnant of the family. But his mother addressed him in the Hebrew tongue, and exhorted him to suffer. Upon this he suddenly exclaimed: "Take off my fetters, for I have something to communicate to the king and all his friends." The king and his nobles, hearing this promise, seemed greatly rejoiced, and his chains were immediately knocked off. Taking the advantage of this circumstance, he thus exclaimed:

"Tyrant! Have you no fears nor apprehensions in your mind after having received at the hands of the Almighty the kingdom and riches you enjoy, than to put to death his servants, and torment his worshippers? Is your conscience touched with no

33

scruples, thus to deprive of their tongues those who share alike the same nature and passions with you? My brothers have undergone a glorious death, and shown how much their piety and uprightness were for the honour of the true religion. For this reason I will suffer death, and in my last pangs discover how much my desire was to follow the brave example of my brothers. I beg and entreat the God of my fathers, that He would be propitious and merciful to our nation." Having finished this address, he instantly threw himself into the boiling cauldron, and, of course, expired.

The dauntless mother of these young men, after being scourged and otherwise severely tortured by order of Antiochus, finished her existence by voluntarily throwing herself into the flames.[1]

[1] This was probably the martyrdom said to be that of the Maccabeus which is described by the Rev. Henry Southwell in *The New Book of Martyrs*, as follows:
"*Antiochus Epiphanes now reigning in Syria*, and having some success against the Jews, went to Jerusalem, where he ordered Eleazer the priest to be put to death in the most cruel manner, for refusing to eat swine's flesh. Then seizing on the family of Maccabeus, consisting of a matron named Salamona, and her seven sons, he carried them all to Antioch. Here he would fain have persuaded them to embrace his idolatry, which they nobly and unanimously refusing, he ordered them all to be put to death.

"Maccabeus, the eldest, was accordingly stripped, stretched on the rack, and severely beaten. He was next fastened to a wheel, and weights hung to his feet till his sinews cracked. Afterwards his tormentors threw him into a fire till he was dreadfully scorched; then they drew him out, cut out his tongue, and put him into a frying-pan, with a slow fire under it, till he died. As long as he had life, and power of expression, under these exquisite torments, he fervently called upon God, and exhorted his brothers to a similar perseverance.

"After the second son had his hands fastened with chains, with which he was hung up, his skin was flayed off from the crown of his head to his knees. He was then cast to a leopard, but the beast refusing to touch him, he was suffered to languish till he expired with the excruciating pain, and loss of blood.

"Machir, the third son, was bound to a globe till his bones were all dislocated; his head and face were then flayed, his tongue cut out, and being cast into a pan he was fried to death.

"Judas, the fourth son, after having his tongue cut out, was beat with ropes, and then racked upon a wheel.

"Achas, the fifth son, was pounded in a large brazen mortar.

"Areth, the sixth son, was fastened to a pillar with his head downwards, slowly roasted by a fire kindled at some distance; his tongue was then cut out, and he was lastly fried in a pan.

"Jacob, the seventh and youngest son, had his arms cut off, his tongue plucked out, and was then fried to death.

"Salamona, the mother, after having in a manner died seven deaths in beholding the martyrdom of her children, was, by the tyrant's order, stripped naked, severely scourged, her breasts cut off, and her body fried till she expired."

The methods employed were very primitive. The mental aspect was in no way considered. If Antiochus had reigned at a later date, the mother, or at least the youngest brother, would have been the first to undergo the torture, and if he proved resolute the others would have been removed and imprisoned separately before they saw him expire. The information, after a few days' contemplation on what they had seen, that the mother and all the remaining brothers had submitted, would have proved more effective than following one another to death each encouraged by a previous example of steadfastness.

The rack used was similar, in my opinion, to the circular racks used in France during the fifteenth and sixteenth centuries, a broad upright wheel to which the hands of the victims were tied, his feet being fettered to the ground. As the wheel revolved the body was strained upwards and backwards.

The Jews, however, were not without a great knowledge of torture. Their chief form of executing capital punishment was by stoning the victim to death,[1] but they also employed other means, amongst which were, burning alive, casting from a rock, and, in the case of prisoners of war, sawing asunder.[2]

In England, as with many nations of antiquity, drowning was a common method of punishment; the Britons four and a half centuries before the birth of Christ dispatched

[1] Lev. xx. 2.

There is one case of stoning to death recorded in England during the reign of Henry VIII:

"One Thomas Sommers, an honest merchant, with three others was thrown into prison, for reading some of Luther's books; and they were condemned to carry these books to a fire in Cheapside; there they were to throw them into the flames; but Sommers threw his over, for which he was sent back to the Tower, where he was stoned to death (Foxe).

[2] The punishment of sawing asunder was also used in Persia, and the sisters of Simeon, the Christian Bishop of Salencia, who were accused of causing the illness of the Empress by means of witchcraft, were sawn alive in quarters, which were afterwards fixed to posts between which the Empress passed as a charm to cure her.

their victims by drowning them in quagmires. Prisoners of war were sacrificed, to appease the Druid's gods, by encasing them in wicker-work and burning them alive.

In Sicily, Phalaris, the tyrant of Agrigentum, ordered Perillus, an artist, to construct a bull of hollow brass, with the object of roasting prisoners to death by means of a fire kindled underneath, their cries representing the roaring of the animal. When the brazen bull was completed the unfortunate artist was chosen as the first victim. Of this Ovid wrote:

> Et Phalaris tauro violenti membra Perilli
> Torruit, infelix imbuit autor opus![1]

As a just retribution Phalaris himself was destroyed in the same manner in 563 B.C.

The tortures in force in Greece and Rome were very similar, and the description of the tortures in use at Rome may be taken to include those practised in Greece. Both Aristotle and Demosthenes were in favour of torture. In early days torture was inflicted in Greece upon slaves only with their master's consent,[2] and, probably, upon resident aliens, but later the rack was employed on free citizens in open court, and Antiphon[3] was put to death by this means.

The Tyrant Nabis of Sparta (205–194 B.C.) put his victims to death by means of an instrument in the form of his wife Apega,[4] a mode of torture, no doubt, resembling "the iron virgin",[5] which will be mentioned later. The instrument is said to have been in the form of a beautiful

---

[1] Perillus, roasted in the bull he made, gave first proof of his own cruel trade.

[2] Torture of free citizens was forbidden by a psephism passed in the archonship of Scarnandrius.

[3] An Athenian orator who flourished 430 B.C. He assisted in establishing the tyranny of the four hundred, for which he was put to death.

[4] Polybius.

[5] Of the Holy Inquisition. Not the "Iron Maiden" of Nuremberg.

Two Sisters of Simeon, Bishop of Salencia, in **Persia,** sawed into
quarters, which were hung up in different parts of the city.

woman, whose rich dress concealed a number of iron spikes in her bosom and arms. When anyone, therefore, opposed his demands, he would say: "If I have not talents enough to prevail with you, perhaps my Apega may persuade you." The automaton statue then appeared; and Nabis taking it by the hand led it to the person, who, being embraced by it, was thus tortured into compliance.

Another interesting anecdote concerning early Greek torture was the Thurian Code, which was drawn up by Charondas[1] who, to check any capricious innovations in his laws, ordained that whoever should propose any alterations in them, should remain in public with a rope about his neck, till the people had formally decided upon their adoption or rejection. In the latter case, the rope was to be tightened and the reformer strangled. There are only three instances recorded of alterations being proposed.

The Thurian Code was a very primitive one and the criminal punishments were chiefly of the *Lex talionis* (eye for an eye, tooth for a tooth) type.

Charondas, having inadvertently broken one of his own laws by appearing armed in a public assembly, plunged his sword into his breast, saying that he would seal his laws with his own blood.

Now for Rome. The Roman system is very important, as it was the basis of all subsequent European systems which recognised torture as part of their procedure, and the rules attained a refinement beyond anything attempted in Greece.

Torture under Roman law was used both in civil and in criminal trials, but in the former only upon slaves, freedmen or infamous persons. With respect to crimes, during the Republic torture was applied only to slaves, but with the Empire it was extended to a free man, if he was an accused, but not if he were merely a witness. However, anyone, whatever his rank, was liable to torture

[1] Fifth century B.C.

for treason and sorcery. A wife could be tortured if accused of poisoning her husband, but only after her slaves had been tortured.

By the Roman law certain persons were exempt from torture, priests, children under fourteen years of age, and pregnant women.

Slaves could always be tortured either as accused or as witnesses for their master, but only in certain cases,[1] against their master. On the same principle a freedman could not be tortured against his patron.

The amount and variety of torture were at the discretion of the judge, but it was to be inflicted so as not to injure life or limb; and torture was to be employed only when the evidence had advanced so that nothing but the confession was wanting to complete it. Repetition of the torture could be ordered only in the case of inconsistent depositions, though there was no limiting the number of repetitions.

Torture was carried out by the *tortores* before the *quaesitor*, who asked the questions and drew up an account of the information obtained.

Roman ladies often hired the *tortores* to perform upon their domestic slaves.

The principal forms of torture were the *equuleus* (rack),[2] the *plumbatae* (scourges to the ends of which were fastened leaden balls),[3] the *ungulae* (barbed hooks or tongs on which were spikes; these were used by the early Germans who knew them as "Klaue"), the *lamina* (hot plate), the *mala mansio*,[4] and the *fidiculae* (compressing the arm with a cord).

The capital punishments included crucifixion,[5] burning alive, decapitation,[6] mutilation and exposure to wild

---

[1] e.g. Treason, adultery, frauds on the revenue, and where a master had bought a slave for the special purpose that he should not give evidence against him, etc.   [2] Mentioned as far back as Cicero.
[3] "Then Decius, moved with anger, commanded him to be beaten with plumbats (which, as says Sabellicus, is a kind of scourging)" (Foxe).
[4] Probably a form of torture similar to the *little ease*.
[5] Abolished by Constantine, 315.
[6] The most honourable form of death.

beasts in the arena, while parricides were sewed up in sacks with venomous serpents and cast into the sea or river.[1]

Burial alive was the fate reserved for Vestal Virgins who violated their vows of chastity. An interesting case of this is mentioned by Seneca, the sole fault of the Vestal Virgin being that she wrote, "Felices Nuptae! Moriar ni nubere dulce est."[2]

The tortures of the Roman consul Regulus[3] by the Carthaginians were ended by his being enclosed in a barrel, studded inside with spikes and nails, in which he was rolled down a hill.[4]

Another form of punishment in Rome was the *furca* (or gallows), an instrument which consisted of a forked piece of timber. This punishment was of three kinds. The first only ignominious, e.g. when a master for some small offence compelled his slave to carry a *furca* on his shoulder about the city. The second was penal, e.g. when the victim was led about the circus, or elsewhere, with a *furca* about his neck, being whipped all the way. The third was capital, and in this case the accused had his head fastened to the *furca* while he was whipped to death.

Such were the punishments employed in Rome up to the Christian era; and it was not till the death of Christ that torture received the impetus which kept it going for so many years. Before the death of Christ torture had been used only as a punishment for a crime, or for the persuasion of an unwilling witness. It had been a legal remedy carried out within legal limits, and it had not been

---

[1] I see it mentioned, in *The Percy Anecdotes*, that Roman parricides were first scourged, then sewed in a leathern sack with a live dog, a cock, a viper and an ape, and then cast into the sea.

[2] "Hail, happy bride! I would I were dead or wedded."

[3] Marcus Attilius Regulus. *Circa* 256 B.C.

[4] A similar fate was ordered for St. Catherine, but after the barrel had been prepared she was miraculously saved by the instrument being destroyed by lightning.

used, except by tyrants, such as the Syrian Antiochus, as a means to alter opinions. The more steadfastly, however, the early Christians maintained their opinions, the more terrible did the methods of torture become, and the more illegal and unrighteous their application. Planted on a barbaric foundation, they slowly grew in ingenuity till they reached the height of cruelty at the time of the Holy Inquisition.

The crucifixion of Christ was a very curious instance of torture, as crucifixion was not a Jewish form of punishment and Christ was not killed by the Romans, unless it can be argued that the Romans did not prevent the infliction of the death penalty when they had it in their power to do so.

From the time of Christ until torture was embodied by Justinian (483–565) in his Code (from which nearly all legal systems in Europe sprang) the instruments with which torture was inflicted increased steadily in barbarity and number. The early persecutions of the Christians fill some of the most terrible pages in history.

The first Christian persecution began under Nero and ended with Vespasian, thousands of Christians suffering the most terrible deaths. The crucifix, the whip, the rack, the cauldron of boiling oil, the red-hot grid, the hoop of steel, the pincers, scraping with shells and flaying alive came into general operation. Special victims suffered by being impaled on sharp stakes thrust through the body lengthwise, torn by wild beasts in the circus, or sewn in the skins of animals and hunted to death by dogs. Others again supplemented the deficient lighting system by having their clothes smeared with combustible materials, being tied to posts and set alight to blaze as torches.

According to Magentius Rabanus-Maurus:

Alii ferro perempti; alii flammis exusti; alii flagris verberati; alii vectibus perforati; alii cruciati patibulo; alii demersi pelagi periculo; alii vivi decoriati; alii vinculis mancipati; alii linguis privati; alii lapidibus obruti; alii frigore afflicti; alii fame

40

cruciati; alii truncatis manibus, alliq, caesis membris, spectaculum contumeliae nudi propter nomen Domini portantes.[1]

Some unusual tortures were used against the Christians at Rome or in Roman provinces. Saturninus, bishop of Toulouse, had his feet fastened to the tail of a bull, which was then driven down the steps of the temple, by which means the bishop's brains were dashed out. A Christian priest of Abitina, of the same name, Saturninus, after the worst tortures (scourging, tearing his flesh with hooks, burning with hot irons, etc.) was stoned to death. Calepodius had a mill-stone tied about his neck and was thrown into the Tiber. Marcus, Bishop of Arethusa, was hung in a basket in the heat of the sun at Alexandria, smeared with honey and stung to death by wasps.

The following extracts taken from Foxe will illustrate the various methods by which the early martyrs met their deaths. The extracts are picked at random from the first ten persecutions of the Church.

Sanctus also, another of the martyrs, who in the midst of his torments endured more pains than the nature of man is thought capable of. . . . And when they had nothing to vex him with, they clapped plates of brass red-hot to the most tender parts of his body, wherewith his body indeed being scorched, yet he never shrunk for the matter, but was bold and constant in his confession. . . . Truly his body was a sufficient witness what torments he suffered; for it was all drawn together, and most pitifully wounded and scorched, so that it had lost the proper shape of a man.

When Maturus, Blandina and Attalus were brought together to the common scaffold, there in the face of the people to be cast to and devoured of the beasts. And Maturus, with Sanctus, being brought the second time to the scaffold, suffered again all kinds of torments, as though hitherto they had suffered nothing at all;

[1] "Some slain with the sword; some burnt with fire; some scourged with whips; some stabbed with forks; some fastened to the cross; some drowned in the sea; some flayed alive; some had their tongues cut out; some were stoned to death; some killed with cold; some starved with hunger; some had their hands cut off, or were otherwise dismembered, and so left naked to the contempt of the world" (Foxe).

yea, rather the adversary being oftentimes put to the worst, they as striving for the crown, suffered again more scourgings, the tearing of wild beasts, and what thing else soever the frantic people on every side cried for and willed. And above all the rest they brought an iron chair in which their bodies being set, were so fried and scorched, as on a gridiron fried on the coals, which filled with the savour of the frying all the people that stood by. . . . And thus these holy men, after they had long continued alive in this most horrible conflict, at the length were slain, being made all that whole day a spectacle unto the world.

And first flying upon a certain priest of ours, named Metra, they apprehended him, and brought him forth to make him speak after their wicked blasphemy; which he would not do, they laid upon him with staves and clubs, and with sharp reeds pricked his face and eyes, and afterwards bringing him out into the suburbs, there they stoned him to death. Then they took a faithful woman, called Quinta, and brought her to the temples of their idols, to compel her to worship with them; which when she refused to do, and abhorred their idols, they bound her feet, and drew her through the whole street of the city upon the hard stones and so dashing her against mill-stones, and scourging her with whips, brought her to the same place of the suburbs, as they did the other before, where she likewise ended her life.[1]

Oh! what tongue is able to express the fury and madness of the tyrant's[2] heart! Now he stamped, he stared, he ramped, he seemed as one out of his wits: his eyes like fire glowed, his mouth like a boar foamed, his teeth like a hell-hound grinned; now not a reasonable man, but a roaring lion he might be called. Kindle the fire, he cried; of wood make no spare. Hath this villain deluded the emperor? Away with him, away with him: whip him with scourges, jerk him with rods, buffet him with fists, brain him with clubs. Jesteth the traitor with the emperor? Pinch him with fiery tongs, gird him with burning-plates, bring out the strongest chains, and the fire-forks, and the grated bed of iron; on fire with it, bind the rebel hand and foot; and when the bed is fire hot, on with him; roast him, broil him, toss him, turn him. On pain of our high displeasure do everyman his office, O ye tormentors! The word was no sooner spoken, but all was done.[3]

[1] The town referred to was Alexandria.
[2] Valarianus.
[3] Martyrdom of St. Laurence.

VINCENT, a Deacon in the Christian Church, tortured and placed on a gridiron over the fire.

Such another was Peter, who among divers and sundry torments, among whom, he being naked, was lifted up, his whole body being so beaten with whips and torn, that a man might see the bare bones; and after they had mingled vinegar and salt together, they poured it upon the most tender parts of his body, and lastly roasted him at a slow fire, as a man would roast flesh to eat.

In this persecution[1] of Trajan, besides the other afore-mentioned, also suffered Phocas, Bishop of Pontus, whom Trajan, because he would not do sacrifice to Neptune, caused to be cast into a hot lime-kiln, and afterwards to be put into a scalding bath, where the constant godly martyr . . . ended his life.

Felicitas, with her seven children, suffered in Rome, under M. Anton. Verus . . . of whom her first and eldest son, Januarius, after he was whipped and scourged with rods, was prest to death with leaden weights. Felix and Philip had their brains beaten out with mawls. Silvanus was cast down headlong, and had his neck broken. Furthermore, Alexander, Vitalis and Martialis were beheaded. Last of all Felicitas, the mother . . . was slain with the sword.

Bergomensis in his eighth book mentions divers martyred under Decius, as Meniatus, who suffered at Florence; of Agatha, a holy virgin of Sicily, who is said to suffer divers and bitter torments under Quintilianus, the pro-consul, with imprisonment, beatings, famine, rackings, rolled also upon sharp shells and hot coals, having moreover her breasts cut from her body.

Furthermore, that the kinds of death and punishment were so great and horrible, as no man's tongue is able to express. In the beginning, when the emperor by his subtlety and cunning rather dallied than showed his rigour, he threatened them with bands and imprisonments; but within a while, when he began to work the matter in good earnest, he devised innumerable sorts of torments and punishments, as whippings, and scourgings, rackings, horrible scrapings, sword, fire, and shipboats, wherein a great number being put were sunk and drowned in the bottom of the sea. Also hanging them upon crosses, binding them to the bodies of dead trees with their heads downwards, hanging them by the middles from gallows, till they died of hunger; throwing them alive to such kind of wild beasts as would devour them, as lions, bears, leopards and wild bulls. Pricking and thrusting in

[1] Third.

43

them with bodkins and talons of beasts, till they were almost dead; lifting them up on high with their heads downward, even as in Thebais they did upon the women, being naked and unclothed, one of their feet tied and lifted on high, and so hanging down with their bodies, which thing to see was very pitiful; with other devised sorts of punishments most tragical or rather tyrannical, and pitiful to describe; at first, the binding of them to trees, and the boughs thereof; the pulling and tearing asunder of their members and joints, being tied to the boughs and arms of trees. The mangling of them with axes, the choking of them with smoke by small and slow fires, the dismembering of their hands, ears and feet with other joints; as the holy martyrs of Alexandria suffered the scorching and broiling of them with coals, not unto death, but every day renewed. With such kinds of torments the martyrs of Antioch were afflicted. But in Pontus, other horrible punishments, and fearful to be heard, did the martyrs of Christ suffer; of whom, some had their finger-ends under the nails thrust in with sharp bodkins; some all besprinkled with boiling lead, having their most necessary members cut from them; some others suffering most filthy, intollerable, and undurable torments and pains in their bowels and privy members.

To conclude . . . everyman might torment the holy martyrs as he pleased, some beat them with cudgels, some with rods, some with whips, some with thongs, and some with cords, and this example of beating was in sundry ways executed, and with much cruelty. For some of them having their hands bound behind their backs, were lifted up upon timber logs and with certain instruments their members and joints were stretched forth, whereupon their whole bodies hanging, were subject to the will of the tormentors, who were commanded to afflict them with all manner of torments, and not on their sides only (like as homicides were) but upon their bellies, thighs and legs, they scratched them with the talons and claws of wild beasts. Some others were seen to hang by one hand upon the engine, whereby they might feel the more grievous pulling out of the rest of their joints and members. Some others were in such sort bound upon pillars with their faces turned to the wall, having no stay under their feet, and were violently weighed down with the weight of their bodies, that by reason of their strict binding, they being drawn out might be more grievously tormented. And this suffered they, not only during the time of their examination, and while the sheriff had to do with them, but also the whole day long. And whilst the judge went thus from one to another, he by his authority appointed certain officers to attend upon those he left, that they might not be let down, until either through the intolerableness of the pain, or by the extremity of cold, they being near the point of death, should be let down, and so were they haled upon the ground. And further they were commanded, that they should show not so much as one spark of mercy or compassion to us; as though our souls and bodies should die together. And therefore yet another torment our adversaries devised, to augment our former plagues; after that they had most lamentably beaten them, they devised moreover a new kind of rack, wherein they lying upright, were stretched by both the feet above the fourth stop or hole, with sharp shells or shares strewed under

them, after  a strange kind
of engine to us here unknown.
Others were cast down upon
the pavement, where they
were oppressed so thick and so
grievously with torments, that
it is scarcely to be credited
what afflictions they endured.

Som burned with Straw tyed about them to cover their nakednefs

CHAPTER II

OF THE CULINARY ARTS

I watch'd a woman burn; and in her agony
The mother came upon her—a child was born—
And, sir, they hurl'd it back into the fire,
That, being but baptised in fire, the babe
Might be in fire for ever. Ah, good neighbour,
There should be something fierier than fire
To yield them their deserts.—TENNYSON, *Queen Mary*

Som Burnt at ſtakes

As we have seen, burning to death was a common punishment in early times. The Romans employed it especially in the case of the Christian martyrs[1] and as a penalty for arson.

After the establishment of Christianity in Rome, burning alive was not recognised as a penalty for heresy under the Imperial code until Frederick II (1222–1223) made it a civil law punishment.

At a later date the Gothic codes used burning as a punishment for adultery, and the Middle Ages extended its use to heresy and witchcraft, and to a lesser degree, to many crimes, such as poisoning or arson.

In England the common law until 1790[2] permitted the

---

[1] Some of whom were more fortunate than others. St. Polycarp was bound to a stake and the fire lighted, "and when the flame began to blaze to a very great height, behold, a wonderful miracle appeared. For the flame making a kind of arch, like the sail of a ship filled with the wind, encompassed as in a circle, the body of the holy martyr. Who stood in the midst of it, not as if his flesh were burnt, but as bread that is baked, or as gold or silver glowing in the furnace. At length, when those wicked men saw that his body could not be consumed by fire, they commanded the executioner to go near to him, and stick his dagger in him" (Foxe).

[2] 30 George III. cap. 28. The last woman burnt in England was Christian Murphy (alias Bowman), who suffered in 1789.

burning of women accused of high or petty treason, as this punishment was considered more decent than hanging, followed by exposure on the gibbet. Concerning this, Sir William Blackstone writes:

For as the decency due to the sex forbids the exposing and publicly mangling their bodies, their sentence (which is to the full as terrible to sensation as the other), is, to be drawn to the gallows, and there to be burnt alive; . . . the humanity of the English nation has authorised, by a tacit consent, an almost general mitigation of such part of these judgments as savours of torture and cruelty, a sledge or hurdle being usually allowed to such traitors as are condemned to be drawn, and there being very few instances (and those accidental and by negligence) of any persons being disembowelled or burnt previously deprived of sensation by strangling.

The Church courts had no power to condemn to death, so that burning for heresy was at first not recognised as a legal penalty, though the Crown reserved the right, probably illegally, of issuing writs *de haeretico comburendo*. However, in 1400 the Statute of *de haeretico comburendo* was passed and burning alive as a legal punishment for heresy became part of the law. This Statute was repealed in 1533, but re-enacted as a punishment for denying transubstantiation in 1539.[1] On the accession of Mary, the Act of 1400 and certain subsidiary Acts were re-enacted, to be abolished again on the accession of Elizabeth in 1558. Therefore the heretics burnt before 1400 and those burnt during the reigns of Elizabeth and James I, were punished illegally under writs issued by the Crown.

In Anglo-Saxon times witches were burnt in England, but after the Norman conquest the punishment was changed to hanging, unlike that in other countries, where burning was the recognised practice, until it became the custom to burn women instead of hanging them.

It is difficult to say who was the first woman burnt

[1] Six Articles Act.

under the Common Law, but the annals of King's Lynn mention a woman suffering this punishment in 1515 for the murder of her husband; and in the same town Margaret Read was burnt for witchcraft in 1590.

In 1722 Eleanor Elsom, who was condemned to be burnt for the murder of her husband, clothed herself in a cloth saturated with tar and with her limbs smeared with the same substance, and a tarred bonnet placed upon her head, "she was brought out of the prison barefoot, and, being put on a hurdle, was drawn on a sledge to the place of execution near the gallows. Upon arrival, some time was passed in prayer, after which the executioner placed her on a tar barrel, a height of three feet, against the stake. A rope ran through a pulley in the stake, and was placed around her neck, she herself fixed it with her hands. Three irons also held her body to the stake, and the rope being pulled tight, the tar barrel was taken aside and the fire lighted. The account in the *Lincoln Date Book* states that she was probably quite dead before the fire reached her, as the executioner pulled upon the rope several times whilst the irons were being fixed. The body was seen amid the flames for nearly half an hour, though, through the dryness of the wood and the quantity of tar, the fire was exceedingly fierce."[1]

The attempts to strangle the victim before she was burnt were not always successful. Catherine Harper was executed at Tyburn on the 3rd of November, 1726. When she was being strangled in the accustomed manner, the fire scorched the hands of the executioner and he released the rope before she became unconscious. She suffered for a considerable time.

Burning alive in England, as a punishment for heresy, commenced illegally with the burning of Alban in 304, and ended, as illegally, with the burnings of Bartholomew Legate, at Smithfield, and Edward Wightman, at Lichfield, in 1610.

[1] William Andrews's *Old-Time Punishments.*

There were isolated instances of the burning of heretics before 1400, but it was not until legal sanction was obtained that the fires really began to blaze in England.

It was a common practice during Mary's reign for the victim to tie a bag of gunpowder to his or her body before being burnt, so that death would follow more quickly. There were so many people burnt alive at this time that it is somewhat difficult to select suitable instances, but Ainsworth in his *Tower of London* gives a good description of such an execution, even though it is historically inaccurate,[1] and, in comparison, there are set out below two extracts from Froude's *Mary Tudor,* the accuracy of which cannot be denied.

As the bell ceased tolling the hour of midnight, a lugubrious procession slowly issued from beneath the gloomy archway of the Coalharbour Gate. First came four yeomen of the guard walking two and two, and bearing banners of black silk, displaying large white crosses. Then twelve deacons in the same order, in robes of black silk and flat caps, each carrying a long lighted wax taper. Then a priest's assistant, in a white surplice, with a red cross in front, bareheaded and swinging a large bell heavily to and fro. Then two young priests, likewise bareheaded, and in white surplices, each holding a lighted taper in a massive silver candlestick. Then an old priest with the mitre. Then two chantry-priests in their robes singing the Miserere. Then four Carmelite monks, each with a large rosary hanging from his wrist, supporting a richly gilt square canopy, decorated at each corner with a sculptured cross, beneath which walked Bonner, in his scarlet chimere and white rochet. Then came Feckenham and other prelates, followed by two more chantry-priests singing the same doleful hymn as their predecessors. Then came a long train of halberdiers. Then the prisoner, clothed in sackcloth and barefooted, walking between two friars of the lowly order of Saint Francis, who besought him, in piteous tones, to repent ere it was too late. And lastly, the rear was brought up by a company of archers of the queen's bodyguard.

As soon as the procession had formed in the order it arrived

[1] This burning never, in fact, took place.

round the place of execution, the prisoner was brought forward by the two friars, who for the last time earnestly exhorted him to recant, and save his soul alive. But he pushed them from him, saying, "Get hence, ye popish wolves! ye raveners of Christ's faithful flock! Back to the idolatrous Antichrist of Rome who sent you hither. I will have none of your detestable doctrines. Get hence, I say, and trouble me no more."

When the friars drew back, he would have addressed the assemblage. But a halberdier, by Bonner's command, thrust a pike into his mouth and silenced him. A wild and uncouth figure, with strong but clumsily formed limbs, coarse repulsive features, lighted up by a savage smile, now stepped forward. It was Wolfytt, the sworn tormentor. He was attired in a jerkin and hose of tawny leather. His arms and chest were bare, and covered with a thick pile of red hair. His ragged locks and beard, of the same disgusting colour, added to his hideous and revolting appearance. He was armed with a long iron pitchfork, and had a large hammer and a pair of pincers stuck in his girdle. Behind him came Mauger and Nightgall.

A deep and awful silence now prevailed throughout the concourse. Not a breath was drawn, and every eye was bent upon the victim. He was seized and stripped by Mauger and Wolfytt, the latter of whom dragged him to the stake, which the poor zealot reverently kissed as he reached it, placed the iron girdle round his waist, and riveted it to the post. In this position, Underhill cried with a loud voice: "God shall preserve Queen Jane and speedily restore her to the throne, that she may deliver this unhappy realm from the popish idolaters who would utterly subvert it."

Several voices cried "Amen!" and Wolfytt, who was nailing the girdle at the time, commanded him to keep silence, and enforced the order by striking him a severe blow on the temples with the hammer.

"You might have spared me that, friend," observed Underhill meekly. And he then added, in a lower tone, "Have mercy upon me, O Lord, for I am weak! O Lord, heal me, for all my bones are vexed!"

While the fagots were heaped around him by Mauger and Nightgall, he continued to pray fervently; and when all was made ready, he cried, "Dear Father, I beseech Thee to give once more

50

Cruel torturing of the REVD. ROBERT SAMUEL.

Burning of the REVD. ROBERT SAMUEL, at Bosford, in Suffolk

to this realm the blessing of Thy word, with godly peace. Purge and purify me by this fire in Christ's death and passion through Thy spirit, that I may be an acceptable burnt-offering in Thy sight. Farewell, dear friends. Pray for me, and pray with me."

As he spoke, Nightgall seized a torch and applied in to the fagots. His example was imitated by Mauger and Wolfytt, and the pile was speedily kindled. The dry wood crackled, and the smoke rose in thick volumes. The flames then burst forth, and burning fast and fiercely, cast a lurid light upon the countenances of the spectators, upon the windows of Saint Peter's Chapel, and upon the grey walls of the White Tower. As yet, the fire had not reached the victim; the wind blowing strongly from the west carried it aside. But in a few seconds it gained sufficient ascendancy, and his sufferings commenced. For a short space he endured them without a groan. But as the flames mounted, notwithstanding all his efforts, the sharpness of the torment overcame him. Placing his hands behind his neck, he made desperate attempts to draw himself farther up the stake, out of the reach of the devouring element. But the iron girdle effectually restrained him. He then lost all command of himself; and his eyes starting from their sockets—his convulsed features—his erected hair, and writhing frame—proclaimed the extremity of his agony. He sought relief by adding to his own torture. Crossing his hands upon his breast, and grasping either shoulder, he plunged his nails deeply into the flesh. It was a horrible sight, and a shuddering groan burst from the assemblage. Fresh fagots were added by Nightgall and his companions, who moved around the pyre like fiends engaged in some impious rite. The flames again arose brightly and fiercely. By this time the lower limbs were entirely consumed; and throwing back his head, and uttering a loud and lamentable yell which was heard all over the fortress, the wretched victim gave up the ghost."[1]

The following is the description of the burning of Bishop Hooper for heresy at Oxford:

He was undressed to his shirt, in the cold; a pound of gunpowder was tied between his legs and as much more under either arm; he was fastened with an iron hoop to the stake, and he assisted with his own hands to arrange the fagots round him.

[1] W. H. Ainsworth's *Tower of London*.

The fire was then brought, but the wood was green; the dry straw only kindled, and burning for a few moments was blown away by the wind. A violent flame paralysed the nerves at once, a slow one was torture. More fagots were thrown in, and again lighted, and this time the martyr's face was singed and scorched; but again the flames sank, and the hot damp sticks smouldered round his legs. He wiped his eyes with his hands, and cried: "For God's love, good people, let me have more fire!" A third supply of dry fuel was laid about him, and this time the powder exploded, but it had been ill placed, or was not enough. "Lord Jesu, have mercy on me!" he exclaimed. "Lord Jesu, receive my spirit!" These were his last articulate words; but his lips were long seen to move, and he continued to beat his breast with his hands. It was not till after three-quarters of an hour of torment that he at last expired."[1]

The following extract relates to the martyrdom of Ridley and Latimer:

A chain was passed round their bodies, and fastened with a staple.

A friend brought a bag of powder and hung it round Ridley's neck.

"I will take it to be sent of God," Ridley said. "Have you more, for my brother?"

"Yea, sir," the friend answered. "Give it him betimes then," Ridley replied, "lest ye be too late."

The fire was then brought. The lighted torch was laid to the fagots. "Be of good comfort, Master Ridley," Latimer cried at the cackling of the flames. "Play the man; we shall this day light such a candle by God's grace, in England, as I trust shall never be put out."

"*In manus tuas, Domine, commendo spiritum meum*," cried Ridley. "*Domine, recipe spiritum meum*."

"O Father of Heaven," said Latimer, on the other side, "receive my soul."

Latimer died first: as the flame blazed up about him, he bathed his hands in it, and stroked his face. The powder exploded, and he became instantly senseless.

[1] A. J. Froude.

His companion was less fortunate. The sticks had been piled too thickly over the gorse that was under them; the fire smouldered round his legs, and the sensation of suffering was unusually protracted. "I cannot burn," he called; "Lord have mercy on me; let the fire come to me; I cannot burn." His brother-in-law, with awkward kindness, threw on more wood, which only kept down the flame. At last someone lifted the pile with "a bill", and let in the air; the red tongues of fire shot up fiercely. Ridley wrested himself into the middle of them, and the powder did its work.

Scotland followed the Roman lead, and in Charles II's day the law still was that witches were to be "worried at the stake and then burnt". A witch was burnt as late as 1708 at Dornoch.

In Jamaica a negro was burnt alive in 1760[1] for taking part in a local rising. The victim was made to sit on the ground, his body chained to an iron stake and the fire was first applied to his feet, "he uttered not a word, and saw his legs reduced to ashes with the utmost firmness and composure; after which, one of his arms by some means getting loose, he snatched a brand from the fire that was consuming him and flung it in the face of the executioner".

Louis IX of France followed the example of Frederick II and sanctioned the punishment of burning alive in his Establishments of 1270.

The method of execution by burning in France was generally as follows: the victim having previously undergone the usual tortures, a stake was erected on the spot specially designed for the execution, and round it a pile was prepared composed of alternate layers of straw and wood, rising to about the height of a man. Care was taken to leave a free space round the stake for the victim, and also a passage by which to lead him to it. Having been stripped of his clothes and dressed in a shirt smeared with sulphur, he had to walk to the centre of the pile through a narrow opening, and then to be tightly bound to the stake with ropes and chains. After this, fagots and straw

[1] Bryan Edward's *History of the British Colonies in the West Indies*.

were thrown into the space through which he had passed to the stake, until he was entirely covered by them, when the pile was fired on all sides at once. Sometimes the sentence was that the culprit should be delivered to the flames only after having been strangled. In this case the corpse was immediately placed where the victim would have been placed alive and the punishment lost much of its horror. As an example of this practice Deschauffours was garrotted previous to being burnt in 1733. It often happened that the executioner, in order to shorten the sufferings of the condemned, when he prepared the pile, placed a large and pointed iron bar amongst the fagots and opposite the stake, breast high, so that directly the fire was lighted the bar was pushed against the victim, giving a mortal blow to the unfortunate wretch, who would otherwise have been devoured by the flames slowly. If, according to the wording of the sentence, the ashes of the criminal were to be scattered in the winds, as soon as it was possible to approach the centre of the pile, a few ashes were taken in a shovel and sprinkled in the air. They were not satisfied in burning the living, they also delivered to the flames the bodies of those who had died a natural death before their execution could be carried out, as if an anticipated death should not be allowed to save them from the punishment which they had escaped. It also happened in cases where a person's guilt was proved only after his decease, that his body was disinterred and carried to the stake to be burnt.

The following description of an execution in France by burning alive is taken from Alexandre Dumas's *Massacres in the South*. The execution took place at the beginning of the eighteenth century. The victims were Protestants, and were sentenced for taking part in the Camisard Rising.

Catinat was thereupon sent back to the palace, where his trial was soon begun and ended. The three others were already con-

Sentence read against the dead bodies of BUCER and PHAGIUS, by
the BISHOP of CHESTER.

The bodies and books of BUCER and PHAGIUS burnt at
Cambridge, three years after burial.

victed, and it only remained to pronounce sentence. Catinat and Ravanel, who were more guilty than the others, were sentenced to be burned alive. Some councillors were in favour of sentencing Catinat to be torn apart by four horses; but the majority were for the stake, because *that punishment was of longer duration and more agonizing than the being torn apart.*

Villas and Jonquet were sentenced to be broken on the wheel alive, but this distinction was made between them: the latter was to be thrown living into the fire at which Catinat and Ravanel were burning. The sentence provided, furthermore, that each of the condemned should first be put to the ordinary and extra-ordinary question. Catinat, who was naturally of a violent disposition, endured the torture with courage, heaping curses upon his executioners. Ravanel endured the most excruciating suffering with superhuman firmness, so that the torturers were the first to grow weary. Jonquet had little to say, and disclosed only matters of the most trifling importance. Villas admitted that the conspirators had formed a scheme to carry off the marshal and M. de Baville when they were out walking, and he further said that the plot was hatched at the house of one Boëton de Saint-Laurent d'Aigorze, at Milland in Rouergue.

On the following day, April 22, 1705, they were taken from the prison and drawn to the place of execution upon two carts, being unable to walk because the bones in their legs were crushed by the extraordinary question. They were arranged in pairs according to the punishment they were respectively to undergo: Catinat with Ravanel, and Villas with Jonquet.

They began by binding Catinat and Ravanel to the same post, back to back, taking care to place Catinat on the side from which the wind was blowing that his agony might last the longer; then they lighted the fire on Ravanel's side.

As was anticipated this precaution was productive of much gratification to those who took delight in human suffering; the wind was blowing with some force, so that the flame rose diagonally and slowly consumed Catinat's legs, who, says the author of the *Histoire des Camisards*, bore the torture with some impatience. Ravanel, however, was a hero to the last, pausing in his singing only to encourage his companions in death, whom he could not see, but whom he could hear cursing and groaning; then resuming his psalms, which he continued to sing until the flames stifled his voice. Just as he breathed his last Jonquet was taken from the wheel with his four limbs shattered and hanging by shreds, and tossed, a shapeless, but still living, mass, upon the half-consumed pile. From the midst of the flames he cried: "Courage, Catinat! We shall meet in heaven!"

A few moments later the post to which the victim was bound burned through at its base and fell, pulling Catinat backwards into the glowing furnace, where he was soon suffocated. This circumstance rendered unavailing the precautions they had taken, and to the intense disgust of the spectators the torture lasted hardly three-quarters of an hour.

Villas lived three hours longer upon his wheel, and died without a single murmur.

Before drawing to a conclusion the subject of burning alive, there is an interesting case to be mentioned which took place at the Cape of Good Hope in 1787. The Cape was then a Dutch settlement, and a dispute arose between the natives and the colonists which ended in the murder of one of the Colonists. The Chief of the tribe to which the murderer belonged was ordered to find the offender and punish him. This was executed in the following manner. The natives made a great fire to which they brought the criminal, attended by all his friends and relations, who took their leave of him, not in sorrowful lamentations, but in feasting, dancing and drinking. When the unfortunate criminal had been plied with liquor till he became insensibly drunk, his friends made him dance till he was spent with fatigue. In that state they threw him into the fire, and concluded the horrid scene with a hideous howl, which they set up immediately he was dispatched.

Some time after this, a Dutchman killed a native, upon which the chief came and demanded justice for the blood of his countryman; but the offender happened to be one of the best accountants and a person whom the Factory could ill spare. However, means were devised to render satisfaction to the natives under a colour of justice. They appointed a day for the execution of the murderer, when the natives assembled in great numbers, little conscious of the trick that was to be played upon them. A scaffold was erected, and the criminal was brought forward, dressed in white and attended by a minister. After praying, singing psalms, etc., the mock executioner presented him with a flaming draught, which was no other than a little burning brandy, and the criminal received it with all the outward signs of horror and dread; his hands shook, his body trembled and his whole frame appeared to be in the most violent agitation. At last he swallowed the fiery drink, and after trembling for a few minutes he fell down dead apparently, and a blanket was thrown over him. The natives raised a shout that rent the air and retired perfectly satisfied, observing, "The Dutch have been more severe than ourselves; for they have put fire into the criminal, whereas we only put the criminal in the fire."

Boiling to death was a favourite form of punishment in the Middle Ages, and was actually sanctioned by English law in 1531 as a penalty for poisoners. This Act remained on the Statute-book for sixteen years. Various people suffered under the Act. Richard Roose was publicly boiled at Smithfield in 1531, and in the same year a maid-servant suffered the same fate at King's Lynn, for poisoning her mistress. In 1542 Margaret Davy suffered death in this way at Smithfield.

Prior to 1531 boiling to death had been used illegally as a punishment for coining or poisoning, and an interesting case is mentioned in the *Chronicles of the Grey Friars*.[1] The victim having been found guilty of poisoning was fastened to a chain and lowered into boiling water several times until he died. This took place at Smithfield in 1522.

As will have been seen from the description of the execution of Francis Ravaillac, which is set out in the preface, tearing the flesh with red-hot pincers as a preliminary to execution was used in France, but it was also used in

[1] Published by the Camden Society, 1852.

57

other countries; and the Earl of Athol was put to death at the Cross at Edinburgh, for the murder of James I of Scotland in 1437, with the most cruel ingenuity a barbarous age could devise. His flesh was lacerated and torn with heated irons, and he was placed on a high pillar, and crowned in derision as the King of Traitors with a red-hot crown.

In France methods of torture by heat varied according to the provinces, but certain punishments were general. Parricides or persons guilty of High Treason were burnt with sulphur fire, and their eyes were often destroyed by the infliction of the *bassin ardent*. Though this latter torture did not involve the loss of life, it was very unpleasant. The victim was strapped in a chair and a red-hot brazier was passed backwards and forwards in front of his eyes until they were destroyed by the scorching heat. This reminds one of the Chinese torture of burning out the eyes with small bags or pads of unslaked lime.[1]

Blinding was quite a common form of punishment in the early days, and was especially used for such crimes as adultery, perjury, or theft. Boiling vinegar was frequently used. A whole army of Bulgarians was said to have been blinded by order of the Emperor Basil. Some of the Eastern emperors suffered this punishment, the eyeballs being torn from their heads.

There were two other tortures in general use in France which cannot be passed over without mention. The first being the placing of hot eggs under the armpits; and the second, the tying of lighted candles to the fingers of the accused, so that candle and flesh burned simultaneously.

In Brittany the culprit was tied to an iron arm-chair and was slowly pushed near to a blazing fire.

At Nuremberg, according to the description of the Rev. A. Wylie, before that famous collection of instruments of torture was purchased by the Rt. Hon. the Earl of

[1] The same result was obtained in China by removing the eyelids of the culprit and binding him to a post with his head facing the sun.

Shrewsbury in 1889, there were to be seen iron ladles designed for "molten lead or boiling pitch to be poured down the throat of the victim and convert his body into a burning cauldron".

The North American Indians bound their captives to stakes and tortured them in the most fiendish manner until they gave no signs of consciousness. To end the performance their favourite device was to heap up gunpowder on the victim's head, which, on being exploded, sent a final thrill of agony through his mutilated frame.

In India the cruel practice of *suttee*, or burning the widows alive with the corpse of their husbands, and the military punishment of tying mutineers to the mouth of a cannon and then firing it, have now both been abolished, but the latter was in practice as late as 1858. Fakirs, or mendicant friars, still sometimes light fires on the tops of their heads until the scalp is burnt through to the bone.

Edward II of England (1307–1327) was tortured to death in Berkeley Castle, but no bruises or wounds were found upon his body. He is said to have been burnt internally with a red-hot iron by Gournay and Ogle.[1]

Ferdinand VII (1810–1859) of Naples carried a small collapsible torture chair about with him on his campaigns. It had pointed legs by which it could be fixed into the ground and a pan underneath for the burning coals.

Branding was a mode of punishment favoured in nearly all countries by the criminal law. Greek slaves were branded with a "$Δ$",[2] and in Rome both robbers and runaway slaves were branded with the letter "F".[3] Under Constantine the branding was inflicted on the hand, arm or calf of the leg and not on the face. In France galley-

---

[1] The execution is said to have taken place under the order of his wife, Isabelle, the She-Wolf of France. Hence Gray says: "She-Wolf of France who tear'st the bowels of thy mangled mate."

[2] Standing for $Δοῦλος$.   [3] Standing for "Fur" or "Fugitivus".

slaves could be branded "TF"[1] as late as 1832. In Germany branding was illegal.

England employed branding in Anglo-Saxon times and the penalty was authorised by law. Under a Statute[2] of Edward VI runaway servants, vagabonds and gipsies were branded with the letter "V" and "fraymakers" with the letter "F". Vagabonds were adjudged to be the slave of any purchaser for two years. If the slave absented himself for fourteen days during the two years, he was branded on the forehead or cheek with the letter "S" and adjudged to be the slave of his master for ever. Severe punishments prevailed for brawling in sacred places. If weapons were used the offender was condemned to lose an ear, or if he had already lost both ears, he was branded as a "fraymaker" on the cheek. As late as the eighteenth century the punishment for being found in possession of clippings or filings of the current coin was a fine of £500 and branding on the right cheek with the letter "R". The punishment of branding slaves with an "S" on their foreheads was abolished in 1636.

From the time of Henry VII until 1822 branding was inflicted for all offences which received "benefit of the clergy",[3] and an Act of 1698 caused criminals convicted of petty theft and larceny, who claimed the benefit, to be "burnt in the most visible part of the left cheek nearest the nose".

During the eighteenth century it became common to evade the law by inflicting the branding with a cold iron, and this finally led to the abolition of the penalty in 1829 for all offences except those under the military law.

It was not until as late as 1879 that branding was totally abolished in England.

Military law enacted that deserters should be branded with a "D" and bad soldiers with the letters "BC",[4]

---

[1] Travaux forcés.   [2] Statute of Vagabonds, 1547.
[3] English justice decreed that those who could read, and who consequently might be presumed to have a knowledge of the law, were only burned in the hand for crimes which were punished by death in those who could not read and who might, therefore, well be supposed ignorant of the law.
[4] Bad character.

but branding in the army was inflicted by tattooing with ink and gunpowder and not with a hot iron. Directions as to the branding of deserters are set out in the British Military Act of 1858.

The method by which branding was inflicted, before the cold iron came into use, was for the prisoner's hand or limb to be held by an iron ring. The brander heated his weapon with the appropriate letter till it was red-hot and then pressed it against the flesh of his victim. The brander then examined the mark and exclaimed, "A fair mark, my Lord."

It was customary to order criminals to hold up their hands before receiving sentence to see if they had been branded previously.

Som Broiled vpon Gridiron

CHAPTER III

A PIECE OF CORD

Hangman, I charge you to pay particular attention to this lady. Scourge her soundly, man; scourge her till her blood runs down! It is Christmas, a cold time for Madam to strip. See that you warm her shoulders thoroughly!—JUDGE JEFFREYS.

IF one had to say which form of torture had been the most popular, it would be difficult to choose between the whip[1] and the rack. These two stand out from all other methods of torture for universal popularity.

The *equuleus* (or rack) was one of the earliest Roman forms of torture and its use was continued until torture was abolished. An interesting case in Roman history was the infliction of the rack on Julietta, a Lyconian, who was seized at Tarsus and brought before Alexander, the governor, to whom she admitted being a Christian. Her son, Cyricus, was taken from her and she was put on the rack and stretched with great severity. The governor, hearing Cyricus crying to get to his mother, noticed his great beauty and took him up on his knee, endeavouring to pacify him. Nothing however could quiet Cyricus and, at length, he lisped out the words in imitation of his mother, "I am a Christian". On hearing this the governor hurled the child down in front of its mother and dashed its brains out. The mother watched the whole transaction from the rack. To complete Julietta's execution, she had boiling

[1] In fact, so common did flogging become in certain countries that the expression "rule by kurbash" became a popular phrase to describe a despotic Government. The kurbash is a strap of about a yard in length made of hippopotamus or rhinoceros hide used for flogging in various Mohammedan countries.

MARTYRDOM OF JULIETTA, a Licenson, who was racked to
death, and her child hurled on the ground before her face, by
which its brains were dashed out.

pitch poured over her feet, her sides were torn with hooks and she was finally beheaded on the 16th of April, 305.[1]

As will have been seen, the object of the rack was to stretch the victim's limbs in as painful a manner as possible, and in England the engine was an oblong frame of wood, raised slightly from the ground, having a fixed bar at one end to which the legs were fastened and a movable bar at the other to which the hands were tied. The latter bar was rounded and could be rolled on its own axis, thus straining the joints of the sufferers till they became dislocated. But there were many different kinds of rack, the most common being similar to the English rack, but with movable bars at both ends, the most terrible being the Austrian ladder, which will be dealt with hereafter.[2]

In England the rack was not so extensively used as in other countries. It was introduced into England by John Holland, Fourth Duke of Exeter, in 1447, and when it was set up in the Tower of London it was popularly known as "the Duke of Exeter's daughter".[3] People undergoing the punishment of the rack were popularly said to be "wedded to the Duke's of Exeter's daughter", just as other unfortunates were wedded to "the scavenger's daughter", which was an instrument exactly opposite in principle. It is believed that the first marriage took place when Hawkins wedded the duke's daughter and the last

[1] The Rev. Henry Southwell's *New Book of Martyrs*.
[2] According to *The Penny Magazine* of 1832, Dr. Lingard is said to have described the English rack as "a large open frame of oak, raised three feet from the ground. The prisoner was laid under it on his back on the floor; his wrists and ankles were attached by cords to two collars at the ends of the frame; then were moved by levers in opposite directions, till the body rose to a level with the frame. Questions were then put, and, if the answers did not prove satisfactory, the sufferer was stretched more and more till the bones started from their sockets." It would appear from this description that a form of rack was used in England with two movable bars, but no such rack has yet been discovered.
[3] "The trial by rack is utterly unknown to the law of England, though once, when the Dukes of Exeter and Suffolk and other ministers of Henry VI had laid a design to introduce the Civil Law into the kingdom as the rule of government, for the beginning thereof they erected a rack for torture, which was called in derision the Duke of Exeter's daughter" (Blackstone).

was the unfortunate Archer, mentioned above, who died in 1640.

The rack came into operation chiefly during the reigns of Mary and James I. Mrs. Anne Askew[1] suffered this torture under Henry VIII, prior to being burnt. Sir Thomas Wyatt, the son of the poet, was racked in the Tower for raising a rebellion against Mary. Father Campian, a deacon who abjured protestantism and became a Jesuit, was, in 1581, put to the rack by order of Elizabeth, to extort a confession, and was afterwards executed at Tyburn. Some of the conspirators of the Gunpowder treason suffered this form of matrimony; Father Oldcorn was racked five times, on one occasion for several hours, and was subsequently hanged at Worcester, cut down while alive, disembowelled and quartered. Guy Fawkes himself suffered the rack amongst other tortures.

The rack was very popular in France, where it was called the "Banc de Torture". There is a good account of a victim undergoing the torture of the rack in the archives of Montauban in France.

In the year 1765, the 7th day of December, we, Dominique, de Sadons, King's Counsellor, &c., Pierre Francois Ayrolle des Angles, Lieutenant Colonel of Cavalry, &c., being at the request of the Royal Prosecutor in attendance in the torture chamber in the prison of the Royal Castle of Montauban, ordered Pierre Delluque, *alias* Toulouse, accused prisoner, to be brought before us, and read over to him the Prevotal Judgment condemning him to do penance and to be hanged after being previously subjected to the ordinary and extraordinary torture.

Thereupon the said Pierre Delluque, having been stripped by the executioner, was laid upon the rack, and his feet attached to an iron hook fixed at one extremity of the said rack, his arms being attached to another hook fixed in a roller at the opposite end, each side of the roller having a wheel, of which the cogs were of the size of six lines. Having repeated to the said Pierre

[1] "Then they did put me on the rack—and thereon they kept me a long time, and because I lay still and did not cry, my lord Chancellor and Mr. Rich took pains to rack me with their own hands till I was nigh dead" (Foxe).

Delluque the oath to speak the truth, we ordered the said executioner to stretch tightly the cords to which were attached the arms and legs of the said Pierre Delluque.

Thereupon having ordered the said executioner to turn three cogs, interrogated the accused as to all the facts relating to his condemnation, answered that he had never committed any robbery, and had no accomplice, and having ordered three more cogs to be turned accused again interrogated, answered he was not a party to any robbery. Having ordered three more cogs to be turned, accused answered he had spoken the truth. Having ordered three more cogs to be turned, accused said if he were released he would speak the truth. Thereupon the said executioner, having by our order released the accused, again urged him to tell us what robberies and offences he had committed since leaving the galleys; who were his accomplices; whether he did not steal a mare at Rousset; whether the said mare was not taken by him or one of his accomplices to the farm of Brousse, near Belfort, answered that he had spoken the truth, had never committed any robbery alone, or with an accomplice.

Thereupon ordered the said executioner to again stretch the cords to the same point at which they were before the prisoner was released; ordered three more cogs to be turned, and the accused, interrogated, answered that the devil might take him, body and soul, if he had been a party to any robbery. And having ordered three more cogs to be turned, again interrogated the accused as to the above facts but he made no reply.

Thereupon called Messrs. Mercadier, father and son, sworn surgeons, whom we had notified to be present during the torture of the said accused, to prevent the happening of any accident, who, being sworn after examining the state of the accused, reported that breathing was suspended, and he was in danger of suffocation unless released for a few moments.

On this report, ordered the accused to be released, he having regained consciousness by the aid of cordials administered by the said Messrs. Mercadier. Interrogated as to the above facts, replied, and still denying being a party to any robbery.

Thereupon, having ordered the cords to be stretched to the same point as before, the accused, interrogated as to the above facts, replied only by loud screams; and, having ordered the executioner to turn two more cogs, the accused, interrogated as to the above facts, still gave no reply, and the said surgeons, having again examined the state of the accused, reported to us that the movement of the diaphragm was stopped by the twisting of the nerves, and that the thumb of his right hand was torn off, and that he was in danger of losing his life if we did not release him entirely.

Thereupon ordered the said executioner to entirely loosen the accused; had him carried on a mattress in front of a fire, where he regained consciousness, with the help of the said surgeons, and the cordials they administered to him. Read over to him the present report, and after having again interrogated him generally as to all the above facts, he again answered that he had not committed any robbery either alone or with accomplices.

The Germans introduced variety into the torments of the rack. In early days the victims were stretched and then whipped until they confessed or died, but later the Germans introduced the following improvement in the infliction of the torture. The victim was first stretched and then a roller was inserted under his back over which he was drawn backwards and forwards. The rollers differed in quality; some had rounded wooden spikes, others pointed wooden spikes; but the roller which tore away the victim's skin, flesh and muscles, leaving him a bleeding, mangled mass, was the one with pointed iron spikes.

The German States also employed the famous *Austrian ladder*, which was rack-like in principle and one of the most terrible tortures ever invented.

Until 1768 not only the governors of a province, but Judges and even Feudal lords, were entitled to inflict torture in Austria and Hungary, but in that year the Empress Maria Theresa passed various laws restricting the use of torture and setting out in detail[1] the instruments to be used. Of these tortures the most effective was the stretching ladder, commonly known as *the Austrian ladder*.

This torture consisted of a wide ladder fixed into the ground and leaning against a wall at an angle of about

[1] *Constitutio Criminalis Theresiana.*

forty-five degrees. At the foot of the ladder was a circular movable bar similar to that used on the rack. The victim was laid on his back on the ladder with his wrists bound behind his back to one of the rungs. His ankles were then attached to a rope running down to the movable bar. The torturers then rotated the movable bar drawing the victim down the ladder, thus twisting his arms upwards from behind till his shoulders were strained to dislocation, and the unnatural backward and upward direction in which his arms and muscles were forced caused the most acute agony. Should the required evidence not be forthcoming, a large bundle of lighted candles was applied to the armpits, one of the most sensitive parts of the body. Struggling was practically impossible and could but add to the fearful tension of the body. First one side was burnt and then the other.

When the *Austrian ladder* was used in Germany the Germans were not bound by the *Constitutio Criminalis Theresiana*, which laid down minute details for the infliction of this torture, so they were at liberty to use torches instead of candles, and to apply red-hot irons to the sides, arms and nails of the victim, privileges which they lost no time in adopting.

The rack was employed in China in conjunction with *the Boots*, which was a torture similar to the French *Brodequins*. Thus, if Marston was right, there ought to be little gout in China.[1]

The other form of torture which obtained universal approval was the whip and all the branches of flagellation. It was used in all countries for dealing with minor offences as well as for some of the major ones. The subject of whipping has had many volumes written on it and can be dealt with only cursorily here.

There were many different ways of using the whip and it took many different forms. In Rome, the *plumbatae*, a

---

[1] "All your empirics could never do the like cure upon the gout as the rack in England on your Scotch boots" (Marston, *The Malcontent*).

scourge consisting of a short piece of wood to which was attached several thongs entwined with leaden or bronze balls, or the *flagellum*, a similar instrument usually with three thongs, having bone knots fastened to them, were generally used as a means of punishment; though, being an infamous punishment, whipping was seldom used on free citizens. Slaves were generally flogged with rods.

In the East, and especially in Turkey, Persia and China, the bastinado was generally employed, though the punishment of the split bamboo was more common in China. The infliction of the bastinado consists in blows given with a light stick or lath of bamboo upon the soles of the feet or on the buttocks. The blows are given gently and the terror of the punishment consists in its long duration. A clever executioner can kill his victim after hours of the most subtle torture.

The Jews were more merciful with regard to flogging than most of the early races, the Jewish law laying down: "And it shall be, if the wicked man be worthy to be beaten, and the judge shall cause him to lie down, and to be beaten before his face, according to his fault, by a certain number. Forty stripes he may give him, and not exceed; lest if he should exceed, and beat him above these with many stripes, then thy brothers should seem vile unto thee."[1] For fear of breaking the law it was customary to give only thirty-nine strokes; three lashes with a thirteen-corded scourge.[2]

Following the Roman lead freemen could not be whipped in England and the punishment was originally reserved for villains. The Anglo-Saxons used a three-corded knotted scourge and in those days it was quite common for mistresses to have their servants whipped to death. King Aethelred was flogged by his mother with candles

[1] Deut. xxv. 2, 3.
[2] In the U.S.A. as late as 1851, at Boston, coloured persons out after hours in the street were arrested, locked up for the night, and sentenced to 39 lashes in the morning. The policeman administering the blows received fifty cents.

so severely, that he became insensible with pain and dreaded candles during the rest of his life.[1]

The abolition of the monasteries in the reign of Henry VIII led to an increase of vagrancy, at which the Statute of Labourers (1350) and its provisions for whipping had been aimed. In the year 1530 the famous Whipping Act was passed which directed that vagrants were to be carried to some market town or other place, "and there tied to the end of a cart naked, and beaten with whips throughout such market town, or other place, till the body shall be bloody be reason of such whipping". This Act remained in force until the thirty-ninth year of Elizabeth's reign, when a Statute was passed under which persons were to be whipped, not entirely naked as formerly, but only from the middle upwards. This Statute caused the introduction of the whipping-post into nearly all the villages in England, but did not prevent the court ordering, in 1684, "certain Scotch pedlars and petty chapmen being in the habit of selling their goods to the greate damage and hindrance of shoppe-keepers" to be stripped naked and whipped.

In England, women were whipped, lunatics were whipped,[2] and one even finds the entry, "1710–1, Pd. Thomas Hawkins, for whipping two people yt had small-pox—8d." The whipping of females was abolished by Statute in 1820.[3]

Two interesting cases of whipping are those of James Nayler, a Quaker, who claimed to be the Messiah and was whipped for blasphemy, and Edward Floyde, who was sentenced to be whipped for insulting the daughter of James I.

The punishment inflicted by Parliament on Nayler for his blasphemy was as follows:[4]

[1] William of Malmesbury.
[2] "1690–1, Paid in charges taking up a distracted woman, watching her and whipping her next day—8s. 6d." (Constable's Account of Great Straughton, Hunts.).
[3] Whipping of Female Offenders Abolition Act, 1820.
[4] *Yorkshire in Olden Times.*

That James Nayler was guilty of horrid blasphemy, and that he was a grand imposter and seducer of the people, . . . that he should be set on the pillory, in the Palace Yard, Westminster, during the space of two hours, on Thursday next, and be whipped by the hangman through the streets from Westminster to the Old Exchange, London; and there, likewise, he should be set on the pillory, with his head in the pillory, for the space of two hours, between the hours of eleven and one, on Saturday next, in each place wearing a paper, containing an inscription of his crimes; and that, at the Old Exchange, his tongue should be bored through with a hot iron, and that he should there also be stigmatised in the forehead with the letter B; and that he should afterwards be sent to Bristol, to be conveyed into and through the city on horseback, with his face backwards, and there also should be whipped the next market-day after he came thither; and that thence he should be committed to prison in Bridewell, London, and there be restrained from the society of all people, and there to labour hard till he should be released by Parliament; and during that time he should be debarred the use of pen, ink and paper, and he should have no relief but what he earned by his daily labour.

The punishment of Edward Floyde was still more severe:[1]

When the news arrived in England, that Prague was taken from the Palsgrave of Bohemia, who had married the Princess Elizabeth, Mr. Edward Floyde, a Roman Catholic gentleman, who happened to be a prisoner at the time in the Fleet, was heard to remark, that Goodman and Goody Palsgrave were now turned out of doors, and to make several other irreverent observations of the same kind.

The expressions were reported abroad, and so sinful were they deemed, that both Houses of Parliament thought it necessary to take them under their serious consideration. Of the proceedings in the Upper House, the only record that remains is the sentence; but those of the Commons have been preserved for the edification of posterity. Witnesses were examined who proved the words, and that Floyde's countenance was in a very indecent degree joyful when he announced them. It was farther proved that he was "a pernicious papist", and "a wicked fellow", so that, in short,

[1] *The Percy Anecdotes.*

the poor gentleman had nothing to say for himself against the charge of having joked at the misfortunes of such high folks as "Goodman and Goody Palsgrave". The crime being thus established, a very strange debate arose as to the punishment to be inflicted on this most heinous offender.

Sir Robert Philips was of opinion, that since his offence had been without limitation, his punishment might likewise be without proportion. He would have him ride with his face to a horse's tail from Westminster to the Tower, with a paper on his hat, wherein should be written, "A Popish wretch that hath maliciously scandalised his majesty's children", and that at the Tower he should be lodged in little ease, with as much pain as he shall be able to endure without loss or danger of life.

Sir Francis Seymour was for standing more "on the *privilege* and power of the house. He would have him go from thence to the Tower at cart's tail with his doublet off, his hands about his neck, and that he should have as many lashes as he hath beads".

Sir Edward Giles thought that besides being whipped, he should stand in the pillory.

Sir Francis Darcy "would have a hole burnt through his tongue, since that was the member that offended".

Sir Jeremy Horsey thought the tongue should be cut out altogether.

Sir George Goring agreed with none of the merciful gentlemen who had preceded him. "He would have his nose, ears, and tongue cut off; to be whipped at as many stages as he hath beads, and to ride to every stage with his face to the horse's tail, and the tail in his hand, and at every stage to swallow a bead; and thus to be whipped to the Tower, and there *to be hanged*"!

Sir Joseph Jephson "would have moved, that a committee might be appointed to consider of the heaviest punishments that had been spoken of; but *because he perceived the house inclined to mercy* (!) he would have him whipped more than twice as far", &c.

The debate was adjourned without anything being definitely agreed on; and before it was resumed, the House of Lords, being resolved to be something more than sharers in the honour of punishing "so vile and undutiful a subject", objected to the power of punishment assumed by the Commons, as an invasion of their *privileges*. The Commons, after long and violent debates, were at last obliged, after inserting a protest in their journals, to give up the point; that Floyde was now left to the Upper House, who equally "inclined to mercy", pronounced the following sentence:

1. That the said Edward Floyde shall be incapable to bear arms as a gentleman, and that he shall be ever held an infamous person, and his testimony not to be taken in any court or cause.
2. That on Monday next, in the morning, he shall be brought to Westminster Hall, and there set on horseback, with his face to the horse's tail, holding the tail in his hand, with papers on his head and breast declaring his offence, and so to ride to the pillory in Cheapside, and there to stand two hours on the pillory, and there to be branded with a letter K on his forehead.
3. To be whipped at a cart's tail, on the first day of the next term, from the Fleet to Westminster Hall, with papers on his head declaring his offence, and then to stand on the pillory there two hours.
4. That he shall be fined to the King in £5,000.
5. That he shall be imprisoned in Newgate *during his life*.

Cowper the poet gives an amusing account of a whipping he witnessed at Olney in 1783 in a letter to the Rev. John Newton:

The fellow seemed to show great fortitude; but it was all an imposition. The beadle who whipped him had his left hand filled with red ochre, through which, after every stroke, he drew the lash of the whip, leaving the appearance of a wound upon the skin, but in reality not hurting him at all. This being perceived by the constable, who followed the beadle to see that he did his duty, he (the constable) applied the cane, without any such management or precaution, to the shoulders of the beadle. The scene now became interesting and exciting. The beadle could by no means be induced to strike the thief hard, which provoked the constable to strike harder; and so the double flogging continued, until a lass of Silver End, pitying the pitiful beadle, thus suffering under the hands of the pitiless constable, joined the procession, and placing herself immediately behind the constable seized him by his capillary club, and pulling him backwards by the same, slapped his face with Amazonian fury. This concentration of

72

events has taken up more of my paper than I intended, but I could not forbear to inform you how the beadle thrashed the thief, the constable the beadle, and the lady the constable, and how the thief was the only person who suffered nothing.

The whip known as the cat-o'-nine-tails was a scourge used for flogging in the Army and Navy, but was restricted to offenders in military prisons by the Army Act of 1881.

Somerville, in his *Autobiography of a Working Man*, gives his experience of the army floggings of his day. He was sentenced, while a private in the Scots Greys, to receive 200 lashes in the usual manner of the regiment. The regiment was formed four deep round the walls of the riding-school. The regimental surgeon, the hospital sergeant and two hospital orderlies were present. The sergeant of the band stood with the *green bag* (the bag containing the "cat") and a farrier and a trumpeter each stood with a "cat" in his hand. The handles of the "cats" were of wood or whalebone, about two feet long, the nine tails about the same length, each tail two, or perhaps three, times the thickness of ordinary whipcord, with six hard knots upon it. A form stood by upon which was a pail of water with some towels in it, to apply to the back of the culprit, and a basin of water for him to drink if he felt faint. A ladder was placed upright against the wall and several strong ropes hung about it. When Somerville was led into the square, the commanding officer read out the minutes of the court-martial and said to the prisoner, "You will take your punishment; strip, sir." He accordingly stripped to his trousers and was fastened by the wrists and ankles to the ladder, so that his arms stretched outwards and his breast and face were brought tightly against the ladder so firmly that he could not move. The regimental sergeant-major, who stood behind with a book and pencil to count each lash and write its number, gave the command, "Farrier Simpson, you will do your duty." The manner in which that duty was done was for the Farrier to swing the "cat" twice round his head, give a stroke, draw the tails of the "cat" through his fingers to rid them of the skin, or flesh and blood, again swing the instrument twice round his head slowly, and so on. In the words of Somerville, "Simpson took the cat as ordered; at least, I believe so; I did not see him, but I felt an astounding sensation between the shoulders under my neck which went to my toe-nails in one direction, my finger-nails in another, and stung me to the heart as if a knife had gone through my body. The sergeant-major called in a loud voice 'One', and I felt as if it would be kind of Simpson not to strike me on the same place again. He came on a second time, a few inches lower, and then I thought the former stroke was sweet and agreeable when compared with that one. The sergeant-major counted 'Two'. The cat was swung twice round the farrier's head again, and he came on somewhere about the right shoulder blade, and the loud voice of the reckoner said 'Three'. The shoulder blade was as sensitive as any other part of the body, and when he came again on the left shoulder, and the voice cried 'Four', I felt my flesh quiver in every nerve, from the scalp of my head to my toe-nails. The time between each stroke seemed so long as to be agonising, and yet the next came too soon. It was lower down, and felt to be the severest. The word 'Five' made me betake myself to mental arithmetic; this, thought I, is only the fortieth part of what I am to get. 'Six' followed, so on up to twenty-five. The sergeant-major then said 'Halt!' Simpson stood back, and a young trumpeter, who had not flogged before, took his cat and began. He had practised often at a stable-post or a sack of sawdust, and could handle the instrument as scientifically as any one. He gave me some dreadful cuts about the ribs, first on one side and then on the other. Someone bade him hit higher up, I do not know who. He then gave them upon the blistered and swollen places where Simpson had been practising. The pain in my lungs was now more severe, I thought, than on my back. I felt

74

as if I would burst in the internal parts of my body. I detected myself once giving something like a groan, and to prevent its utterance again I put my tongue between my teeth, held it there, and bit it almost in two pieces. What with the blood from my tongue and my lips, which I had also bitten, and the blood from my lungs or some other internal part ruptured by the writhing agony, I was almost choked, and became black in the face. It now became Simpson's second turn to give twenty-five. One fifty had been inflicted, and the time since they began was like a long period of life; I felt as if I had lived all the time of my real life in pain and torture, and that the time when existence had pleasure in it was a dream, long, long gone by. Simpson got up amongst the old sores: the strokes were not so sharp as at first: they were like blows of heavy weights but more painful than the fresh ones. It was now that he, probably more inclined to remember that he was my friend than a farrier, was commanded in a loud voice in these words, 'Farrier Simpson, do your duty.' He travelled downwards, and came on heavier than before but, as I thought, slower. It seemed a weary slowness for the sergeant-major to be only counting the fifteenth and the sixteenth of the third twenty-five. When the other youngster had reached his five-and-twenty, which made a hundred, the commanding officer said, 'Stop, take him down; he is a young soldier.' " Somerville was then unbound, a wet towel spread on his back, his jacket placed loosely over that and he was led to the hospital between two men. There a cloth dipped in a lotion was put on the skin and he was laid on his back.

A common practice among soldiers to correct inter-regimental offences was *booting and bottling*. This consisted of each soldier of the regimental jury giving twelve blows with a boot-jack and then pouring a bottle of cold water down the sleeves of the culprit.

In Russia a form of military punishment, which was also inflicted upon Polish civilians, was "Running the

Gauntlet". The victim was first shaved and stripped to the waist. His wrists were tied to the barrel of his musket, the bayonet of which pressed into his stomach to prevent his hurrying, and he was slowly led through ranks of soldiers, while each struck him with a whip as he passed. Peter the Great humanely limited the number of blows to be given in this form of punishment to 12,000, but as it was seldom that anybody survived 2,000 lashes, his nobleness of heart was not very effective.

Captains of ships have power under the Common law to whip undutiful seamen, but the power was largely restricted, if not removed, by the Merchant Shipping Act. The following description of a whipping at sea is taken from a book published privately at London in 1885 called *Experiences of Flagellation*.

Amongst the recruits consigned to his command on his passage outwards was an unfortunate man named Green, who formerly kept a hatter's shop in Catherine Street, Strand, and who, under a conviction for some crime, was sentenced to transportation for fourteen years. His wife, an amiable, but heart-broken, woman, was permitted to accompany him on the voyage; and shortly after the vessel sailed from the Downs symptoms of mutiny were discovered amongst the convicts; several had sawed off their irons; and Green was charged, not with any act of mutiny, but with furnishing the convicts with money to procure the implements for taking off their irons. The unfortunate man stated in his vindication, that he had only lent some of the wretches a few shillings to take some sheets and other necessaries out of pawn. But his defence would not do. He was brought to the gangway by order of the Governor, without drum-head, or any other court-martial, and flogged with a boatswain's cat, until his bones were denuded of flesh. Still the unfortunate man never uttered a groan. The Governor, who superintended the punishment, swore he would conquer the rascal's stubbornness, and make him cry out, or whip his guts out. The surgeon remonstrated on the danger of the man's death, but in vain. Ensign Wall, the governor's brother, a humane young man, on his knees entreated that the flogging should cease; but also in vain; and his importunity only served to provoke a

76

threat of putting himself in arrest. He then entreated the unfortunate Green to cry out, and save himself. But the unhappy man said it was now too late, as he felt himself dying, and unable to cry out; and that he had not avoided it from stubbornness, but concealed his pangs, lest his wretched wife, who was down below and knew nothing of his situation, should hear his cries, and die with anguish. The flogging was continued until the convulsions of his bowels appeared through his lacerated loins, when he fainted under the lash, and was consigned to the surgeon.

The cat or birch can still be inflicted under English law in certain cases.[1]

Whipping was common in Denmark and whipping-posts were to be seen at the entrance of many towns; they were surmounted by the figure of a man holding a whip in his right hand. The punishment for those convicted of child murder used to be that the accused was condemned to work in a spinhouse for life and to be whipped annually on the day when, and at the place where, the crime was committed.

Whipping slaves, often to death, was very frequently employed in the Southern States of America. The following extract will show how this was put into execution in the year 1823:

The first article of the Ohio constitution declares, that "All men are born equally free and independent". This is the law; at Cincinnati Mr. Fearon discovered the practice.

"Many persons in this state", says he, "have coloured people, whom they call *their property*. The mode in which they effect this perpetuation of slavery, in violation of the spirit of the Ohio constitution, is to purchase blacks, and have them apprenticed to them. Some are so base as to take these negroes down the river, at the approach of the expiration of their apprenticeship, *and sell them at Natchez for life*."

Of the manner in which the slaves are treated, the following proof, so afflicting to humanity, is related by the same author:

"A few minutes before dinner, my attention was excited by the

[1] See (*inter alia*) Convict Prison Rules (82–85) and Local Prison Rules (88–91).

piteous cries of a human voice, accompanied with the loud crackling of a whip. Following the sound, I found that it issued from a log-barn, the door of which was fastened. Peeping through the logs, I perceived the bar-keeper, together with a stout man, more than six feet high, who was Colonel ——, and a negro boy about fourteen years of age stripped naked, receiving the lashes of these monsters, who *relieved* each other in the use of a horse-whip: the poor boy fell down upon his knees several times, begging and praying that they would not kill him, and that he would do anything they liked; this produced no cessation in their *exercise*. At length Mr. Lawes arrived, told the valiant Colonel and his humane employer, the bar-tender, to desist, and that the boy's refusal to cut wood was in obedience to his (Mr. L.'s) directions. Colonel —— said that he did not know what the *nigger* had done, but that the bar-keeper requested his assistance to whip Caesar; of course he lent him a hand, being no more than he should expect Mr. Lawes to do for him, under similar circumstances.[1]

An American Act of Legislature of 1740 states: "In case any person shall wilfully cut out the tongue, put out the eye, or cruelly scald, burn, or deprive any slave of any limb or member, or shall inflict any other cruel punishment, other than by whipping, or beating with a horse-whip, cow-skin, switch, or small-stick, or by putting irons on, or confining or imprisoning such slave, every such person shall for every such offence, forfeit the sum of one hundred pounds current money." It will be seen, therefore, that before the War of Independence efforts were being made to alleviate the lot of the unfortunate slaves. The Code of Louisiana incorporated the same idea when it contained the following: "The slave is entirely subject to the will of his master, who may correct and chastise him, though not with unusual rigour, nor so as to maim or mutilate him, or to expose him to the danger of loss of life, or to cause his death." Let us see the American Southerner's interpretation of "unusual rigour".

[1] *The Percy Anecdotes.*

Every variety of instrument that has been invented was used to inflict the utmost degradation and torture on both male and female slaves. They were put in "slings" (i.e. suspended by their arms) and swung whilst heavy battledores crushed their flesh; they were skewered up into frightful distortions that the distension of their muscles might aggravate the pains of the blows; they were fastened naked to four stakes in the ground and flogged till they fainted or died; husbands were made to beat their naked wives in public; and they were buried in holes in the ground just large enough to receive their bodies, a door put upon the top, and in this position they were sometimes kept for a month, if they survived as long.

A Mr. Faraby used to stretch his slave girls on the ground, their arms and legs stretched and fastened to stakes, and lash them till they screamed. When they screamed he used to kick them in the face with his heavy boots. After he had tired of this amusement he used to send for sealing-wax and a lighted lamp and dropped the blazing wax into the gashes. When his arm was rested he used to lash the hardened wax out again. His two grown-up daughters were interested spectators of the proceedings.

Colonel James Castleman was indicted for killing a slave. He was acquitted. He had merely fastened his slave by a chain round his neck to a beam above his head. If the slave bent or moved his body he would be strangled. After some time he did, and was.

American slavery after the time of the Union is merely degrading and disgusting. Enough has been said of it already, but mention might be made of "cobbing", as this has become a not uncommon word in the English language. Whipping slaves with a lash, even when followed by the happy practice of rubbing red pepper into the wounds, decreased the market value of a slave when put up for sale. The ingenuity of the Southern members of the Union substituted a pliant leather strap or paddle of wood in which small holes were bored. The holes acted like diminutive cups and inflicted great pain. The use of the strap and the paddle, which were called "cobbing", left no mark on the back of the slaves to deteriorate their value.

The most celebrated form of whipping and undoubtedly the most savage was the Russian torture of the *knout*. The *knout* is said to have been introduced into Russia by Ivan III (1462–1505) and consisted of various forms. One was a lash of raw hide, sixteen inches long, attached to a wooden handle nine inches long; the lash ended in a metal ring, to which was attached a second lash, nine inches long, ending also in a ring to which was attached a few inches of hard leather, ending in a beak-like hook. Another kind of *knout* consisted of plaited thongs of skin interwoven with wire and ending with wired ends. The commonest form of *knout* was a wooden handle a foot long with several thongs about two feet in length, twisted together, to the end of which had fastened a single tough thong a foot and a half in length, tapering towards a point and capable of being changed by the executioner when too much softened by the blood of the criminal. The point was often dipped in milk and allowed to freeze.

According to *The Percy Anecdotes*, when the philanthropic Howard was in Petersburg, he saw two criminals, a man and a woman, suffer the punishment of the *knout*. They were conducted from prison by about fifteen hussars and ten soldiers. When they had arrived at the place of punishment, the hussars formed themselves into a ring round the whipping-post; the drum beat a minute or two, and then some prayers were repeated, the populace taking off their hats. The woman was taken first, and after being roughly stripped to the waist, her hands and feet were bound with cords to a post made for the purpose. A servant attended the execution, and both he and his master were stout men. The servant first marked the ground and struck the woman five times on the back; every stroke seemed to penetrate deep into her flesh; but his master, thinking him too gentle, pushed him aside, took his place and gave all the remaining strokes himself, which were evidently more severe. The woman received twenty-five blows and the man sixty. "I", continues Mr. Howard, "pressed through the hussars, and counted the numbers as they were chalked on a board for the purpose. Both the criminals seemed but just alive, especially the man, who had yet strength enough remaining to receive a small present with some signs of gratitude. I saw the woman in a very weak condition some days after, but could not find the man any more."

There are many examples of famous people *knouted* in Russia. Peter the Great is accused of *knouting* his son Alexis to death, and the Empress Eudoxia, in the same reign, was sentenced to undergo this punishment on a charge of infidelity; she no sooner saw the dreadful apparatus than she readily confessed every species of criminality laid to her charge. She owned to every amorous intrigue with which she was accused, and of which, to all appearances till that terrible moment, she had not the least idea. Eudoxia was, however, condemned to undergo the discipline, and was afterwards imprisoned in a dungeon, deprived of her servants and reduced to the necessity of performing the most menial offices herself.[1]

The Emperor Nicholas abolished the *knout* and substituted the *pleti*, which was a three-thonged scourge, in its place.

A special type of whipping used to be practised at Rome as a punishment for minor offences. This was called the *cavaletto*. The victim was tied breast-downward to a table, his clothes being drawn tight by his position, and he received the number of strokes ordered in his sentence. The more hardy offenders were so little affected by this punishment that they named a different saint at every blow.

In France, a special form of whipping was applied in 1816 to the female Protestants, a terrible description of

[1] There are, of course, many incidents of perfectly innocent people confessing to guilt under torture.

which is given in Mark Wilks's *History of the Persecution endured by the Protestants of the South of France*, 1821.

At Nismes, as in all France, the inhabitants wash their clothes either at the fountains or on the banks of streams. There is a large basin near the fountain, where every day a great number of women may be seen kneeling at the edge of the water, and beating the linen with heavy pieces of wood in the shape of battledores. This spot became the scene of the most cruel and indecent practices. The Catholics vented their fury on the wives, widows, and daughters of Protestants, by a newly-invented punishment. They turned their petticoats over their heads, and so fastened them as to favour their shameful exposure, and their subjection to chastisement; and nails being placed in the wood of the *battoirs* in the form of *fleurs-de-lys*, they beat them till the blood streamed from their bodies, and their screams rent the air. The 14th and 15th of August were especially signalised by these horrors; and thus the fête of the Assumption, professedly designed by the Catholics to recall the most exalted purity and the Divine benevolence, was observed by those of Nismes, by the most revolting violation of female modesty, and by brutal gratifications at which even savages might blush. Often was death demanded as a commutation of this ignominious punishment; but death was refused with malignant joy; murder was to perfect, and not prevent, the obscene and cruel sport. To carry their outrages to the highest possible degree, they assailed in this manner several who were in a state of pregnancy.

Madame Rath, when near her confinement, was attacked by about sixty of the *purest* Catholics, armed with knotted cords, *battoirs* and stones. It was with difficulty she escaped instant death, and only by extraordinary skill that her life was preserved in premature child-birth. Her babe just breathed and expired. Her mother had already lost an eye from the discharge of a pistol, fired at her by Trestaillon. The loss of her child, the distressing situation of her mother, and her own agony and shame, were the punishments inflicted on her for being guilty of—Calvinism.

Madame Gautiere and Madame Domerque, in a similar critical period, were treated with similar indignity. Madame Reboul died in a few days of the injuries she had received. The daughter Benouette was beaten and torn with nails, by a young

A PIECE OF CORD

man named Merle, assisted by an inhuman rabble of both sexes.
One of the daughters of Bigonnette (who was thrown into a well
and drowned) died of the ill-treatment she experienced; one
orphan sister, in terror, had become a Catholic, but the other,
although at the risk of her life, refused to abandon her religion.
A female servant was stripped of all her clothes, and left on the
public road, covered with blood, and exposed to the jests of a
degraded populace—a soldier took off his great-coat, threw it on
her, and conducted her to the town. A young woman, about
twenty years of age, had engaged to marry a Catholic poorer than
herself, but she made it a condition, that the marriage should be
celebrated in the Protestant temple: this was during the 100 days.
Circumstances changed, and the relations of the young man
persuaded him to break off the connection. He went to the young
female and demanded that their union should be celebrated in
the Catholic Church; she refused to alter her resolution, and the
compact was dissolved. Vengeance was threatened; she was
seized in the street, and her intended husband joined the assailants:
she was dragged to the fountain, and there whipped amidst cries
of "*Vive le roi*", and indecencies, both of language and conduct,
which it is impossible to relate.

The wife and daughter of Barignon were stripped before their
own door, and the daughter received a blow from a knife, which
has become an incurable wound.—Francoise was cruelly flogged;
and after being placed backward on a donkey, with one of her
hands tied to its tail, she was finally exposed in a most shameful
attitude, and covered with mud to the sound of "*Vive le roi*". The
widow Driole was stripped and flogged in her own house; the
brigands then took away in a cart, all her goods, and a quantity of
corn she had gleaned, and afterwards set them on fire. Chabanelle
was treated in the same manner in her apartments, when near
confinement; and Isabeau Calours, also, before her dwelling in
the *Place de Bachelas*. These miserable beings were so lacerated,
that both they and their executioners weltered in blood. A female,
called the *great Marie*, was whipped and brought into Nismes to the
Place de Justice on an ass: she died soon after. The daughter of
Allerd died of the wounds she received. Madame Pic was carried
in a hand-barrow to the hospital, and for two years did not
recover from the effects of her injuries.

The scandalous nature of these outrages prevented many of

83

the sufferers from making them public, and especially from relating the most aggravating circumstances; but the dames Gibelin, Bragouse, Gervier, Gourdoux, Audizer and daughter, Gregoire, Frequolle, Portier, Rigaud, Durante, Gas and many others are known to have been the victims of these barbarities;— the practice continued for several months. "I have seen", sayd M. Durand, a Catholic avocat, "the assassins in the faubourg Bourgade, arm a *battoir* with sharp nails in the form of *fleur-de-lys*; I have seen them raise the garments of females, and apply with heavy blows to the bleeding body this *battoir* to which they gave a name, which my pen refuses to inscribe. The cries of the sufferers —the streams of blood—the murmurs of indignation, which were suppressed by fear—nothing could move them. The surgeons who attended on those who are dead, can attest by the marks of their wounds, and the agonies which they endured, that this account, however horrible, is most strictly true."

As an instrument of torture the Germans used a whip consisting of a short wooden handle to which was attached a bunch of iron cords, with a spiked circle at the end of each lash for tearing the flesh from the back till the bones and sinews were laid bare. Some German executioners are said to have dipped their whips into poison before applying them to their victims.

Whipping was commonly practised, among other punishments, on the inhabitants of the Philippine Islands by the priest and friar during the Spanish ownership. "I have known", says Jorge Gracia del Fierro, in his answers to interrogatories (dated 11th of September, 1900)[1] by the United States Commissioner, "many Dominican, Augustinian, Recolletto, and Franciscan friars; perhaps 200 of them, and having been in rather intimate relations with some of them, I can assert that the best of them were tyrants, who found much pleasure in saying: 'The Filipino must be given bread with one hand and rattan beatings with the other.'" An example of such a beating is given in the answer of Franco Gonzales (7th of October, 1900)[2]:

[1] U.S. Senate Document 190, Church Lands in the Philippines.   [2] *Ibid.*

The principal cause for the hostility against the friar curates in the said provinces has been egotism, unbridled license, ill-treatment, and contempt for the Philipino.

As a sample of what a displeased parish priest is capable of, I shall relate what I witnessed about the year 1867 or 1868 in Rosales (Neuva Ecija) on a feast day after high mass at the very moment in which the people were leaving the church. The curate of this pueblo, Fr. Raimundo Gallardo, a Franciscan, with his sleeves rolled up, was in front of the principal entrance to the church belabouring the shoulders of a man standing, though strongly tied to a step-ladder, with a rattan. I left that repugnant spectacle, which lasted, as I subsequently learned, until the curate no longer had strength to continue. The cause for so brutal a punishment was due to his having dared to collect in the said town for Masses for the famous Virgin Manauag (Pangasenan). That unhappy man was agent of the parish priest of Manauag.

Though it is hardly a subject which comes within the scope of this book, but of which more will be said hereafter, mention may be made of the voluntary infliction of whipping. Nearly every ancient religion introduced voluntary whipping as part of its ceremonial, either as a sacrifice or a penance. The most famous sect of whippers were the Flagellants, who established themselves at Perouse about 1260. They maintained that there was no remission of sin without flagellation, and publicly lashed themselves, in processions preceded by a cross, until the blood flowed from their naked backs. They were suppressed and their leader, Conrad Schmidt, burnt in 1414.

CHAPTER IV

SOME MORE PIECES OF CORD

The result of the torture is simply a matter of calculation. Given the force of the muscles and the sensibility of the nerves of an innocent person, it is required to find the degree of pain necessary to make him confess himself guilty of a given crime.—BECCARIA.

A woman hang'd and her daughter in her haire

UNTIL modern times hanging could not be described as one of the humane methods for destroying life.

Hanging first became a legal punishment in England under the Saxon law, by which an adulteress was compelled to hang herself before being burnt on the funeral pile of her paramour. From those days hanging continued in England as a legal punishment, though it is possible that it was suspended during the reign of William the Conqueror in favour of mutilation; but it was certainly in force in the time of Henry I, when thieves caught in the act were hanged without trial.

The method of hanging, originally, was to suspend the culprit to the nearest tree, but, later, the criminal was driven to the place of execution in a cart. On arrival, the noose was placed round his neck and the cart drove away, leaving him suspended in the air, struggling, until he was dead. It was customary to leave the body hanging for not less than one hour.

The following report of an execution by hanging is taken from *The Times*, of the 25th March, 1829:

Yesterday morning, at the usual hour, four unhappy criminals underwent the extreme penalty of the law, opposite the Debtor's door, Newgate, viz.: Joseph Redguard, aged 23, William Kelly,

86

aged 21, Thomas Birmingham, aged 21, and Charles Goodlad, aged 22. The first three culprits were convicted at the last Old Bailey sessions of a daring highway robbery, attended with great aggravation. Goodlad was convicted for robbing his master of plate and other property to the value of £170.

A few minutes before eight o'clock the bell of St. Sepulchre's commenced tolling, at which time the mournful procession left the Press-room, and proceeded to the gallows. Birmingham first ascended the platform, and was instantly greeted by a vast number of girls of dissolute character in the mob, who most indecorously called out repeatedly: "Good-bye, Tom! God bless you, my trump!"

A most painful sensation was enacted by the rope having slipped under Birmingham's chin, and which was occasioned by the sufferer giving a sort of jump just before the drop fell. This prolonged his sufferings to a considerable extent. The miserable being breathed in agony for nearly five minutes. Shouts and screams from the mob caused the executioner to hang on his legs till life was extinct.

Executions by hanging took place in public, usually near to the spot where the crime was committed until recognised places for hanging were introduced; and it was not until 1868,[1] that public executions ceased in England. Between 1752 and 1832 part of the sentence was, that the bodies of executed criminals should be given to the surgeons as subjects for dissection. In this way a considerable number of criminals had remarkable escapes from death by being revived after they had been hanged. A curious example of this is given by Dr. Plot's *Natural History of Oxfordshire*, as follows:

In the year 1650, Anne Green, a servant of Sir Thomas Read, was tried for the murder of her new-born child, and found guilty. She was executed in the Castle-yard, where, when they opened the coffin, notwithstanding the rope still remained unloosed and straight about her neck, they perceived her breast to rise; whereupon one Mason, a tailor, intending only as an act of charity, set foot upon her; and, as some say, one Orum, a soldier,

[1] The last public execution was that of Michael Barret on the 26th of May, 1868.

struck her again with the butt-end of his musket. Notwithstanding all this, when the learned and ingenious Sir William Petty, ancestor of the present Marquis of Lansdowne, then anatomy professor of the University, Dr. Willis, and Dr. Clark, then president of Magdalen College, and vice-chancellor of the University, came to prepare the body for dissection[1] they perceived some small rattling in her throat; thereupon desisting from their former purpose, they presently used means for her recovery, by opening a vein, laying her in a warm bed, and also using divers remedies respecting her senselessness, insomuch that within fourteen hours she began to speak, and the next day talked and prayed very heartily.

Another case was reported from Ireland in 1767, and is referred to in the *Gentleman's Magazine* of February of that year:

Saturday, January 24th, 1767.—One Patrick Redmond having been condemned at Cork, in Ireland, to be hanged for a street robbery, he was accordingly executed, and hung upwards of twenty-eight minutes, when the mob carried off the body to a place appointed, where he was, after five or six hours, actually recovered by a surgeon, who made the incision in his windpipe called bronchotomy, which produced the desired effect. The poor fellow has since received his pardon, and a genteel collection has been made for him. It is recorded that the man had the hardihood to go to the theatre the same evening.

In 1814 hanging became the only method of inflicting the capital sentence in England, apart from sentences carried out under Military law.

Persons guilty of High Treason were given no opportunity of escaping death by being revived after execution as their sentence ran somewhat as follows:

That you be carried hence to the place from whence you came, and from thence you shall be drawn upon a Hurdle to the Place

[1] Before the Act in 1752 came into force giving the bodies of executed criminals to the surgeons for dissection it was often customary to acquire, by purchase or otherwise, the bodies of deceased criminals.

of Execution,[1] where you shall be hanged by the Neck, and, being alive, cut down; Your Privy Members shall be cut off, and burned before your face, your Head severed from your Body and your Body divided into four quarters,[2] and they to be disposed at the Pleasure of the King. And the God of infinite mercy have mercy upon your Soul.[3]

There were certain privileges and customs with respect to hanging of which mention may be made. Gentlemen sometimes craved the right to be hanged by a silken cord. When Carlile and Irving, the murderers of John Turner, in the reign of James I, were hanged in Fleet Street, Carlisle, being a gentleman, insisted on being hanged on a higher gibbet than his companion, who was of a lower station than himself.[4]

In various parts of the country there were customs dealing with the process of criminals to the place of execution. In London, the cavalcade halted at two places—once, when the sexton of St. Sepulchre's pronounced a solemn exhortation after he had rung a handbell, and again, when the whole party were regaled at "The Crown" for a draught from St. Giles's bowl. In York, the party was also regaled on the way to execution, and a rather curious story is told about this. A saddler refused to stop for his ale and was driven on to execution. His reprieve

[1] In former times the criminal was tied to the tail of a horse and dragged along the ground.

[2] Quartering was introduced from France during the reign of Richard III, though it had been used previously in extraordinary cases.

[3] This sentence was passed upon Algernon Sydney by the Rt. Hon. Sir George Jeffreys, Lord Chief Justice of England. "Tryal and Condemnation of Algernon Sydney", London 1684. Sentences of death varied. The executioner sometimes cut out the heart from the living man and held it aloft, exclaiming, "Behold the heart of a traitor". "Lord Ellenborough used to say to those condemned, 'You are drawn on hurdles to the place of execution, where you are to be hanged, but *not* till you are dead; for, while still living, your body is to be taken down, your bowels torn out and burnt before your face; your head is then cut off, and your body is divided into quarters."—*Gentleman's Magazine*, 1803, part 1, pp. 177, 275.

The first person hanged, drawn and quartered in England was Maurice, the son of a nobleman, in 1241, for piracy.   [4] A Scottish custom.

arrived a few minutes later, and had he taken the usual refreshment, no doubt his life would have been saved. Prohibitionists please note!

Sometimes especial brutality was shown towards the condemned. The populace pelted unpopular criminals with dirt and other missiles on their way to execution, and the executioners themselves did not refrain from making the last minutes of the culprit unpleasant. A case of this is seen in the execution of some of the Regicides. When Hugh Peters was drawn on a sledge to the scaffold, he was made to sit within the rails so that he could see the execution of his friend Cook. When the latter was cut down to be quartered, Colonel Turner ordered the Sheriff's men to bring Peters near, that he might see the operation performed; and when the hangman rubbed his bloody hands together, he tauntingly asked, "Come, how do you like this work, Mr. Peters?" Harrison, at the same execution, is said to have risen and boxed the ears of the hangman after being disembowelled.

After the execution of a notorious criminal the body was often hanged in chains, as a warning to would-be malefactors. This was known as "Gibbeting" and was not abolished till 1834.[1] The bodies were occasionally painted with tar as a means to their preservation. Gibbeting, for offences done on the high seas, was carried out near the harbour at which the ship landed.

It has often been said that criminals were hanged alive in chains and left to starve; Holinshed bears this out in his *Chronicle of England*, in which he states:

In wilful murder done upon pretended malice, or in anie notable robbery, the criminal is either hanged alive in chains near the place where the act was committed, or else, upon compassion taken, first strangled with a rope, and so continueth till his bones come to nothing.

Apart from this statement by Holinshed and some local

[1] The last criminal to be gibbeted in England was James Cook in 1832.

folk-lore, there is no evidence that hanging alive in chains was ever carried out in England.

Hanging in Ireland was similar to the execution in England, with the exception that the place of execution was usually the gaol where the prisoner was kept. A description of an Irish place of execution about 1850 is given in Trench's *Realities of Irish Life*. Most prisons were said to have scaffolds consisting of a balcony or cage permanently fixed to the gaol wall. There was a small door in the wall opening onto the balcony, the bottom of which was so constructed that on the withdrawal of a bolt within the gaol, a trap-door upon which the prisoner was placed dropped from under his feet. The upper end of the rope attached to the prisoner's neck was fastened to an iron bar which projected over the trap-door. There were often several trap-doors on the same balcony, so that two or three persons could be hanged simultaneously.

There is a curious case of an Irish weaver named Michael Carmody who was hanged in the county of Cork on the 3rd of June, 1734. His business had declined owing to the wearing of cotton instead of wool and he determined to do his best to revive the declining industry. He was dressed in cotton, and not only the hangman, but the gallows, were decorated with the same material. His dying speech included the following words:

I confess I have been guilty of many crimes that necessity obliged me to commit; which starving condition I was in, I am well assured was occasioned by the scarcity of money that has proceeded from the great discouragement of our woollen manufactures.

Therefore, good Christians, consider, that if you go on to suppress your own goods by wearing such cottons as I am now clothed in, you will bring your country into misery, which will consequently swarm with such unhappy malefactors as your present object is, and the blood of every miserable felon that will hang, after this warning from the gallows, will lie at your doors.

And if you have any regard for the prayers of an expiring mortal, I beg you will not buy of the hangman the cotton garments that now adorn the gallows, because I can't rest quiet in my grave if I should see the very things worn that brought me to misery, thievery, and this untimely end; all which I pray of the gentry to hinder their children and servants, for their own characters' sakes, though they have no tenderness for their country, because none will hereafter wear cottons, but oyster-women, criminals, hucksters, and common hangmen.

Hanging and quartering (l'esquartellage) were both practised in France on criminals guilty of minor offences before the guillotine became the sole method of punishment. Some of the French gallows were made to carry several scores of bodies. The following is a description of the Paris gibbet which was situated at Montfaucon:

For several centuries and down to the Revolution, hanging was the most common mode of execution in France, consequently in every town and almost in every village there was a permanent gibbet, which, owing to the custom of leaving the bodies to hang till they crumbled to dust, was very rarely without having some corpses or skeletons attached to it. These gibbets were generally composed of pillars of stone, joined at their summit by wooden traverses, to which the bodies of the criminals were tied by ropes or chains. The gallows, the pillars of which varied in number according to the will of the authorities, were always placed by the side of frequented roads, and on an eminence. The gallows of Paris, which played such an important part in the political as well as the criminal history of that city, were erected on a height north of the town near the high road leading into Germany. Montfaucon, originally the name of the hill, soon became that of the gallows itself. This celebrated place of execution consisted of a heavy mass of masonry composed of ten or twelve layers of rough stones, and formed an enclosure of forty feet by twenty-five or thirty. At the upper part there was a platform, which was reached by a stone staircase, the entrance of which was closed by a massive door. On three sides of this platform rested ten square pillars about thirty feet high, made on blocks of stone a foot thick. These pillars were joined to one another by double bars of wood, which were fastened into them and bore iron chains three feet and a half long, to which the criminals were suspended. Underneath, halfway between these and the platform, other bars were placed for the same purpose. Long and solid ladders riveted to the pillars enabled the executioner and his assistants to lead up criminals or to carry up corpses destined to be hanged there. Lastly, the centre of the structure was occupied by a deep pit, the hideous receptacle of the decaying remains of the criminals. One can easily imagine the strange and melancholy aspect of this monumental gibbet if one thinks of the number of corpses continually attached to it, and which were feasted upon by thousands of crows. On a single occasion it was necessary to replace fifty-two chains which were useless, and the accounts of the City of Paris prove that the expenses of executions were more heavy than that of the maintenance of the gibbet. Montfaucon was used not only for executions, but also for exposing corpses which were brought there from various places of execution in every part of the country. The mutilated remains of criminals who had been boiled, quartered, and beheaded were also hung there in sacks of leather or wickerwork. They often remained hanging for a considerable time, as in the case of Pierre des Essarts, who had been beheaded in 1413, and whose remains were handed over to his family for Christian burial after having hung on Montfaucon for three years. The criminal condemned to be hanged was generally taken to the place of execution sitting or standing in a wagon with his back to the horses, his confessor by his side, and the executioner behind. He bore three ropes round his neck, two the size of the little finger and called "Tortouses," each of which had a slip-knot, and the third called the "jet" was only used to pull the victim off the ladder, and so to launch him into eternity. When he arrived at the foot of the gallows the executioner first ascended the ladder backwards, drawing the culprit after him by means of the ropes and forcing him to keep pace with him. On arriving at the top he quickly fastened the two tortouses to the arm of the gibbet, and by a jerk of his knee he turned the culprit off the ladder, still holding the jet in his own hand. He then placed his feet on the tied hands of the condemned, and clutching him by repeated jerks, insured complete strangulation."[1]

In a previous chapter the torture by burning of a negro, for taking part in a rising in Jamaica, was mentioned.

[1] Lacroix, *Manners, Customs, and Costumes of the Middle Ages.*

Some of his companions were gibbeted alive. Two of these were indulged, at their own request, with a hearty meal before being suspended at Kingston. One survived eight days and the other nine.

New York, at the time of the protectorate of Cromwell, supplies another curious example of hanging. A cobbler killed an Indian and was tried, found guilty, and condemned to be hanged. The criminal was very popular, so means were taken to save him; and an old, bedridden weaver was substituted and hanged instead of the real offender. Thus justice was satisfied.

In Germany, in later days, no method of execution was permitted other than hanging, the body being suspended for twelve hours to prevent any chance of revival, but in former times the methods of execution varied in the different states. Some of the German customs with respect to hanging were curious and were more brutal than those of contemporary nations. In Morryson's *Account of Germany*, it is stated:

Near Lindau I did see a malefactor hanging in iron chains on the gallows, with a mastive dogge hanging on each side by the heels, as being nearly starved, they might eat the flesh of the malefactor before himself died of famine; and at Frankforte I did see the like punishment of a Jew.

A description of a Prussian execution in 1819 is given in *The Percy Anecdotes* as follows:

The execution of criminals is distinguished by a species of cruelty worthy of the worst days of the Inquisition; yet Prussia is a country that boasts a high degree of civilisation. A traveller who was at Berlin in 1819 gives the following account of the execution of a man for murder: "The executions of the Prussian capital take place about a quarter of a mile from the gate of Orianesberg. A triangular gibbet is raised in the centre of an extensive plain, commanding a view of the city; attached to this gibbet is a stone platform, lightly railed in with iron, so as to admit of all that takes place being distinctly viewed by the spectators. A large

94

grave was dug in front of it. The ground was kept by a detachment of lancers, formed in hollow squares, and enfiladed round the execution place by an inner square of the infantry guard. About half an hour before the appearance of the criminal, twelve persons—executioners, officers of police, and two little boys as assistants—mounted the scaffold, and fixed the strangling cords. At length the buzz of the surrounding multitude, the flourishing of naked sabres, and the galloping of the officers, announced the slow approach of the criminal upon a hurdle drawn by six horses. On his approach, the word of command flew through the ranks, arms presented, drums beat, and colours and lancers' flags were raised, until he had mounted the scaffold. During the yet short space that remained for him to make his last, his expiring peace with his offended Maker, no ecclesiastic, as in England, appeared to gild the horrors of eternity in those awful moments, when religion arrays itself in her brightest robes, and bids the expiring criminal sink into her everlasting arms with hope, if not with security; no dying and repentant prayer closed the quivering lips of the blood-stained murderer. Never (continues the narrator), never shall I forget the one bitter look of imploring agony that he threw around him, as almost immediately on stepping on the scaffold, his coat was rudely torn from off his shoulders. He was then thrown down, the cords fixed round his neck, which were drawn by the executioner until strangulation almost commenced, or at least until luxation of the neck was effected. Another executioner then approached, bearing in his hands a heavy wheel bound with iron, with which he violently struck the legs, stomach, arms, and chest, and lastly the head of the criminal. I was unfortunately near enough to witness his mangled and bleeding body still convulsed. It was then carried down for interment, and in less than a quarter of an hour from the beginning of his torture, the corpse was completely covered with earth! Several large stones which were thrown upon him hastened his last gasp: he was mangled into eternity."

Before closing the subject of hanging by the neck mention may be made of the famous German secret society of the *Fehmgericht*, which acquired an immense influence, especially in Westphalia. This much maligned society certainly abused its privileges, but less so than many other secret societies. The refusal to obey the thrice-served summons was dealt with by the first of the free judges (*freischoffen*) who met the accused and hanged him to a tree. The members of the society (*wissende*) were reputed to number over a hundred thousand. This society was not suppressed until 1811 by order of King Jerome Bounaparte.

So far this chapter has dealt with hanging by the neck, but there were other ways by which people could be hanged in a more painful, if a less dangerous, manner.

The *picquet* (or *puntale*) has already been mentioned, but a similar form of torture was used in the Tower of London. This was known as *the gauntlets* and consisted of two iron gloves which hung from a column about nine or ten feet from the ground. They were fastened onto the hands of the victim by means of screws which caused excruciating pain, the victim being placed upon blocks of wood so as to be able to reach them. The blocks were then removed one by one until the victim was suspended by his crushed hands and fingers. Father Gerard, of Gunpowder Treason fame, is said to have suffered this torture on two occasions. On the first he was left hanging for five hours. On the second he fainted but was revived by having vinegar poured down his throat. It was twenty days before he recovered the use of his limbs.

A description of this torture is given by Ainsworth in his *Guy Fawkes*; the victim in this case being a Viviana Radcliffe:

"You are Jasper Ipgreve?" said Viviana, rising.

"Right," replied the jailor. "I am come to take you before the lieutenant and the council. Are you ready?"

Viviana replied in the affirmative, and Ipgreve, quitting the cell, outside which two other officials in sable habiliments were stationed, led the way down a short, spiral staircase, which brought them to a narrow vaulted passage. Pursuing it for some time, the jailer halted before a strong door, cased with iron, and opening it, admitted the captive into a square chamber, the roof of which was supported by a heavy stone pillar, while its walls were garnished with implements of torture. At a table on the left sat the lieutenant and three other grave-looking personages. Across the lower end of the chamber a thick, black curtain was stretched, hiding a deep recess; and behind it, as was evident from the glimmer that escaped from its folds, there was a light. Certain indistinct but ominous sounds issuing from the recess proved that there were persons within it, and Viviana's quaking heart told her what was the nature of their proceedings.

She had ample time to survey this dismal apartment and its occupants, for several minutes elapsed before a word was addressed to her by her interrogators, who continued to confer together in an undertone, as if unconscious of her presence. During this pause, broken only by the ominous sounds before mentioned, Viviana scanned the countenances of the group at the table, in the hope of discerning in them some glimpses of compassion; but they were inscrutable and inexorable, and scarcely less dreadful to look upon than the hideous implements on the walls.

Viviana wished the earth would open and swallow her, that she might escape from them. Anything was better than to be left at the mercy of such men. At certain times, and not unfrequently at the most awful moments, a double current of thought will flow through the brain, and at this frightful juncture it was so with Viviana. Whilst shuddering at all she saw around her, nay, dwelling upon it, yet another and distinct train of thought led her back to former scenes of happiness.

These reflections were suddenly dispersed by the lieutenant, who, in a stern tone, commenced his interrogations.

As upon her previous examination, Viviana observed the utmost caution, and either refused to speak or answered such questions only as affected herself. At first, in spite of all her efforts, she trembled violently, and her tongue clove to the roof of her mouth. But after a while she recovered her courage, and regarded the lieutenant with a look as determined as his own.

"It is useless to urge me farther," she concluded. "I have said all I will say."

"Is it your pleasure, my lords," observed Sir William Waad to the others, "to prolong the examination?"

His companions replied in the negative, and the one nearest him remarked, "Is she aware what will follow?"

"I am," replied Viviana resolutely, "and I am not to be intimidated."

Sir William Waad then made a sign to Ipgreve, who immediately stepped forward and seized her arm. "You will be taken to that recess," said the lieutenant, "where the question will be put to you. But, as we shall remain here, you have only to utter a cry if you are willing to avow the truth, and the torture shall be stayed. And it is our merciful hope that this may be the case."

Summoning up all her resolution, and walking with a firm footstep, Viviana passed with Ipgreve behind the curtain. She there beheld two men and a woman—the latter was the jailer's wife, who instantly advanced to her and besought her to confess.

"Mind your own business, dame," interposed Ipgreve angrily, "and assist her to unrobe."

Saying this, he stepped aside with the two men, one of whom was the chirurgeon, and the other the tormentor, while Dame Ipgreve helped to take off Viviana's gown. She then tied a scarf over her shoulders, and informed her husband she was ready.

The recess was about twelve feet high and ten wide. It was crossed near the roof, which was arched and vaulted, by a heavy beam, with pulleys and ropes at either extremity. But what chiefly attracted the unfortunate captive's attention was a couple of iron gauntlets attached to it, about a yard apart. Upon the ground under the beam, and immediately beneath that part of it where the gauntlets were fixed, were laid three pieces of wood of a few inches in thickness and piled one upon another.

"What must I do?" inquired Viviana, in a hollow voice, but with unaltered resolution, of the old woman. "Step upon those pieces of wood," replied Dame Ipgreve, leading her towards them.

Viviana obeyed, and as soon as she had set foot upon the pile, the tormentor placed a joint-stool beside her, and, mounting it, desired her to place her right hand in one of the gauntlets. She did so, and the tormentor then turned a screw, which compressed the iron glove so tightly as to give her excruciating pain. He then got down, and Ipgreve demanded if he should proceed.

A short pause ensued, but, notwithstanding her agony, Viviana made no answer. The tormentor then placed the stool on the left side and fastened the hand which was still at liberty within the other gauntlet. The torture was dreadful—and the fingers appeared

98

crushed by the pressure. Still Viviana uttered no cry. After another short pause, Ipgreve said:

"You had better let us stop here. This is mere child's play compared with what is to come."

No answer being returned, the tormentor took a mallet and struck one of the pieces of wood from under Viviana's feet. The shock was dreadful and seemed to dislocate her wrists, while the pressure on the hands was increasing in a tenfold degree. The poor sufferer, who was resting on the points of her feet, felt that the removal of the next piece of wood would occasion almost intolerable torture. Her constancy, however, did not desert her, and, after the question had been repeated by Ipgreve, the second block was struck away. She was now suspended by her hands, and the pain was so exquisite that nature gave way and, uttering a piercing scream, she fainted.

A similar form of torture was used on the Continent and especially by the Holy Inquisition. In the Continental form the gauntlets were dispensed with; the hands of the victim were tied behind his back and attached to these was a rope running over a pulley. He was raised from the ground, his arms being strained unnaturally upwards and backwards. If no confession was forthcoming, his joints were jerked by letting the rope loose and allowing him to fall a short distance. At Orleans this torture was slightly varied. For the ordinary torture the accused was stripped half naked and his hands were tied behind his back with a ring fixed between them to which was fastened the cord running over the pulley. A weight of 180 lb. was attached to his feet and he was raised from the ground by means of a windlass. For the extraordinary torture, which was given the name of *estrapade*, the victim was raised with 250 lb. tied to his feet; he was allowed to tall suddenly, several times in succession, nearly to the level of the ground, by which means his arms and legs were completely dislocated. The Germans improved upon this torture according to the Rev. Dr. A. Wylie's description of Nuremberg:

There was the iron chain which wound over a pulley and hauled up the victim to the vaulted roof; and there were the two great stone weights, which, tied to his feet and the iron cord let go, brought him down with a jerk that dislocated his limbs, while the spike rollers, which he grazed in his descent, cut into and excoriated his back, leaving his body a bloody dislocated mass.

The dislocation of the shoulders and arms of labourers and artisans at Rome led to many cases of suicide, as they were unable to earn their bread after the application of this form of torture; and the *cavaletto* was substituted in its place.

A more merciful form of torture was practised at Avignon as an ordinary torture, which was to suspend the victim by the wrists with a heavy iron ball attached to his feet. For the extraordinary torture at Avignon the Italian form of torture known as the *veglia* was used. The *veglia* was a very common form of torture throughout Italy. The body of the victim was stretched horizontally by means of ropes attached to his wrists and ankles which were drawn tight through rings in the walls, the only support for the body being a pointed stake just touching the backbone.

A torture common in China said to be very effective was suspending the victim by his ankles and swinging him continually backwards and forwards.

Som hung vpon Tenterhooks

CHAPTER V

SHAME

Cropped! aye, and the luckiest thing that could happen to you! Why, I would not give twopence for an author who is afraid of his ears!—SAMUEL FOOTE

MANY means were employed in ancient times to punish minor offences by bringing their perpetrators into public contempt.

We have seen that the Romans employed the *furca* in the first degree as a purely ignominious punishment; and branding, under European law, served a similar, if more lasting, purpose.

The object of these forms of punishment was to humiliate the culprit and set him up as an example to others. The humiliation sometimes lasted a lifetime.

The most obvious examples are the pillory and stocks, but branding, and the deprivation of a limb or two, served the same purpose. Pike, in his *History of Crime in England*, writes that men branded on the forehead, men without hands, without feet, without tongues, lived as an example of the danger which attended the commission of petty crimes, and as a warning to all men who had the misfortune to hold no higher position than that of a churl.

One of the worst forms of these punishments by ignominy, and one which attained great popularity in France during the reign of Louis XI, was "the cage".

It is difficult to trace the first instance of the use of the cage as a punishment, but it was employed in 1306, when the Countess of Buchan, who had been extremely active in the cause of Bruce, and even placed the crown on his head, was, by the order of King Edward, shut up in a wooden cage in one of the towers of Berwick Castle. The order to the Chamberlain of Scotland, or his lieutenant in Berwick, for making the cage was by writ of privy seal, by which he was directed to make in one of the turrets of Berwick-upon-Tweed, which he should find the most convenient, a strong cage of lattice-work, constructed with posts and bars and well strengthened with iron. This cage was to be so contrived that the Countess might have therein the necessary convenience, proper care being taken that it did not lessen the security of her person; that the said Countess, being put in this cage, should be so carefully guarded that she should not by any means go out of it; that a woman or two of the town of Berwick, of unsuspected character, should be appointed to administer her food and drink, and attend her on other occasions; and that she should be so strictly guarded in the said cage as not to be permitted to speak to any person, man or woman, of the Scottish nation, or any other, except the woman or women assigned to attend her and her other guards.[1] Mary, the sister of Bruce, suffered a similar fate in Roxburgh Castle.

Another instance of the early use of the cage was when Tamerlane the Great (1335–1405) captured Bajazet, Emperor of the Turks, and ordered him to be enclosed in an iron cage and exposed like a wild beast. The cage was carried along in the train of the conqueror for three years, until the great Bajazet, despairing of ever being released, thrust his head with such violence against the iron bars that he died.[2]

Louis XI of France greatly utilised the cage, and he was assisted in their construction by the Bishop of Verdun,

[1] According to Matthew of Westminster, the King ordered that as she (the Countess) did not strike with the sword, she should not die by the sword, but ordered her to be shut up in an habitation of stone and iron, shaped like a crown, and to be hung out at Berwick in the open air, for a spectacle and everlasting reproach, while living or dead, to all that passed by.

[2] In 1403.

who himself suffered for fourteen days in one of them. Louis specialised in three forms of punishment, though he certainly did not neglect the others.[1] The three were hanging, drowning with a stone tied to the victim's neck, and exposing the culprit in a cage attached to the walls of one of his castles.[2]

The cage was employed even as late as the reign of Louis XIV, who caused the publisher of a Leyden gazette to be enclosed in a cage at St. Michael. The cage was made of wood and was about nine feet long, six broad, and eight high. The wretched prisoner employed his time in carving landscapes and figures on the bars with his nails.

To bring variety into the punishment of the cage, prisoners were occasionally given the companionship of one or two wild cats; and to stir these ferocious animals into activity the cage was heated.

The cage is still used as a means of punishment for robbery in Afghanistan. The criminal is placed in a cage on the top of a post and is left to starve to death.

A simpler form of punishment, similar in idea to the cage, was merely to chain up the prisoner in some exposed place, so that he could be ridiculed by passers-by. Agrippa was punished in this way by Tiberius, who ordered him to be chained to the palace gates.

In England, and, more especially, in Scotland, this punishment was very common under the name of the *jougs*.[3] The *jougs* consisted of an iron collar attached to a chain by which means the prisoner was fastened in some exposed position, generally to the cross in the market-place, the door of the church, or a tree in the churchyard.

[1] See Philip de Comines, *Life of Louis XI.*
[2] Of this monarch Mesaria writes, "that he had put to death above four thousand by different punishments, which he sometimes delighted to see. Most of them had been executed without form of law; several drowned with stones tied to their necks; other precipitated, going over a swipe, from whence they fell upon wheels armed with spikes and cutting instruments; others were strangled in dungeons; Tristan, his companion and provost of his palace, being at once judge, witness, and executioner."
[3] In Ayrshire the name given to the *jougs* was *bregan* or *bradyeane.*

An instance of the punishment of the *jougs* in England is given in the *Diary of Henry Machyn, Citizen and Merchant-Taylor of London, from* A.D. *1550 to* A.D. *1563*:

The 30th day of June, 1553, was set a post hard by the Standard in Cheap, and a young fellow tied to the post with a collar of iron about his neck, and another to the post with a chain, and two men with two whips whipping them about the post, for pretended visions and opprobrious and seditious words.

Another interesting case of the infliction of the *jougs* is given in Charles Rogers' *Social Life in Scotland*.[1]

David Leyes, who struck his father, was sentenced by a Kirk-Session of St. Andrews, in 1574, to appear before the congregation "bairheddit and bairfuttit, upon the highest degree of the penitent stuool, with a hammer in ane hand and ane stane in the uther hand, as the twa instruments he mannesit his father—with ane papir writin in great letteris about his heid with these wordis, 'Behold the onnaturall Son, punished for putting hand on his father, and dishonouring of God in him.' " Nor was this deemed sufficient humiliation, for the offender was afterwards made to stand at the market cross two hours in the jaggs, and thereafter cartit through the haill toun.

The most common use of the *jougs* in England and Scotland was as a punishment for persons who neglected to attend church, or who caused a disturbance during the service.

Sometimes the punishment of the *jougs* exceeded punishment merely by ignominy. In 1541 Bishop Bonner ordered John Porter to Newgate for reading the Bible.

The young man had a chain put round his neck, and was tied to a post several days, at the end of which he was found dead.[2]

In early days prisoners of war were frequently led in triumph through the principal towns of their conquerors; and in the Middle Ages persons convicted of petty offences

[1] See Andrews, *Old-Time Punishments*.
[2] The Rev. Henry Southwell's *New Book of Martyrs*.

were often similarly treated as an example to would-be wrong-doers. Sometimes the victim was led by a rope held by the public hangman; sometimes a drummer headed the procession to attract attention; sometimes the culprit was whipped through the town; and sometimes he was carried on a chair,[1] or led through the town on a donkey, his face towards its tail.

An instance of riding the stang was given in the Liverpool *Mercury* as recently as the 15th of March, 1887:[2]

That ancient Welsh custom, now nearly obsolete, known as riding the ceffyl pren—*anglice*, "wooden-horse"—and intended to operate as a wholesome warning to faithless wives and husbands, was revived on Saturday night in an Anglesey village some three miles from Llangefni. The individual who had drawn upon himself the odium of his neighbours had parted from his wife and was alleged to be persistent in his attentions to another female. On Saturday night a large party surrounded the house, and compelled him to get astride a ladder, carrying him shoulder-high through the village, stopping at certain points to allow the womankind to wreak their vengeance upon him. This amusement was kept up for some time until the opportune arrival of a sergeant of police from Llangefni, who rescued the unlucky wight.

The repentance stool and public penance were frequent punishments for ecclesiastical offences, but in most cases the offender acted voluntarily in submitting to these acts. There were, of course, exceptions; and public penance was ordered by ecclesiastical courts.[3]

A few minor forms may be noted as interesting, forming examples of this type of punishment, but, when one remembers that each lord of the manor, each monastery and each village claimed rights of punishing local offenders in its own way, it is impossible to go into great detail in a

[1] This was known as "riding the stang" and was usually inflicted for matrimonial offences.
[2] W. Andrews, *Old-Time Punishments*.
[3] E.g. Jane Shore, mistress of Edward IV.

single chapter. However, the following are a few of the more general forms of punishment by ignominy.

The Cucking-Stool was a chair in which the offender was bound outside his or her dwelling. It is mentioned as far back as the Domesday Book. It was common in Scotland in very early days, chiefly as a punishment for Ale-wives who sold bad ale.[1] In 1555 it was enacted by the Queen Regent of Scotland that itinerant singing women should be put on the "Cuck-stules". The Cucking-Stool later got confused with the Ducking-Stool, which was a method of dealing with "scolds" or nagging women; and the two words became synonymous. The Ducking-Stool was a chair fastened to the end of a beam which could be swung out over a river or pond. The offender was usually immersed three times.

> There stands, my friend, in yonder pool,
> An engine call'd a ducking-stool;
> By legal pow'r commanded down,
> The joy and terror of the town.
> If jarring females kindle strife,
> Give language foul, or lug the coif;
> If noisy dames should once begin
> To drive the house with horrid din,
> Away, you cry, you'll grace the stool,
> We'll teach you how your tongue to rule.
> The fair offender fills the seat,
> In sullen pomp, profoundly great.
> Down in the deep the stool descends,
> But here, at first, we miss our ends;
> She mounts again, and rages more
> Than ever vixen did before.
> So, throwing water on the fire,
> Will but make it burn the higher.

[1] "Wemen quha brews aill to be sauld, gif she makes gude ail, that is sufficient; but gif she makes evill ail, contrair to the use and consuetude of the burgh, and his convict thereof, she sail pay ane unlaw of aucht shillinges, or sal suffer the justice of the burgh, that is, she sall be put upon the cuck-stule, and the ail sall be distributed to the pure folke" (Sir John Skene, *Regiam Majestatem*).

If so, my friend, pray let her take
A second turn into the lake;
And, rather than your patience lose,
Thrice and again repeat the dose.
No brawling wives, no furious wenches,
No fire so hot but water quenches.[1]

The Ducking-Stool survived until 1809, when a woman known as Jenny Pipes was paraded through the streets of Leominster, and ducked on the town Ducking-Stool by order of the magistrates.

The Ducking-Stool was in common use in America, a woman, Mary Davis, being publicly ducked in 1813; and its use continued to a much later date than it did in England. According to W. Andrews, a woman named Miss Annie Pope was charged on the 8th August, 1890, with being a common scold, and was committed for trial at the assizes at Ottawa as the magistrate had no Ducking-Stool.

Abroad, an improvement was made on the Ducking-Stool by the invention of Ducking-Cages, which were used for various offences. These cages, usually made of oak and about six feet high, were employed in the same manner as the Ducking-Stool. The victim was enclosed in the cage, which was sometimes provided with a seat, and was ducked, the cage being drawn up and down in the water till the wretched occupant was nearly drowned.

Another method of dealing with scolds was the "Brank" or "Scold's Bridle", which was an iron mask that fitted over the victim's face, with a protruding piece pressing upon her tongue to prevent her from speaking. Thus masked she was led through the town. This punishment was common all over Europe.[2] The protruding bar was generally a blunt piece of iron, but there are Continental examples with spiked bars, which lacerated the tongue;

[1] Benjamin West.
[2] This was a punishment for scolds only in England, but for various minor offences abroad.

and there is a terrible Brank in Ludlow Museum which
was described by W. J. Bernard Smith;[1] as follows:

The powerful screwing apparatus seems calculated to force the
iron mask with torturing effect upon the brow of the victim;
there are no eye-holes, but concavities in their places, as though
to allow for the starting of the eye-balls under violent pressure.
There is a strong bar with a square hole, evidently intended to
fasten the criminal against a wall, or perhaps to the pillory; and
I have heard it said that these instruments were used to keep
the head steady during the infliction of branding.

The female sex was not the only one to have punishments
by ignominy selected for it. There was a special punishment for drunkards known as the "Drunkard's Cloak".
This was a barrel without a bottom and through the top
was a hole for the head of the victim. The barrel was
placed over his head and rested on his shoulders; small
slots were made at the sides through which the culprit
could put his hands. Bearing this weight he was led through
the town. This punishment was very popular in the time
of the Commonwealth.

Ralph Gardener, in his *England's Grievance Discovered in
Relation to the Coal Trade* published in 1655, gives depositions of various witnesses to support his charges against
the magistrates of Newcastle-upon-Tyne. One of these
refers to the branks and to the drunkard's cloak.

John Willis, of Ipswich, upon his oath said that he, and this
deponent, was in Newcastle six months ago, and there he saw
one Ann Bridlestone drove through the streets by an officer of the
same corporation, holding a rope in his hand, the other end
fastened to an engine called the branks, which is like a crown, it
being of iron, which was musled over the head and face, with a
great gag or tongue of iron forced into her mouth, which forced
the blood out; and that is the punishments which the magistrates
do inflict upon chiding and scolding women; and he hath often
seen the like done to others.

[1] *Archæological Journal*, September 1856. See Andrews, *Old-Time Punishments*.
108

He, this deponent, further affirms that he hath seen men drove up and down the streets with a great tub or barrel opened in the sides, with a hole in one end to put through their heads, and so cover their shoulders and bodies, down to the small of their legs, and then close the same, called the new-fashioned cloak, and so make them march to the view of all beholders; and this is their punishments for dunkards and the like.

The Drunkard's Cloak was known all over the Continent. John Evelyn wrote in 1634 that he had seen one in the Senate house at Delft and he describes it as—

A weighty vessel of wood, not unlike a butter-churn, which the adventurous woman that hath two husbands at one time is to wear on her shoulders, her head peeping out at the top only, and so led about the town, as a penance for her incontinence.

Pepys mentions a similar barrel at The Hague in 1660. John Howard, in his *The State of Prisons in England and Wales*, 1784, writes:

Denmark—some (criminals) of the lower sort, as watchmen, coachmen, etc., are punished by being led through the city in what is called "The Spanish Mantle". This is a kind of heavy vest, something like a tub, with an aperture for the head, and irons to enclose the neck. I measured one at Berlin, 1 ft. 8 in. in diameter at the top, 2 ft. 11 in. at the bottom, and 2 ft. 11 in. high.

The Drunkard's Cloak was used in the United States of America, but for a different kind of offence. American drunkards were usually led through the streets with a wooden board suspended from their necks, upon which was painted a large red "D". The author of a paper published in 1862, under the title of *A Look at the Federal Army*, writes:[1]

I was extremely amused to see a "rare" specimen of Yankee invention in the shape of an original method of punishment drill. One wretched delinquent was gratuitously framed in oak, his

[1] Andrews, *Old-Time Punishments*,

head being thrust through a hole cut in one end of a barrel, the other end of which had been removed; and the poor fellow "loafed" about in the most disconsolate manner, looking for all the world like a half-hatched chicken. Another defaulter had heavy weights fastened to his wrists, his hands and feet being chained together.

In China a similar punishment was used for various offences such as robbery, defamation, gambling, etc. This was the "wooden collar", or *Cangue*, which was a large, heavy, square piece of woodwork with an opening in the centre for the neck. Once fixed, the culprit was compelled to wear it for a period which varied according to the nature of his offence, the framework being sealed to prevent tampering, as it was only to be taken off in the presence of a magistrate at the expiration of the sentence. Insolvent debtors were sometimes ordered to wear the *Cangue* until they had satisfied their creditors. One of the points to note about this torture was that the accused could not reach his mouth with his hands, and was thus unable to obtain food and drink unless it was given to him. An unpopular victim often died of thirst or starvation.

The Pillory or "Stretch Neck" was the commonest form of ignominious punishment. It consisted of a wooden post and frame fixed on a platform raised several feet from the ground, behind which the culprit stood, his head and hands being thrust through holes in the frame and exposed in front of it. This frame, in the more complicated forms of the instrument, consisted of a perforated iron circle, which secured the heads and hands of several persons at the same time.

The severity of the punishment depended upon whether the criminal was popular or not. In some cases the crowd pelted the victim with refuse until he died; in others, his punishment was a public triumph.

In 1364 John de Hakford was sentenced to a year's imprisonment and to stand in the pillory for three hours every three months "without hood or girdle, barefoot and unshod, with a whetstone hung by a chain from his neck and lying on his breast, it being marked with the words, A FALSE LIAR, and there shall be a pair of trumpets trumpeting before him on his way". His offence was that he told a friend there were ten thousand men ready to rise and slay the chief men of London.

The punishment of the pillory frequently included mutilation. The ears were sometimes nailed to the woodwork when the victim was set in the pillory and sliced off before he was released, or the nose of the culprit was slit, or his face branded.

Fog's Weekly Journal for June 12, 1731, gives an account of the punishment of the pillory being put into execution:

Thursday, Japhet Cook, *alias* Sir Peter Stringer, who was, some time since, convicted of forging deeds of conveyance of two thousand acres of land belonging to Mr. Garbet and his wife, lying in the Parish of Claxton, in the County of Essex, was brought by the keeper of the King's Bench, to Charing Cross, where he stood in the pillory from twelve to one, pursuant to his sentence. The time being near expired, he was set on a chair on the pillory, when the hangman, dressed like a butcher, came to him, and, with a knife like a gardener's pruning-knife, cut off his ears and, with a pair of scissors, slit both his nostrils; all which Cook bore with great patience, but, at the searing with hot irons of his right nostril, the pain was so violent that he got up from his chair. His left nostril was not seared, so he went from the pillory bleeding.

Another example is given in the *Morning Herald*, of the 28th of January, 1804:

The enormity of Thomas Scott's offence, in endeavouring to accuse Captain Kennah, a respectable officer, together with his servant, of robbery, having attracted much public notice, his conviction that followed the attempt could not but be gratifying to all lovers of justice. Yesterday, the culprit underwent a part of his punishment: he was placed in the pillory at Charing Cross for one hour. On his first appearance he was greeted by a large mob with a discharge of small shot, such as rotten eggs, filth, and dirt from the streets, which were followed up by dead cats, rats, etc., which had been collected in the vicinity of the Metropolis by the boys in the morning. When he was taken away to Cold Bath Fields, to which place he was sentenced for twelve months, the mob broke the windows of the coach and would have proceeded to violence had not the police officers been at hand.

The pillory was abolished in England at the end of the reign of William IV, in 1837, the last victim being Peter James Bossy, who suffered on the 22nd of June, 1832.

In France the pillory was known as the *carcan* and was often a large permanent structure in which many persons could be pilloried at the same time. Sometimes these pillories were made to revolve slowly. W. H. Ainsworth, in his *John Law*, gives the following description of a French pillory:

On the following day, the first part of this rigorous sentence was carried into effect. Stripped to the shirt, with ropes round their necks, lighted candles in their bound hands, the two miserable men were attached to a tumbrel. On the back of each hung a label, inscribed, "Robber of the People". In this wretched condition they were dragged through the streets, amid the hootings of the rabble, to the Pillori des Halles—an octangular turret, built of stone and having a tall pointed roof, which stood on one side of the picturesque old market-place. At each angle of the structure was a lofty unglazed window, so that a large horizontal wheel, turning upon a pivot, could be distinctly seen inside. Within the bands of this revolving wheel, which in fact formed the pillory, were holes destined to receive the head and hands of the sufferers. Fixed to this machine, in the painful and degrading position alluded to, poor Laborde and his faithful servant were exposed for several hours to the insults and outrages of the mob, who pelted them incessantly with mud, rotten eggs, and other missiles.

The pillory was abolished in France in 1832.

In the United States of America the pillory was abolished in 1839, except in the State of Delaware, where it survived as late as 1905.

There was another kind of pillory of which mention must be made. This was the finger-pillory which

In order to preserve as much as possible the degree of decorum that was necessary (at manorial festivals during the fifteenth century) there were frequently introduced a diminutive pair of stone stocks of about eighteen inches in length, for confining within them the fingers of the unruly.

There is an example of this kind of pillory in the parish church of Ashby-de-la-Zouch, which was described in *Notes and Queries* of the 25th of October, 1851, as:

Fastened at its right hand extremity into a wall, and consists of two pieces of oak; the bottom and fixed piece is three feet eight inches long; the width of the whole is four-and-a-half inches and, when closed, it is five inches deep: the left hand extremity is supported by a leg of the same width as the top, and two feet six inches in length; the upper piece is joined to the lower by a hinge, and in this lower and fixed horizontal part are a number of holes varying in size; the largest are towards the right hand: these holes are sufficiently deep to admit the finger to the second joint, and a slight hollow is made to admit the third one, which lies flat; there is, of course, a corresponding hollow at the top of the movable part, which, when shut down, encloses the whole finger.

Plot, in his *History of Staffordshire*, 1686, gives a further description of a finger-pillory:

I cannot forget a piece of art that I found in the Hall of the Right Honourable William Lord Paget, at Beaudesart, made for the punishment of disorders that sometimes attended feasting in Christmas time, etc., called the finger-stocks, into which the Lord of Misrule used to put the fingers of all such persons as committed misdemeanours, or broke such rules as, by consent, were agreed on for the time of keeping Christmas among the servants and others of promiscuous quality; there being divided in like manner as the stocks of the legs, and having holes of different sizes to fit for scantlings of all fingers, as represented in the table.

The stocks, which date from Anglo-Saxon times, may be described as the local form of pillory. They were used either as a means of detaining a prisoner before trial or as a punishment for petty offences.

The culprit sat on the ground, or on a bench, with his ankles, and sometimes his wrists, or even his neck, thrust through holes in movable boards. Sometimes intentional cruelty was used in the confinement.[1]

Attempts were made at various times to induce every village to erect its own stocks.[2]

The stocks were used as a punishment for various petty offences, but chiefly as the penalty for drinking not wisely but too well. Cardinal Wolsey was a distinguished sufferer, being put in the stocks about the year 1500 at Lymington, near Yeovil, for overstepping the bounds of moderation!

The use of the stocks declined early in the nineteenth century, though they were never abolished by law. They were employed at Rugby as late as 1867.[3]

Many villages had a combination of pillory, stocks, and whipping-post all in one.

The stocks were frequently used in the United States, in the New England States, during the eighteenth century, and in the Southern States, as a common method of punishing slaves.

To conclude, the following is a poem taken from Andrews's *Old-Time Punishments*, by a Mr. John Cotton, of Birmingham:

[1] King and his companions, who burned the image at Devonport in 1532, were among his (Rose's) constant hearers; and the Romanists at that time were eager for his destruction. He was sent to London and confined for many months in Bishop Langley's house in Holborn, being kept in the stocks for several weeks; at which his sufferings were very severe, as they laid him with his back upon the ground, while his feet were raised up. See *Annals of Queen Mary*.
[2] See Acts of 1350 and 1405 and Prayer of the Commons to King Edward III, 1376.
[3] See letters to *The Times* from Lord Warrington of Clyffe and Mr. A. Scott, 31st of January, 1929. A later case has been reported from Cardiganshire. A man named John Foster is stated to have been put in the stocks at Newcastle Emlyn on the 19th of January, 1872.

View of the Inside of Lollard's Tower, with the manner of torturing the Protestants, by order of BISHOP BONNER, during the reign of QUEEN MARY.

SHAME

Thus, times and customs, men and manners change,
And so all institutions have their day;
Like instruments of torture, out of range
Of memory, the stocks will pass away,
And with them those that 'neath yon tree decay.

. . . . . .

The ducking-stool is done with, and the helm,
Contrivances ordained for scolding wives;
The pillory is banished from the realm,
And corporal punishment no longer thrives,
Save through the cat, which now alone survives.

. . . . . .

Each mode has served its turn, and played a part
For good or ill with man; but while the bane
Of drunkenness corrupts the nation's heart—
Discrediting our age—methinks the reign
Of stocks, at least, were well revived again.

. . . . . .

CHAPTER VI

COMPRESSION

Of all the monsters that the world pollute,
None is so savage as a human brute;
Man, when benevolence is once forgot,
Is one gross error, one prodigious blot.

Som Prest to Death with
Great weights of Leade

THERE are many forms of torture which come under the heading of "Compression", but none more terrible than that practised until comparatively quite a recent date in England.

Despite the fact that torture was not permitted by English law to force an accused person to confess, it was often used to compel him to plead, and it was not until 1772 that he could be tried by a jury without his express consent!

In early times trial was by compurgation and the ordeal, until the Normans introduced trial by combat. The ordeal was forbidden by the Lateran Council, and trial by inquest, which is the form of trial subsisting to-day, made its appearance. An inquest had to be authorized by the king, and, unless the accused was prepared to waive the king's authorization by pleading to the indictment, there was no right in law to adopt this procedure. By an Act passed in 1772, a person refusing to plead was taken to be convicted, and it was not until 1827 that his refusal was taken to be a plea of "Not Guilty".

Before 1772, if an accused refused to plead, the jury had to decide whether he was "mute of malice"[1] or

[1] The meaning of the legal word "malice" is "intent".

"mute by the visitation of God".[1] If he was found to be "mute of malice", means of persuasion were adopted to compel him to plead. Before (about) 1406, the prisoner was starved until he complied or died; this was given the name of *prison forte et dure*.[2] After that date various means of persuasion came into force; sometimes the victim's thumbs were tied with cord and twisted,[3] or he was suspended by a cord from the rafters, but the more usual method and the one which became the normal procedure was the infliction of the *peine forte et dure*.

There were very few cases in which the accused refused to plead, and of these only a small number failed to submit under the infliction of the *peine forte et dure*. The usual reason for the refusal was that by dying under the torture, instead of being found guilty and hanged, the accused saved his goods from forfeiture and his family from penury. It was only the goods of a convicted felon that were forfeited to the State.

The torture of the *peine forte et dure* (pressing to death) originated in England, and was not widely adopted elsewhere, though it was used in America at Salem, in 1692, on Giles Cory, who refused to plead when arraigned for witchcraft,[4] and it was one of the punishments used by the Ku-Klux-Klan. It was also used in Ireland, the last reported case being in 1740. The victim was stripped and tied to the ground with his arms and legs extended; a square board was then placed on his chest, upon which

[1] The findings of the jury were not always just. At the Nottingham Assizes in 1735 a man who had been deaf and dumb from his infancy was pressed to death, continuing, says the register of the times, "obstinately dumb to the last"!

[2] In the reign of Edward III a prisoner lived forty days' starvation under the *prison forte et dure* and was pardoned.

[3] In 1721 Mary Andrews, after bearing the first three whipcords, which broke from the violence of the twisting, submitted to plead at the fourth. In 1741 Baron Carter, at the Cambridge Assizes, and Baron Thompson, at the Sussex Assizes, ordered prisoners who refused to plead to have their thumbs twisted with cords.

[4] Bouvier.

weights[1] were laid until he pleaded or life became extinct. The torture occasionally lasted three days. A triangular board was sometimes placed under the victim's back, which had the effect of breaking his spine, thus bringing the torture to a more rapid termination.

The infliction of the torture is described by Ainsworth in his *Jack Sheppard* as follows:

Blueskin, having been indicted by Wild for several robberies, and true bills found against him, was placed at the bar of the Old Bailey to be arraigned; when he declared that he would not plead to the indictment, unless the sum of five hundred pounds, taken from him by Jonathan Wild, was first restored to him. This sum, claimed by Wild under the statute 4th and 5th of William and Mary, entitled "*An Act for Encouraging the Apprehending of Highwaymen*", was granted to him by the court.

As Blueskin still continued obstinate, the judgment appointed to be executed upon such prisoners as stood mute was then read. It was as follows, and, when uttered, produced a strong effect upon all who heard it except the prisoner, who in no respect altered his sullen and dogged demeanour.

"Prisoner at the bar," thus ran the sentence, "you shall be taken to the prison from whence you came, and put into a mean room, stopped from the light; and shall there be laid on the bare ground, without any litter, straw, or other covering, and without any garment. You shall lie upon your back; your head shall be covered; and your feet shall be bare. One of your arms shall be drawn to one side of the room, and the other arm to the other side; and your legs shall be served in the like manner. Then there shall be laid upon your body as much iron, or stone, as you can bear, and more. And the first day you shall have three morsels of barley bread, without any drink; and the second day you shall be allowed to drink as much as you can, at three times, of the water that is next to the prison-door, except running-

[1] In 1721 Nathaniel Hawes, after the cord had proved inefficacious, bore weights of 250 pounds before he was willing to plead. Thomas Spiggot, according to the Rev. Mr. Willette (*Annals of Newgate*, 1776), bore 400 pounds before pleading, and Burnworth is said to have borne 4 cwt. before pleading at Kingston in 1726.

water, without any bread. And this shall be your diet till you die."

"Prisoner at the bar," continued the clerk of the court, "he against whom this judgment is given, forfeits his goods to the king."

An awful silence prevailed throughout the court. Every eye was fixed upon the prisoner. But, as he made no answer, he was removed.

Before the full sentence was carried into execution, he was taken into a small room adjoining the court. Here Marvel, the executioner, who was in attendance, was commanded by Wild to tie his thumbs together, which he did with whipcord so tightly that the string cut to the bone. But as this produced no effect, and did not even elicit a groan, the prisoner was carried back to Newgate.

The Press Room, to which Blueskin was conveyed on his arrival at the jail, was a small, square chamber, walled and paved with stone. In each corner stood a stout, square post reaching to the ceiling. To these a heavy wooden apparatus was attached, which could be raised or lowered at pleasure by pulleys. In the floor were set four ring-bolts, about nine feet apart. When the prisoner was brought into this room, he was again questioned; but, continuing contumacious, preparations were made for inflicting the torture. His great personal strength being so well known, it was deemed prudent by Marvel to have all four partners, together with Caliban, in attendance. The prisoner, however, submitted more quietly than was anticipated. He allowed his irons and clothes to be taken off without resistance. But just as they were about to place him on the ground, he burst from their hold and made a desperate spring at Jonathan, who was standing with his arms folded near the door watching the scene. The attempt was unsuccessful. He was instantly overpowered and stretched upon the ground. The four men fell upon him, holding his arms and legs, while Caliban forced back his head. In this state he contrived to get the poor black's hand into his mouth, and nearly bit off one of his fingers before the sufferer could be rescued. Meanwhile, the executioner had attached strong cords to his ankles and wrists and fastened them tightly to the iron rings. This done, he unloosed the pulley, and the ponderous machine, which resembled a trough, slowly descended upon the prisoner's breast. Marvel then took two iron weights, each of a hundred pounds, and placed them in the press. As this seemed insufficient, after a lapse of five minutes he added another hundred-weight. The prisoner breathed with difficulty. Still, his robust frame enabled him to hold out. After he had endured this torture for an hour, at a sign from Wild, another hundred-weight was added. In a few minutes an appalling change was perceptible. The veins in his throat and forehead swelled and blackened; his eyes protruded from their sockets and stared wildly; a thick damp gathered on his brow, and blood gushed from his mouth, nostrils, and ears.

"Water!" he gasped.

The executioner shook his head.

"Do you submit?" interrogated Wild.

Blueskin answered by dashing his head violently against the flagged floor. His efforts at self-destruction were, however, prevented.

"Try fifty pounds more," said Jonathan.

"Stop!" groaned Blueskin.

"Will you plead?" demanded Wild harshly.

"I will," answered the prisoner.

"Release him," said Jonathan. "We have cured his obstinacy, you perceive," he added to Marvel.

"I will live", cried Blueskin, with a look of the deadliest hatred at Wild, "to be revenged on you."

And as the weights were removed he fainted.

The most remarkable case of the infliction of the *peine forte et dure* was that of Major George Strangeways in 1657–8.

Major Strangeways was a Royalist who, to avoid his estate being sequestered at the end of the Civil War, leased it to his sister, with whom he lived, for her life. His sister, Mabellah Strangeways, became engaged to be married, and Major Strangeways became so infuriated that he murdered the would-be husband and was arrested. He refused to plead to avoid the forfeiture of the family estate and the court[1] directed:

That the prisoner be sent back to the place from whence he came and there put into a mean room where no light can enter, that

[1] Lord Chief Justice Glynn.

he be laid upon his back with his body bare, save something to cover his privy parts, that his arms be stretched forth with a cord, one to each side of the prison, and in like manner his legs shall be used, that upon his body shall be laid as much iron and stone as he can bare and more, that the first day he shall have three morsels of barley bread and the next day he shall drink thrice of the water in the next channel to the prison door, but no fountain or spring water, and this shall be his punishment till he dies.[1]

A request was made that Major Strangeways should be placed on boards with a projecting piece so that he should die more quickly. The request was refused. No sooner had the weights been placed on the board than he begged his friends, who were standing beside him, to end his sufferings by adding their weights to the board. They jumped on the board and a corner, placed over his heart, pressed down and ended his pain.

Whether his friends were guilty of murder or not is difficult to say, but one must bear in mind that at this time it was a common practice for the friends of a felon who was being hanged to end his sufferings by jerking his legs when he was suspended from the gallows.

There is a picture of a Roman Catholic being tortured by the infliction of the *peine forte et dure* in the *Theatrum Crudelitatum Haereticorum*, printed at Antwerp in 1592. According to the heading, "Persecutiones aduersus Catholicos a Protestantibus Caluinistis excitae in Anglia", it would appear that this torture was applied to religious offenders in this country, but, despite this picture, it is doubtful if it was ever used except for the purpose set out above. The "martyr of York", a lady named Margaret Clitheroe (or Clitherow), the step-daughter of the Mayor of York, who was accused of harbouring a Roman Catholic priest and was pressed to death on the 25th of March, 1586,

[1] *The Unhappy Marksman. Or, A Perfect and Impartial Discovery of That Late Barbarous and Unparallel'd Murther Committed by Mr. George Strangeways.* London, 1659.

for refusing to plead to the indictment, is probably the subject of the illustration. The scene is described as follows:[1]

> After she had prayed, Fawcett (one of the sheriffs) commanded them to put off her apparel, when she, with the four women, requested him on their knees that, for the honour of womanhood, this might be dispensed with, but they would not grant it. Then she requested that the women might unparrel her, and that they would turn their faces from her during that time. The women took off her clothes and put on her the long linen habit. Then very quietly she laied her down upon the ground, her face covered with a handkerchief, and most part of her body with the habit. The dore was laied upon her, her hands she joined upon her face. Then the sheriff said: "Naie, ye must have your hands bound!" Then two sergeants parted her hands, and bound them to two posts in the same manner as the feet had been previously fixed. After this they laied weight upon her, which, when she first felt, she said: "Jesu, Jesu, Jesu, have mercye upon mee"; which were the last words she was heard to speake. She was in dying about one quarter of an hower. A sharp stone as big as a man's fist had been put under her back. Upon her was laied to the quantity of seven or eight hundredweight, which, breaking her ribs, caused them to burst forth of the skinne.

The procedure under the Irish law appears, from the following account, to have been somewhat different; for when the accused was found guilty of being "mute of malice", he was ordered to be pressed to death publicly, without being given the option of pleading.

At the Kilkenny Assizes in 1740, one Matthew Ryan was tried for highway robbery. When he was apprehended, he pretended to be a lunatic, stripped himself in the gaol, threw away his clothes and could not be prevailed upon to put them on again, but went as he was to the court to take his trial. He then affected to be dumb and would not plead; on which the judges ordered a jury to be impanelled, to inquire and give their opinion whether he was mute and

[1] Dr. Lingard's *History of England*.

lunatic by the hand of God, or wilfully so. The jury returned in a short time and brought in a verdict of "Wilful and affected dumbness and lunacy". The judges on this desired the prisoner to plead; but he still pretended to be insensible to all that was said to him. The law now called for the *peine forte et dure*; but the judges compassionately deferred awarding it until a future day, in the hope that he might in the meantime acquire a juster sense of his situation. When again brought up, however, the criminal persisted in his refusal to plead; and the court at last pronounced the dreadful sentence—that he should be pressed to death. This sentence was accordingly executed upon him two days after, in the public market-place of Kilkenny. As the weights were heaping on the wretched man he earnestly supplicated to be hanged; but it being beyond the power of the sheriff to deviate from the mode of punishment prescribed in the sentence, this was an indulgence which could not be granted him.

A different form of pressing to death is said to have been used at Lissa. It was known as "The Iron Coffin of Lissa." The prisoner was laid in the coffin, the iron lid of which was slowly lowered upon him, crushing him to death. The gradual descent of the lid took some days.

The torture of the "Scavenger's Daughter" has been alluded to above. It derived its name from the inventor, Sir William Skeffington, a Lieutenant of the Tower of London, in the reign of Henry VIII, who introduced it into the Tower. It consisted of a broad hoop of iron which opened on a hinge, and was forcibly closed on the victim, who was made to kneel inside the hoop, his legs, thighs and body being compressed together in the smallest possible space, the legs being pressed against the thighs, and the thighs against the stomach. So great did the pressure become when the ends of the hoop were made to meet by means of a screw, that blood frequently poured from the tips of the fingers, toes, nostrils and mouth; and often the breast-bone and ribs were crushed in. A description of the infliction of this torture is given below in the chapter on collective punishments.

In Germany a similar punishment was inflicted by frames of wood or iron in which were holes to admit the hands and feet, so contrived that the person put in them had his body bent into unnatural and painful positions and his agony became greater and greater by moments, and yet he did not die.

A French torture which was introduced into Scotland, where it became very popular, was the torture of the *brodequins* or "boots".[1] As will be seen from the Preface, Ravaillac suffered this torture in an attempt to compel him to disclose the names of his accomplices.

The torture of the boots took various forms, but the most common was to place the prisoner in a sitting position on a chair or bench and fix his legs, from the knees to the ankles, between two upright planks, which were then securely held together by a framework of iron rings and ropes. Having got the legs compressed in this fashion, wooden wedges were hammered with a mallet, some between the planks on the inner side of the legs and some between the planks on the outer side of the legs and the surrounding framework. The legs were thus tightly jammed and reduced to a jelly. Another common method of inflicting this torture was to set the prisoner in a sitting posture on a massive bench, with his arms tied behind him and with strong narrow boards fixed inside and outside of each leg, which were tightly bound together with strong rope; wedges were then driven in between the central boards with a mallet, four wedges for the ordinary and eight wedges for the extraordinary torture. Not infrequently in the latter operation the bones and legs were literally burst, and the marrow spurted out. A less common method was to encase the victim's legs in stockings made of parchment, in which it was easy to thrust the feet and legs when wet, but which shrunk so considerably when

[1] Often referred to as the "Scottish Boots".

they were held near the fire that they caused insufferable agony to the wearer. At Autun the French employed yet another method of the boots. The victim was first bound to a large bench or table, and had his feet placed in high boots made of spongy leather, over which was poured a large quantity of boiling water, which penetrated the leather, ate away the flesh and is said to have even dissolved his bones.

The boots were employed in Scotland in 1579 on a clergyman and a notary, and, by order of Walsingham, on William Holt in 1583 and on Hurbey in 1584.

An interesting case was that of Fian, a schoolmaster of Saltpans, who was accused of witchcraft in 1591. Among other things he was supposed to have raised a storm at sea to wreck James (who afterwards ascended the English Throne as James I) on his voyage to Denmark to visit his future queen. He suffered the boots, the thumbscrews, a tightened cord twisted round his forehead and finally was burnt at the stake. Henry Neville Payne, the instigator of the "Montgomery Plot", was ineffectually tortured under the direct orders of William III, in 1690, by the boots and the thumbscrews.[1]

Two forms of the torture of the boots were common in Spain, each called the "Spanish Boots". One consisted of two metal boots which reached up to the calves of the legs. The legs of the victim were placed in them, and they were then filled up with boiling water, pitch or boiling oil. These were the kind of boots ordained for use in Austro-Hungary under the *Constitutio Criminalis Theresiana*, which also authorised an instrument called a "Shin-crusher". This latter torture is badly named as it was not used for crushing the shins, but consisted of an instrument similar to a large pair of hedging-shears with wide flat blades, which were studded with nails and were applied to the calves of the sufferer. The real shin-bone crushers were

[1] A special form of Scottish boots was known as the *cushielaws*. This consisted of an iron boot into which the foot was thrust and then applied to the fire.

used as a torture of the second degree[1] in Germany. They were similar in form to thumbscrews, only of a larger size, and were screwed on to the ankles of the victim until the bones became pulp.

The other form of boots employed in Spain, also known as the "Spanish Boots", consisted of two strong pieces of heavy wood fitted with protruding iron knobs or buttons. The boards were made to screw up so tightly into the foot and leg as completely to break them, and at the same time to inflict the most agonising torture.

In China, as has been mentioned above, the torture of the boots was employed in conjunction with the rack.

The thumbscrews were one of the most universal forms of torture used for the purpose of eliciting information. They were generally the first instrument tried, and, if they failed, other and more complicated methods were used. However, in many cases the thumbscrews alone played their part successfully. Thumbscrews took many forms, the object being to crush the bones of the fingers and thumb. Primitive examples were similar to nut-crackers, but the form which became most usual was two iron slots in which the thumbs were placed and an iron bar which could be screwed on to the thumbs and thus crush them. William Carstairs, a Scottish divine, accused of participating in the Rye House Plot, was, in 1682, tortured with the thumbscrews for an hour and a half, but firmly refused to disclose any secrets. Carstairs was a personal friend of William of Orange, and after the Revolution the thumbscrews were presented to Carstairs by the Council. It is said that William asked to see them and had the effect tried on his own thumbs, but quickly expressed the belief that another turn would make him confess *anything*.

The recognised practice for the ordinary torture in Normandy was the crushing of one thumb in the screws, and both for the extraordinary.

[1] Tortures in Germany were classified into three degrees.

Thumbscrews were authorised under the *Constitutio Criminalis Theresiana*, and blunted or spiked thumbscrews were employed in Germany. According to the Rev. Dr. Wylie's account of Nuremberg, there were "instruments for compressing the fingers till the bones should be squeezed to splinters".

Skull-crushers were also used in Germany, and consisted of a cone-shaped piece of iron which was fixed on to the top of the skull, attached to a plate at the bottom which fitted under the chin. It was then screwed tightly until the victim's teeth were forced out of his jaws, and the pressure on the brain became utterly intolerable. The pain was intensified by tapping on the cone, each tap sending a thrill of acute agony through the wretched sufferer's body.

Another method of uncomfortably compressing the body was by the torture of the "little ease" in the Tower of London, where it can still be seen and which is said to have resembled the Roman torture of the *mala mansio*. It consisted of a dark prison so narrow and small that the wretched prisoner confined in it was unable either to stretch himself at full length in any direction or to stand upright. He was thus compelled to remain doubled up in a cramped and painful position. This torture lasted for several days.

An Indian form of executing capital punishment was by driving an elephant over the accused, who was tied to the ground, or by making the elephant kneel on him. An account of an execution in India is given in a Bombay journal for 1814. The accused was a slave who had murdered his master at Baroda. About eleven o'clock in the morning the elephant was brought out with only the driver on its back, surrounded by natives with bamboos in their hands. The criminal was placed three yards behind on the ground, his legs tied by three ropes, which were fastened to a ring on the right hind leg of the animal. At every step the elephant took it jerked him forwards, and eight or ten steps must have dislocated every limb, for they were loose and broken when the elephant had proceeded five hundred yards. The criminal, though covered with mud, showed every sign of life, and seemed to be in the most excruciating torment. After having been tortured in this manner for about an hour, he was taken to the outside of the town, where the ele-phant, which is instructed for such purposes, was backed, and put its foot on to the head of the criminal, thus ending his life.

CHAPTER VII

BODY BREAKING

That mother beautiful and kind and pure,
Who stands upon a trap, with look demure,
Her arms on hinges, and her holy side
Worked by machinery, and opening wide
To clasp the unwary in its fell embrace.
Once there, the arms are locked, and in his face,
His limbs, his tortured body, and his heart
The spikes are driven with remorseless art.
The grasp is then relaxed, and thus let go,
The victim falls into the depths below.

H. Grattan Guinness

Som Throne
Downe From
Rocks And
Broken to
Peeces

As a method of dispatching heretics, burning alive, before or after strangulation, must unquestionably be given the first place; but following close upon it in popularity, especially in France, was the torture of "breaking on the wheel". This punishment was unknown in England. Its name is not descriptive of the process. The victim was not broken on the wheel, the wheel merely being the place on which the mangled body was exposed for exhibition.

Breaking on the wheel does not appear to have originated earlier than 1534, when it was the subject of an edict of Francis I. The instrument of punishment consisted of two separate parts, a St. Andrew's Cross and a large wheel. The victim was laid on the cross, his legs and arms being bound to the four joists. Two places were hollowed out in the woodwork of the cross under each limb, in order that they might be more easily broken, only the joints being allowed to touch the wood. The executioner would advance and strike the limb over each hollow in the cross

I

with an iron bar. This bar was usually square in shape, about two inches broad and rounded at the handle. Each limb was thus broken in two places. To the eight blows required for this the executioner generally added one or two blows on the chest, which ended the execution and from which the term *coups de grâce* is said to have originated. Just before or after the delivery of the *coups de grâce* the mangled body was taken off the cross and placed on the wheel, which was constructed to turn on a pivot so that the onlookers could have a good view. Sometimes, as in the case of burning, but not nearly so frequently, the victim was strangled before execution.

The following description of the punishment of breaking on the wheel is taken from Alexandre Dumas's *Massacres in the South*:

Boëton, who was a Protestant of moderate views, but steadfast and devout, professed doctrines somewhat akin to those of the Quakers, and objected to drawing his sword, but consented to assist the cause in every other way. He was awaiting, with his customary trust in God, the day appointed for putting the plot in execution, when his house was suddenly invaded by the king's troops in the night time. Faithful to his peaceful creed, he made no resistance, held out his hands for the cords, and was taken in triumph to Nîmes, and transferred thence to the citadel of Montpellier. On the road he was overtaken by his wife and son, who were on their way to Montpellier to solicit indulgence for him. They were both riding upon the same horse; they dismounted, and falling upon their knees in the road asked the blessing of the husband of one, and the father of the other. He raised his fettered hands, and gave his wife and son the blessing they craved, after which the Baron de Saint-Chatte, who was deeply moved by the episode—he was Boëton's cousin by marriage—permitted the prisoner to embrace them. For an instant the ill-fated family stood in the road, heart to heart; but Boëton himself gave the signal for departure, and put an end to the heart-breaking embrace, commanding his wife and son to pray for M. de Saint-Chatte, who had allowed them this last solace, and setting the example by striking up a psalm, which he sang aloud from beginning to end.

On the day following his arrival at Montpellier, Boëton, despite the entreaties of his wife and son, was condemned to die upon the wheel, after undergoing the ordinary and extraordinary question. His tranquillity and his courage did not fail him when the sentence was pronounced, inhuman as it was, and he declared his readiness to suffer all the ills it might please God to inflict upon him to prove the steadfastness of his faith.

Boëton endured the torture with such unflinching constancy that M. de Baville, who was present to hear such avowals as he might make, seemed to suffer more than the victim himself. His annoyance carried him so far that he forgot his sacred character as a magistrate, and insulted and even struck the prisoner. Thereupon Boëton, without other reply, raised his eyes and cried: "O Lord, Lord, how long wilt Thou suffer the impious to triumph? How long wilt Thou suffer him to shed innocent blood? That blood cries to Thee for vengeance; wilt Thou delay yet a long while to do justice? Arouse Thy jealousy, as of old, and remember Thy compassion!"

M. de Baville withdrew, ordering him to be taken out to execution.

The scaffold was erected upon the Esplanade, as was usually the case for that variety of execution. It consisted of a platform five or six feet from the ground, on which was laid flat a Saint-Andrew's cross, made of two joists fastened together in the middle, and crossing diagonally. In each of the four branches grooves were cut about a foot apart, in order that the limbs, having no support at those points, would be more easily broken. At one of the corners of the scaffold, near the cross, a small carriage wheel hung upon a pivot, its upper edge being cut so that it resembled a saw. Upon this bed of agony, which allowed the spectators to enjoy his last convulsions, the victim was stretched when the executioner had performed his part, and it only remained for death to perform his.

Boëton was taken to the place of execution upon a cart, surrounded by drums, so that his exhortations should not be heard. His voice was so powerful, however, that it constantly rose above the beating of the drums, as he exhorted his brethren to remain steadfast in the communion of Jesus Christ.

At the corner of the first street he perceived the scaffold; he immediately held his hand aloft, and exclaimed joyously, with smiling face: "Courage, my soul! I see the place of thy triumph, and soon thou wilt enter the heavenly kingdom, released from thy sorrowful bondage!"

When he reached the foot of the scaffold, they were obliged to assist him to ascend; for his legs, lacerated by the torture of the *brodequins*, would not bear his weight, and during the whole time he exhorted and comforted the Protestants, who wept as if their hearts would break. As soon as he stepped upon the platform he voluntarily stretched himself on the Saint-Andrew's cross, but the executioner told him that he must undress. He rose with a smile, and the executioner's assistant removed his doublet and his trousers; as he wore no stockings, but simply the linen bandages wrapped around his wounded legs, he removed the bandages, turned back the sleeves of his shirt to the elbow, and bade him lie down again upon the cross in that condition. Boëton complied as calmly as before; the assistants then bound him with cords at every joint, and, having completed the preparations, withdrew. The executioner then came forward, holding in his hand a square iron bar, an inch and a half square, three feet long, and rounded at the handle. As his eyes fell upon it, Boëton struck up a psalm, but almost immediately interrupted it with a faint cry; the executioner had broken the bone of his right leg. He resumed his singing, however, an instant later, and kept it up without remission, although the executioner proceeded to break, one after another, the right thigh, the other leg and the other thigh, and each arm in two places. He then took the shapeless, mutilated trunk, still living and singing the praises of God, detached it from the cross and laid it upon the wheel, with the poor, mangled legs folded beneath the body, so that the heels were touching the back of the head; and throughout this whole atrocious performance the victim's voice never for one instant ceased to sing the praise of the Lord.

Never perhaps did an execution produce such an effect upon the crowd; and the Abbé Massilla, observing the prevalent feeling, informed M. de Baville that the spectacle was very far from terrifying the Protestants, and intended rather to strengthen them in their convictions, as it was easy to see by the tears they shed, and the praise they lavished upon the dying man.

M. de Baville, appreciating the force of the suggestion, ordered the victim to be put out of misery. The order was at once trans-

Mr. John Calas, a French Protestant merchant, broke on the wheel by order of the Parliament of Thoulouse.

mitted to the executioner, who approached Boëton to beat in his breast with a final blow; but at that, an archer who was upon the scaffold stepped between the executioner and the sufferer, saying that he did not propose that the Huguenot should be killed, because he had not suffered enough. The victim, overhearing the hideous discussion, which took place close beside him, ceased his praying for an instant, and raised his head, which was lying on the wheel. "My friend," he said, "you think that I am suffering, and you are not mistaken; I am suffering, indeed; but He who is with me, and for whom I suffer, gives me strength to endure my suffering with joy."

At that moment, M. de Baville's order being renewed, and the archer daring no longer to oppose his execution, the executioner drew nigh the sufferer.

"My dear brethren," said Boëton, realising that the end was at hand, "let my death aid you by its example to maintain the purity of the Gospel, and be ye my witnesses that I die in the religion of Christ and His blessed apostles."

The last words were hardly uttered when the iron bar crushed in his chest. A few inarticulate sounds, which retained the accent of prayer, were heard; then the victim's head fell back. The martyr had breathed his last.[1]

Another anecdote relating to the torture of breaking on the wheel is given in *The Percy Anecdotes* as follows:

In the year 1770, a person of the name of Monthaille, without any accuser, witness, or any probable or even suspicious circumstances, was seized by the superior tribunal of Arras, and condemned to have his hand cut off, to be broken on the wheel, and to be afterwards burnt alive, for killing his mother. This sentence was executed, and his wife was on the point of being thrown into the flames as his accomplice, when she pleaded that she was *enciente*, and gave the Chancellor of France, who was informed of the infernal iniquity that was perpetrated in the sacred name of justice, time to have the sentence as to her reversed. "The pen trembles in my hand", says Voltaire, "when I relate these enormities! We have seen, by the letters of several French lawyers,

[1] M. Boëton de Saint-Laurent d'Aigorse, the victim whose punishment is described, was a Camisard, at whose house at Milland the Camisard rebellion was planned in 1705.

that not one year passes in which one tribunal or another does not stain the gibbet or the rack with the blood of unfortunate citizens, whose innocence is afterwards ascertained when it is too late."

Breaking on the wheel was employed so late as 1805 in Holland, when five persons were put to death by this method for murdering a family near Delft.

Occasionally breaking on the wheel was followed by disembowelling, and permission was sometimes given for the victim to remain clothed. A case of this is related in M. de la Place's Memoirs. The criminal was a young girl who had stabbed her husband. She was sentenced to be broken on the wheel at Brussels, but pleaded to be allowed "to appear upon the scaffold with that decent degree of covering which may screen my naked limbs". The request was granted and she was executed in a dress "which consisted of a jacket and pantaloons of white satin".

The torture from which breaking on the wheel had its origin was a circular wheel with a projecting iron flange. This was laid on the prostrate form of the victim and the executioner struck down on this framework commencing at the ankles and working upwards, the bones thus being splintered into small fragments. The *coups de grâce* for which the victim had often to wait in unendurable anguish was delivered on the neck or chest. This torture, which somehow got the name of "the bone-breaking bed", owing to the fact that the victim was generally placed on a wooden bench of bed-like appearance, prior to the infliction of the torture, is said to have been employed first by Commodus, who died in A.D. 192.

The cradle was a popular German torture, consisting of a large iron cradle about the size of an ordinary bath, but slightly more rounded and studded inside with nobs and, sometimes, spikes. The victim was bound hand and foot and rocked in the cradle till he was a mass of bruises and wounds.[1] When he was brought forth his body was discoloured, swollen and bleeding, but he was still living.

[1] Some German cradles are said to have had spiked wooden movable pillows.

Other forms of German tortures were:

The Spiked Hare, which consisted of a long wooden roller studded with numerous spikes. The victim was laid on a bench or stretched on a ladder, and the spiked hare was rolled over his naked body, or, to vary the punishment, he was rolled over the spiked hare.

The Spiked Collar, which was an iron collar with spikes on the inside, was locked onto the neck of a prisoner so as to prevent his adopting any attitude than an upright one. Prisoners were compelled to wear this for long periods to increase the misery of their incarceration.

Numerous smaller instruments which gained popularity in Germany were pincers and tongs, which were heated and then used for tearing the flesh, wrenching out the tongue and slitting the nose and ears. Sharp spoon-like instruments for scooping out the eyes, or grubbing up the ears, were also common, and sharp, pointed instruments were used for pinching, probing or tearing the most sensitive parts of the body and continuing the pain up to the verge where reason, or life, gave way.

Shooting has very seldom been used for the purpose of torture, though we have seen that mutineers in India were tied to the mouths of cannons before they were discharged. In early days, Danish pirates are said to have tortured their prisoners by binding them to posts or trees and firing their arrows at them, striking the body as often as possible without wounding a vital part.[1] In 1817 Ciro Annichiarico, an outlaw of Calabria, who had been a priest, was pursued by a Major Bianchi, who captured him. He was sentenced to be shot and received twenty-one bullets without being mortally wounded. The twenty-second ended his life.

A case in which mental torture was allied with shooting is related in *The Percy Anecdotes*, as follows:

In Queen Anne's reign, a soldier belonging to a marching regi-

[1] Edmond, the last king of East Anglia, was shot to death in this way by the Vikings in 870.

ment that was quartered in the city of W——, was taken up for desertion, and, being tried by a court-martial, was sentenced to be shot. The colonel and lieutenant-colonel being both in London, the command of the regiment had devolved in course to the major, who was accounted a very cruel and obdurate man. The day of the execution being come, the regiment, as usual upon those occasions, was drawn up to witness it; but when everyone present who knew the custom at these executions expected to see the corporals cast lots for the ungracious office, they were surprised to find it fixed by the Major upon the prisoner's own brother, who was also a soldier in the regiment, and was at the moment taking his last leave of the unfortunate culprit.

On this inhuman order being announced to the brothers they both fell down on their knees; the one supplicated in the most affecting terms that he might be spared the horror of shedding a brother's blood; and the other brother, that he might receive his doom from any other hand than his. But all their tears and supplications were in vain; the Major was not to be moved. He swore that the brother, and the brother only, should be the man, that the example might be the stronger, and the execution the more terrible. Several of the officers attempted to remonstrate with him, but to no purpose. The brother was prepared to obey. The prisoner having gone through the usual service with the minister, kneeled down at the place appointed to receive the fatal shot. The Major stood by, saw the afflicted brother load his instrument of death, and this being done, ordered him to observe the third signal with his cane, and at that instant to do his office, and dispatch the prisoner. But behold the justice of Providence! When the Major was dealing his fatal signals for the prisoner's death, at the last motion of his cane the soldier, inspired by some superior power, suddenly turned about his piece, and shot the tyrant in a moment through the head. Then throwing down his piece, he exclaimed: "He that can show no mercy, no mercy let him receive. Now I submit, I had rather die this hour, for this death, than live a hundred years, and give my brother his." At this unexpected event, nobody seemed to be sorry; and some of the chief citizens, who came to see the execution, and were witnesses of all that passed, prevailed with the next commanding officer to carry both the brothers back to prison, and not to execute the first prisoner until further orders, promising to in-

ADALBERT, BISHOP of PRAGUE, murdered with darts in the City
of Dantzick by the pagans.

demnify him from the consequences, as far as their whole interest could possibly go with the queen. This request being complied with, the city corporation, that very night, drew up a most pathetic and moving address to their sovereign, humbly setting forth the cruelty of the deceased, and praying her majesty's clemency towards both prisoners. The Queen, upon the perusal of this petition, which was presented to her majesty by one of the city representatives, was pleased to promise that she would inquire a little further into the matter. On doing so, she found the truth of the petition confirmed in all its particulars; and was graciously pleased to pardon both the offending brothers, and discharge them from her service. "For which good mercy in the queen", says a chronicle of that period, "she received a very grateful, and most dutiful, address of thanks from her loyal city."

The "Spider" was a terrible instrument of torture much used by the Holy Inquisition, but as it was used to a greater extent as a punishment for civil offences on the Continent, it can be dealt with here. This atrocious device was for the infliction of the most fearful mutilation and suffering upon helpless women, whose breasts were gripped with the spider's hideous claws. The spider consisted simply of two iron bars, projecting from the wall, on which were curved iron spikes in the shape of claws, over which the naked bodies of the female sufferers were dragged, till they were literally torn to pieces. The palm must be awarded to this comparatively insignificant-looking instrument for horrible and malignant cruelty. So far as sheer brutality goes, for it possessed none of the subtlety of some other of the tortures, it may well be doubted whether a more repulsive instrument of torture has ever been devised. A similar instrument was used on the thighs and buttocks of men, but not nearly to so great an extent as the real spider, which may well be regarded as a prerogative of the female sex.

A French punishment for sacrilege or forgery which proved very effective was a bench at the side of which was a vice for securing the hands. The hands were held in a perpendicular position, the tips of the fingers appearing above the surface of the bench. The executioner then crushed the tips of the fingers one after another with blows from his mallet. Very few were able to stand the ordeal of having each finger slowly mutilated in this fashion. The palms of the hands, and the wrists, were often smashed by blows from a mallet in a similar manner.

There were two distinct tortures of "The Chair", each differing in form and principle. One of these was used for civil offences in Spain and under the Holy Inquisition. For simplicity, the torture here described will be called the torture of "The German Chair"; and when the other is described under the chapter dealing with the Holy Inquisition, it will be called "The Spanish Chair".

The German Chair consisted of a heavy[1] iron chair, the seat of which was studded with spikes.[2] The victim was bound to the chair, the whole weight of his naked body resting on the spikes. After he had recovered from the effect of this, a heavy lead or iron collar was fixed round his neck to increase the pressure, and, finally, weights were heaped onto his knees. Every writhing, agonised movement of the wretched man could cause only fresh bruises and wounds; yet it was not possible for him to sit still with the terrible spikes penetrating farther and farther into his flesh.

There was a Spanish military punishment for desertion, insubordination or pillaging, called "The Donkey", signs of which are to be seen in some of the feudal castles of Germany. The torture consisted in setting the victim astride a wall, $\wedge$-shaped at the top, and then attaching weights to his feet, the weights being slowly increased until the body was split in two. If a suitable wall was not available, small walls about four feet long and six feet high were erected, some on portable stands.

Impaling alive was a torture very dear to the hearts of

[1] To prevent the victim upsetting it in his agonised struggles.
[2] Sometimes the chair had also spiked arm and feet rests.

the Ancient Romans, whose example was followed by the inhabitants of the East. This was one of the principal tortures inflicted by the Turks during the Bulgarian atrocities in 1876.

The assassin of General Jean Baptiste Kleber[1] was a Turkish peasant of the name of Solyman Illeppy. The murderer was captured, and suffered death by having the flesh burned off his right hand, and by being impaled; in which position he lived one hour and forty minutes, dying without showing any fear.

The instrument of torture about which most has been written, and which is generally the best known, is the *Eiserne Jungfrau* of Nuremberg. Some writers have translated this as the "Iron Virgin", others as the "Iron Maiden".[2] But, to save confusion, the latter name is the better of the two, as there was another torture known by the name of the "Iron Virgin" which was employed by the Holy Inquisition at Toledo, and to which reference will be made hereafter. These, again, must not be confused with the Virgin of Baden-Baden, from the use of which we get the expression *"baiser de la vierge"*. The Baden-Baden Virgin was a figure which the victim was ordered to kiss. When he advanced to do so he fell through a trap-door onto a spiked wheel.

The Iron Maiden was a terror-inspiring instrument of torture, and was made of strong wood, bound with iron bands. The front consisted of two doors which opened to allow the prisoner to be placed inside. The whole interior was fitted with long, sharp, iron spikes, so that, when the doors were closed, these sharp prongs forced their way into various portions of the victim's body. Two entered his eyes, others pierced his back, his chest, and, in fact, impaled him alive in such a manner that he lingered in the most agonising torture. When death relieved the

---

[1] Who was murdered on the 14th of June, 1800.

[2] The word *Jungfrau* is correctly translated as "virgin", though it can be used to describe a maiden, for which the German word is *Mädchen*.

poor wretch from his agonies, perhaps after days, a trap-door in the base was pulled open and the body was allowed to fall into the water below.

Death by the Iron Maiden was inflicted for various offences civil and ecclesiastical, but chiefly for major offences, such as plots against the State, parricide or religious unbelief.

The Rev. Dr. Wylie visited Nuremberg, and in his *History of Protestantism* he describes the Iron Maiden as follows:

The person who has passed through the terrible ordeal of the Question Chamber, but has made no recantation, would be led along the tortuous passage by which we had come, and ushered into this vault, where the first object that would greet his eye, the pale light of a lamp falling on it, would be the IRON VIRGIN. He would be bidden to stand right in front of the image. The spring would be touched by the executioner—the Virgin would fling open her arms, and the wretched victim would straightway be forced within them. Another spring was then touched—the Virgin closed upon her victim; a strong wooden beam, fastened at one end to the wall by a movable joint, the other placed against the doors of the iron image, was worked by a screw, and as the beam was pushed out the spiky arms of the Virgin slowly but irresistibly closed upon the man and did their work.

When the dreadful business was ended, it needed not that the executioner should put himself to the trouble of making the Virgin unclasp the mangled carcase of her victim; provision had been made for its quick and secret disposal. At the touching of a third spring, the floor of the image would slide aside, and the body of the victim drop down the mouth of a perpendicular shaft in the rock. Down this pit, at a great depth, could be discerned the shimmer of water. A canal had been made to flow underneath the vault where stood the Iron Virgin, and when she had done her work upon those who were delivered over to her tender mercies, she let them fall, with quick descent and sullen plunge, into the canal underneath, where they were floated to the Pegnitz, and from the Pegnitz to the Rhine, and by the Rhine to the ocean, there to sleep beside the dust of Huss and Jerome.

Mr. Walter Besant treats the subject of the Iron Maiden in a more humorous light.

It was the spirit of one who had suffered; he proved to have been one of those who had been embraced by the Iron Maiden of Nuremberg. "They condemned me to death", he said, "because I was a Jew. Some of my friends were grilled, roasted, and fried, and done to death very slowly. This was disagreeable. Others were tortured with refinements, as the Chief Inquisitor called it—that is to say, in fancy fashion by some of the things which are now hanging on these walls. Art, imagination, and fancy, applied to torture, means a lingering which one would rather avoid. So that when I learned that it had been decided that I was to step inside the Iron Maiden, I inwardly rejoiced, outwardly I showed every sign of horror, I shrieked, I knelt, I prayed, I shrieked again, but I saw my brother Ezekiel slowly turning round and round on the spit while they basted him with lard; and I saw my cousin Nathaniel bubbling and boiling in oil; and another cousin screaming while they put on the red-hot gloves; and I laughed, gentlemen—I laughed to myself. They got me in; they stood me upright in the Iron Maiden; and then—ha, ha! they were clumsy torturers; they did not know their own business; they should have closed the door slowly—slowly, so that every spike should produce its own agony. They *slammed the door*. The hundred and fifty spikes all went right through me. And in an instant I was as dead as a door-nail. My friends joined me an hour or two later, one after the other, when the roasting and boiling were over. They had a much more disagreeable time.

Som Stoned to Death

CHAPTER VIII

ODDS AND ENDS

It may be asked, Why rake up these horrors of the past, these tortures inflicted upon innocent women and children in times long since past and gone? Simply because they are matters of history, which cannot be ignored or suppressed. They may be horrible to relate, it is true; but they were far more horrible to suffer. And, however revolting they may now appear, any description of them, no matter how vivid or how detailed, must necessarily fall far short of the dreadful reality to those who endured them.—SMILES

Som were set in the ground up to the chin to be starved to death

THERE were many methods of torture and their accompanying instruments which cannot be classified under the previous chapter headings. As space does not permit a separate chapter to each form of torture, they will need to have a general chapter to themselves. So far as France is concerned, torture can be divided into two definite classes. One was called the *préparatoire*, and the other the *préalable*. The former was to elicit a confession and the latter was inflicted as part of the punishment. The *préparatoire* was called either ordinary or extraordinary, according to the duration or violence of the torture employed. In Paris, the usual torture used for the *préparatoire* was the *brodequins*, which have been described, but before these came into general use the water torture was very common. About sixteen pints were given for the ordinary torture, and double that quantity for the extraordinary. This torture was inflicted in the following manner: The victim, having been stripped, was bound to a bench or table and a funnel was inserted into his mouth and pressed down into his throat. The water was

The torturing of DANIEL RAMBAUT by daily cutting off the fingers, toes, etc.

PICHEL'S DAUGHTER leaping into the bosom of her husband, who was ordered to be drowned by her father.

then poured down the funnel in jugfuls, his nose being pinched to induce him to swallow. A less common form of water torture in France was to bind the accused in an immovable position and to let water trickle, drop by drop, onto a part of his body, usually the stomach. The constant dripping was said to prevent the blood pulsating through the vein on which it dropped. This torture was sometimes applied to the victim's head, which was first shaved, and often resulted in the sufferer's insanity.

Water was used in various other ways as a torture. In Turkey unfaithful wives were tied up in sacks and dropped into the Bosphorus. Thirst and starvation were often used to force a confession. The following two descriptions of the effects of thirst and hunger are interesting, though the former may not be considered to be an intentional torture, but merely torture by neglect to give definite orders for the comfort of the captive.

During the travels of the celebrated Mungo Park into the interior of Africa, he was made a prisoner and conveyed to the Moorish camp at Benown, on the borders of the Great Desert, and the residence of Ali, the Moorish chief or sovereign, at Ludemar. The first night he was compelled to sleep on a mat that was spread upon the sand before the tent, and where he was summoned before the curious multitude and subjected to continued insult and irritation.

The Moors, though very indolent themselves, are rigid task-masters and keep every person under them in full employment. To Mr. Park was assigned the respectable office of barber; but happening in his first essay to make a slight incision in the head of the young Prince of Ludemar, the king concluded that his son's head was in very improper hands; he was ordered to resign his razor and walk out of the tent.

When Ali quitted the camp of Benown, Mr. Park was compelled to form part of his suite. During the journey, and on their arrival at Jarra, he suffered much from hunger and thirst; the barbarous Moors would not suffer his boy to fill the skin at the well, but often beat him for his presumption; everyone being astonished that the slave of a Christian should attempt to draw water from the wells which had been dug by the followers of the Prophet.

"This treatment," says Mr. Park, "at length so frighted the boy, that I believe he would sooner have perished with thirst than attempt again to fill the skin; he therefore contented himself with begging water from the Negro slaves that attended the camp; and I followed his example, but with very indifferent success, for though I let no opportunity slip, and was very urgent in my solicitations both to the Moors and the Negroes, I was but ill supplied and frequently passed the night in the situation of Tantalus. No sooner had I shut my eyes, than fancy would convey me to the streams and rivers of my native land; there, as I wandered along the verdant brink, I surveyed the clear stream with transport and hastened to swallow the delightful draught; but, alas! disappointment awakened me, and I found myself a lonely captive, perishing of thirst amidst the wilds of Africa!

"One night, having solicited in vain for water at the camp, and being quite feverish, I resolved to try my fortune at the wells, which were about half a mile distant from the camp. Accordingly I set out about midnight, and being guided by the lowing of the cattle, soon arrived at the place, where I found the Moors were busy drawing water. I requested permission to drink, but was driven away with outrageous abuse. Passing, however, from one well to another, I came at last to one where there was only an old man and two boys. I made the same request to this man, and he immediately drew me a bucket of water; but as I was a Christian, and fearing that his bucket might be polluted by my lips, he dashed the water into the trough, and told me to drink from thence. Though this trough was none of the largest, and three cows were already drinking in it, I resolved to come in for my share; and kneeling down, thrust my head between two of the cows, and drank with great pleasure, until the water was nearly exhausted and the cows began to contend with each other for the last mouthful." [1]

Readers will be glad to hear that Mr. Park finally effected his escape. The treatment of Mr. Park by the Moors was, to a certain extent, justified by the treatment which the

[1] *The Percy Anecdotes.*

Moors received at that time, when they had the misfortune to fall into Christian hands:

The cruelties of the Algerines to their slaves is amply retaliated by the Genoese on such Algerines as fall into their hands. Dupaty, in his *Letters on Italy*, in 1785, gives an affecting picture of the galleys of Genoa, where "poverty and criminality are fettered by the same chain; those who serve the republic partaking of the misery of those who betray it". Speaking of the Algerine Turks taken at sea, who are condemned to the galleys at Genoa, he says:

"What have we here?" said I to a person who conducted me to a kind of prison or receptacle; "how low, dark, and humid! What, too, I pray you, are those animals lying on the ground, whose hideous heads appearing from beneath their wretched rugs are covered with long and matted hair? They seem unable to crawl; yet what ferocity in their looks! Ah! do they eat only that black and hard bread?"

"Nothing else."

"Drink only that turbid water?"

"That alone."

"Do they always lie in that state?"

"They do."

"How long have they been here?"

"*Twenty years.*"

"How old are they?"

"Seventy."

"What are they?"

"Algerine Turks."

These unhappy Mahometans are, indeed, so entirely thrust out from humanity that they frequently lose the spontaneous movement of their limbs; and, indeed, enclosed as it were in a tomb, harden into idiotism.

Captives under sixty, when brought from labour, are chained in small open niches in a long wall, six feet asunder, in such a way as scarcely to be able either to sit or recline; in this state they breathe the little air which is given them, or rather which they steal.

Let me add a conclusive trait for a picture of the galleys of Genoa. I have seen the bones and garbage abandoned by the dogs in the streets carried from bench to bench, and sold to the galley slaves, who disputed for their possession with all the rage and selfishness of extreme hunger.[1]

Starvation was often used, as has been seen from the infliction of the *prison forte et dure*, and from the punishments permitted to the aristocracy of Aragon. An interesting case was that of Ugolino, Count of Gheradesca, who was cast into prison in the Tower of Gualandi, in 1288, with his two sons and two grandsons, all of whom were starved to death for deserting the Pisans in their war against Genoa in 1284. Dante, in his *Inferno*, has immortalised the story.

In Winchester debtors were often starved to death until quite recent times. They were imprisoned over the city gates and were not provided with food or drink until their debts were paid. They had, however, this privilege: there was a small hole in the floor through which they were permitted to fish with a string in the hopes that some charitable passer-by might attach a parcel of food or a can of water to the end.

The tortures of the North American Indians are rather a problem, as it is very difficult to get accurate facts, and to divide them from the fictitious ones, as to what tortures were actually inflicted.

Tortures naturally varied among the different tribes. The Cheyennes, according to Captain Clark in his *Sign Language*, did not inflict torture at all.[2] But there can be no question that torture was inflicted by North American Indians to a very great extent on prisoners of war, either white or other Indians. The following is a description of torture said to have been inflicted by the Indians as given in *The Percy Anecdotes*, which may be of interest to those suffering from partial paralysis:

On the breaking out of the last Cherokee war, prior to the American revolution, Colonel Sinclair sent Dr. David Menzies, a

[1] *The Percy Anecdotes.*
[2] "There is no good evidence that captives have been burned at the stake, flayed alive, or any other excruciating torture inflicted on persons captured by these fierce, war-loving and enterprising barbarians."

146

surgeon, to visit a gang of negroes at a new settlement situated on the Oconie River, which is a stream of the Alatamahaw, and joins a branch of the Savannah, about seventy miles from the town of Augusta, in Georgia, and about one hundred miles distant from the nearest town of the Indians. The following account of the sufferings which Mr. Menzies endured is from his own pen, and has been confirmed by the celebrated Logan, who rescued him.

"On the night I arrived at Colonel Sinclair's plantations, we were surrounded by a party of Cherokees, and, as we made no resistance, were all taken alive. We were then driven away before them, laden with pillage, into their own country, excepting two negroes, who, being sick and unable to keep pace with us, they scalped and left on the path. In proceeding to the Indian town, I understood (having some knowledge of their language) that these Cherokees had lost in the expedition one of their head warriors, in a skirmish with some of our rangers, and that I was destined to be presented to that chief's mother and family in his room; at which I was overjoyed, as knowing that I had thereby a chance, not only of being secured from death and torture, but even of good usage and caresses. I perceived, however, that I had much overrated my matter of consolation as soon as I was introduced to the mother of their hero. She sat squat on the ground, with a bear's cub in her lap, as nauseous a figure as the accumulated infirmities of decrepitude, undisguised by art, could make her; and instead of courteously inviting her captive to replace, by adoption, her slain child, she fixed her bloodshot haggard eyes upon me; then, riveting them on the ground, gurgled through her throat my rejection and destruction.

"The famous Logan, a chief of another territory, some of whose hunters were in the party who took us, sent in to interpose for my life, and offered a great supply of gunpowder, shot, flints, provisions, and rum for my ransom; but his offers were refused —the feast of revenge was too delicious for the old ferocious savage.

"My head ran on nothing now but stones, sticks, pitch-pine, scalping-knives, tomahawks, and the other instruments of savage cruelty; but I was mistaken in that too, and reserved, alas! for new and unheard-of torments. These Indians, in one of their late excursions into South Carolina, had met, it seems, with some larded venison, which pleased their taste; in consequence of which they had carried off some larding pins, as well as a quantity of bacon; and my cannibal mistress had determined to make, by means of an Indian who had seen the operation in Carolina, an application of this discovery to human flesh.

"When it was evening these barbarians brought me, entirely naked, before a large fire, kindled in the midst of the diabolical heroine's hut, around which the three or four other families, who were also inmates of this Indian house, with other savages, were collected, with store of rum before them, and every other preparation towards a feast. Two young torturers, having first bound me to a stake, began to experiment on me the culinary operation of larding. After they had larded my left side so as to exhibit a complete hemiplegia of bacon, they turned it close to the fire and proceeded on the other. This performance took up much time, on account of the inexperience of the operators, as well as my struggling, in which I afforded infinite merriment to the old hag and her company—the pin not merely going through the insensible epidermis, but lacerating also the pyramidal papilæ of the cutis, which anatomists agree to be the seat of feeling; and as the savages all the while plied their rum impatiently, the whole assembly were soon intoxicated.

"Fortunately at this moment an alarm was given that Logan had arrived, and had set fire to the town; my executioners fled, leaving me roasting, and the old hag and some others fast asleep. I did not let this providential opportunity slip me: but instantly disengaged my right arm (at the expense of the palmaris brevis muscle, and with a dislocation of the eighth bone of the carpus), and fell to untying myself with expedition. I then escaped into the town, whence I dashed into the woods, having only stayed just long enough to place some of the fire-brands in a position to fire the cabin, and not having forgotten to lay a small one in the lap of my inhuman she-tyrant.

"When I perceived that I was not pursued, I looked back, and saw with great satisfaction the Indian town in flames. I continued my flight through the wilderness, chiefly by night, steering southeast; but was soon alarmed at the immediate danger I found myself in of starving, unprovided as I was with firearms; yet from the imminent danger I was preserved by the very cruelty of the Indians; nor am I ashamed to express that I sustained famished nature by the bacon that was saturated with the juices of my own body.

"I penetrated at last through all difficulties to Augusta, where I was entertained with great humanity and civility by Justice Ray, and was cured of my wounds, and of the fever, their symptomatic consequence. And so far am I from experiencing any material detriment by this Indian treatment (for I am above accounting a few scars on my cheek such), that I have received, I imagine, a momentous benefit from it, as I have got entirely rid of paralytic complaint with which I have been for years afflicted in my left side, which was roasted."

The history of torture among the Indians does not commence till after the arrival of the white races in America, as, previous to this, enemies not killed in battle were adopted into the tribe and in very rare instances tortured. No tortures were used by the Indians, even in the later days, other than those which had been used by the Europeans.[1]

The most common tortures which the Indians are said to have inflicted were scalping (which was in the nature of a rite and consisted of removing the skin from the skull with the hair attached),[2] mutilation, burning at the stake, and inserting dry pine needles all over the naked body of the victim and then igniting them.

So much has been written in fiction about the extraction of the teeth of Jews by our Feudal Barons to compel disclosures of hidden wealth, that it is rather refreshing to find this torture used in comparatively modern times by the Turks. Hussein, Capitan Pasha, called in a Jewish physician to relieve him from an aching tooth. The Jew extracted the wrong tooth and Hussein ordered the arrest

[1] "There was no torture used by the Indians that was not also used by the Spaniards" (Ernest Thomas Seton).

[2] Scalping was a form of mutilation used from the earliest times in Europe, Herodotus mentions the practice among the Scythians; it was employed by the ancient Germans under the name of *decalvare*, and the Anglo-Saxons and Franks used it as late as 879. It was also common among the negro tribes in Africa. American history shows that scalping has often been used by the white races in their wars with the Redskins.

of the unfortunate dentist and had every tooth in his head drawn!

The cruelties of the Feudal Barons in Stephen's reign are well described in Ingram's *Saxon Chronicle*, where they are summarised as follows:

The Barons took those supposed to have any property, and inflicted on them unutterable tortures. Some they hanged up by the feet, and smoked with foul smoke; some they hung by the thumbs, and weighted with coats of mall. They tied knotted cords about the heads of others, and twisted the cords till the pain went to the brains; others they kept in dungeons with adders and snakes. Some they tore in pieces by fastening them to two trees; and some they placed in a crucet house, i.e a chest short and narrow, in which were spikes; the victims being forced into the chest, all their limbs were crushed and broken.[1]

The torture of bending two adjacent trees and tying the legs of the victim to them had the effect of tearing the sufferer in half when the trees were released. It was of very early origin, and Sinis (or Sinnis), a Corinthian robber, received the nickname of "The Pine Bender", for putting his captives to death in this way. It is also said to have been used against the French in the guerrilla warfare in Spain.

A rather unusual torture was introduced by Bishop Bonner in the examination of a Deacon, Cuthbert Simpson, in 1558, who was punished for suppressing a list of his Protestant congregation.

The persecutors were very anxious to obtain an accurate account of the members of the congregation. As Sympsom refused to discover their names, he was put upon the rack, and kept there for three hours. On the Sunday following, he was again examined; the Lieutenant of the Tower swore that he should tell. They bound his two fore fingers together, and drew a barbed arrow backwards and forwards between them; they then racked

[1] In France a similar torture was used known as the "*chambre à crucer*". This was a chest filled with sharp stones or studded with spikes, into which the sufferer was packed and buried alive.

him twice, but he still refused to give the information they required. He relates:

"Five weeks after, I was sent unto the high-priest (Bonner), where I was greatly assaulted, and at whose hand I received the Pope's curse, for bearing witness of the resurrection of Jesus Christ." Bonner bore testimony that he was the most patient sufferer of all that came before him. He also was tortured by being inclosed in Skeffington's gyves,[1] an engine which kept the body in an agonising posture.[2]

The torture of the Arrow seems to have been invented by Bonner, or the Lieutenant, and only used on this one occasion.

The "Awaken" was a torture commonly used in the Holy Inquisition which was popular on the Continent and was in use in Scotland. It consisted of preventing a prisoner from going to sleep until the necessary confession was forthcoming. He was placed in a cell with guards who were constantly changed, and he was roughly flung about or shaken if he showed any signs of drowsiness. Victims often went mad under this torment.

Mention is made of the infliction of the "Awaken" in Bishop Burnet's *History of His Own Time*, as follows:

When any are to be stuck in the boots, it is done in the presence of the council; and upon that occasion almost all offer to run away. The sight is so dreadful, that without an order restraining such a number to stay, the boards would be forsaken. But the Duke of York,[3] while he was in Scotland, was so far from running away that he looked on all the while with an unmoved indifference, and with an attention as if he had been to look on some curious experiment. This gave a terrible idea of him to all that observed it, as a man that had no bowels of humanity in him. Lord Perth observing this, resolved to let him see how well qualified he was to be an inquisitor-general. The rule about the

[1] The Scavenger's Daughter.
[2] This description is taken from an early nineteenth-century book called, apparently, *The Annals of the Days of Queen Mary*. My copy has no title-page, so I cannot give the correct name or the date.
[3] Afterwards James II.

boots in Scotland was, that upon one witness and presumptions, both together, the question might be given. But it was never known to be twice given, or than any other species of torture besides the boots might be used at pleasure. In the Court of Inquisition, they do upon suspicion, or if a man refuses to answer upon oath as he is required, give him the torture, and repeat it as often as they think fit, and do not give over till they have got out of their mangled prisoners all that they have a mind to know from them.

This Lord Perth now resolved to make his pattern, and was a little too early in letting the world see what a government we were to expect under the influence of a prince of that religion. So upon his going to Scotland, one Spence, who was a servant of Lord Argyle's and was taken up to London only upon suspicion, and sent down to Scotland, was required to take an oath to answer all the questions which should be put to him. This was done in direct contradiction to an express law, obliging men to swear that they will answer *super inquirendis*. Spence likewise said, that he himself might be concerned in what he might know, and it was against a very universal law, that excused all men from swearing against themselves, to force him to take such an oath. So he was stuck in the boots, and continued firm in his refusal. Then a new species of torture was invented; he was kept from sleep eight or nine nights. They grew weary of managing this, so a third species was invented. Little screws of steel were made use of that screwed the thumbs with that exquisite torture, that he sunk under this, for Lord Perth told him that they would screw every joint of his whole body, one after another, till he took the oath.

When the torture had this effect on Spence, they offered the same oath to Carstairs; and upon his refusing to take it, they put his thumbs into the screws, and drew them so hard, that as they put him to extreme torture, so that they could not unscrew them, till the smith that made them was brought with his tools to take them off.

Two more forms of torture by mutilation may be mentioned. The first was a very early form and consisted in stretching a victim on an upright rack and tearing his flesh with iron claws fastened to the ends of poles. These were given the name of "The Flesh Tearers". A more subtle form of the same torture common in Germany, which sometimes took the place of the spiked hare, was the racking of a sufferer on a horizontal rack, then drawing backwards and forwards over the fleshy parts of his naked body a framework of barbed wire, the barbs all being made to point downwards.

A rather curious form of leg-screw, or boots, was in use in Germany, which consisted of an instrument which screwed tightly onto the leg, and in the centre, at the back, was a drill or auger, which was twisted by means of a screw through the leg with such force that it entered the calf and forced its way through the bone. This would permanently cripple the victim unless he stopped the slow progress of the drill by a confession.

Sometimes the imprisonment of offenders or accused persons awaiting trial amounted to torture. While in prison, Damiens, the murderer of Louis XV, was bound to his bed in an immovable position with eleven separate bands to prevent his injuring himself before his torture and execution.

The sufferings of secret prisoners of the Bastile have so often been described that it would be mere repetition to go into them, but the miseries of the captives enclosed in the castle of Konigstein in Germany are less known. Trenck describes this fortress as follows:

This vast rock is not a fortress that an enemy must subdue before he can conquer Saxony. It contains but a small garrison, incapable of making a sally; and serves only to secure the records of the country, and prisoners of state. Konigstein is the Bastile of Saxony, in which many a brave man has pined out his life in durance. When I was there, part of the rock was blown up to form casemates. In doing this there was found a dungeon bored in the solid stone, to the depth of sixty fathoms. At the bottom of this dungeon appeared a bedstead, on which a skeleton reposed, and by its side the remains of a dead dog. Mournful sight for a heart possessed of the feelings of a man! How savage the tyrant that can invent such tortures for his fellow-creatures, and can lie down on his pillow, conscious that in a hole like this a man is slowly consuming the lamp of life, feebly supported by vain hopes of compassion. Even now the walls of this prison confine three persons not unworthy of notice. One of these was a private secretary of the Court of Saxony, and in the year 1756 betrayed the secrets of the Dresden archives to the King of Prussia. He was taken in Poland; and has now been four-and-thirty years in a dungeon; he still lives—but his appearance is more that of a wild beast than of a man.

Another is Colonel Acton. He who is acquainted with the secret history of Dresden will remember the horrid poison scheme which was detected, but was thought proper to be kept secret. Acton was chief in this conspiracy.

The third is a fine young Swede. Six years ago he was arrested at Leipsic, at the private request of the King of Sweden, and brought to Konigstein in a mask. When he was taken, he defended himself like a lion, claiming his right to be protected by the law of nations. This man is excluded from the light of day. No one sees him; no one speaks to him; and, on pain of death, no one must know what is his name, who he is, or even that he is there. From what I could learn, he is no criminal; he has had no trial; but some state or love intrigue at the Swedish Court had brought on him his fate. Pity him, reader! he has no deliverance to hope for, but in death; for the Elector has promised the King of Sweden that he shall never behold the beams of the sun. He is now under thirty years of age, and the worthy governour cannot speak of him without the tear of compassion in his eyes; he shrugs up his shoulders, looks up to Heaven, and says, "It is the Elector's order, and I must obey. God help him!"

Imprisonment was just as terrible in Switzerland at the beginning of last century, and the following is a description of a Swiss prison taken from *The Percy Anecdotes*:

In Switzerland the prisoners who have not been tried, and consequently punished on presumption of guilt, are most severely treated. They are not only a long time in being brought to trial, but their places of confinement are most cruel. In a visit to one of these prisons, in 1818, a man was found shut up in a tower

situated in the middle of a river. He was its only human inhabi-
tant. His gaoler came three times a day in a boat to examine his
chain and bring him food; and his judges from time to time, as
they proceeded in his examination. He was chained to his bed,
from which he could not move far, and had neither chair, table,
fire, nor comfort, nothing but a few old books. He could indeed
see the sky, but that only. He had been in this situation for twelve
months, and even then it was not determined whether he was
guilty or not. In the same tower was a room, about sixteen feet
square, without light altogether, or air, except what passed
through a narrow funnel. In this place a man had been on one
occasion confined eleven months. In another prison, a large
apartment in the tower of an ancient convent, a man was found
who had been taken up on suspicion, and had been confined
forty-eight days. The window was unglazed, but not large enough
to admit light. The room was very cold. The straw on which the
prisoner lay was almost black with use, and his clothes had not
been changed since his confinement. These are, it is to be hoped,
singular cases; yet it is the general treatment of untried prisoners
in Switzerland.

The prison at Antwerp is described as having—

Two rooms for citizens, and above there is a cage about six feet
and a half square, into which criminals are put before the torture.
A criminal, while he suffers the torture, is clothed in a long shirt,
has his eyes bound, and a physician and surgeon attend him.
When a confession is forced from him, and he has had some
wine, he is required to sign his confession; and about forty-eight
hours afterwards he is executed.

In a small dungeon is a stone seat, such as is often seen in old
prison towers, on which it is said that formerly prisoners were
suffocated by brimstone, when their families wished to avoid the
disgrace of a public execution.

Prisoners on the Continent were sometimes stripped and
enclosed in cells, the floors and walls of which were made
of small diamond-shaped pieces of hard oak—the points
being placed upwards. The victim thus found it difficult
to take his rest. The Princess who could not sleep on a

pea placed under her many mattresses would have found this type of confinement exceptionally uncomfortable.

A rather curious punishment was used at Nuremberg for parents of a child born out of wedlock. The two victims were yoked together by a long wooden yoke, their hands being manacled together by means of a long chain, and they were forced to draw water up the steep hill to the castle on top. Yokes were also used as instruments of ignominy, and it was common in Switzerland to yoke couples together who had been found guilty of an act against public morals.

Flaying or skinning alive was a very common form of punishment on the Continent, and was also popular in Turkey, where pirates suffered this fate. The process was begun at the head and continued downwards till the victim died, which was generally about the time the tormentors reached the breast.

In Sweden a very unusual torture was employed which was called "The Cave of Roses". In this torture the prisoner was enclosed in a cave in which were kept numerous snakes and other poisonous reptiles and he was stung to death. This cave was closed by Gustavus III in 1772.

It is rather curious to note that all the tortures which have been described have at times been unsuccessful in eliciting the necessary information or effecting a change in the opinions, generally religious, of the victim. There seems to have been only one form of torture invariably proficient, and that was the French torture of soaking the victim's feet in salt water and letting a goat lick them! Other minor methods of torment which the French found successful and which were more or less common were the injection of water, vinegar or oil into the body of the accused, pouring boiling pitch over the naked body, starvation and forcing dice under the skin and flesh.

Implements of torture have been used in heraldry and architecture. The Scottish family of Dalziel formerly bore a "Man hanging on a gallows", but this was later changed to "*sable* a hanged man with his arms extended *argent*". Several aristocratic German and Spanish families bear wheels, block and axes, racks and other instruments of torture on their coats of arms. Philip II of Spain erected a palace called the Escurial, in honour of St. Lawrence to commemorate his victory of St. Quentin on the 10th of August, 1557. The Escurial took some twenty-four years to build and cost eight millions. In memory of the Martyrdom of St. Lawrence the ground plan resembled a gridiron, the palace representing the handle and various courts formed the bars. In front was a silver statue of St. Lawrence holding a golden gridiron in his hand. "*Gridirons*", says one who examined it, "are met with in every part of the building. There are *sculptured* gridirons, *iron* gridirons, *painted* gridirons, etc. There are gridirons *over* the doors, gridirons in the *yards*, gridirons in the *win-*dows, gridirons in the *galleries*. Never was an instrument of martyrdom so multiplied, so honour-ed, so cele-brated; and thus much for gridirons."[1]

Som buried alive

CHAPTER IX

THE HOLY INQUISITION

I have seen heretics of the poorer sort,
Expectant of the rack from day to day,
To whom the fire were welcome, lying chain'd
In breathless dungeons over steaming sewers,
Fed with rank bread that crawl'd upon the tongue,
And putrid water, every drop a worm,
Until they died of rotted limbs; and then
Cast on the dunghill naked, and became
Hideously alive again from head to heel,
Made even carrion-nosing mongrel vomit
With hate and horror.

TENNYSON, *Queen Mary*

Som Rosted vpon spits by a soft fire

THE subject of the Holy Inquisition in general is far too vast to be covered by one chapter, and it is therefore intended to consider the workings of the Holy Inquisition merely in Spain and her colonies, commonly known by the name of the Spanish Inquisition, as it was there that the chief tortures originated. It is, however, somewhat important to understand the history of the Holy Inquisition and the founding of the Spanish branch, which was an almost entirely separate institution.

The word "Inquisition" means an "inquiry" and all modern courts of law are inquisitions. The Holy Inquisition was a court set up by the Church of Rome to inquire into cases of heresy, though its use was later extended to include such crimes as witchcraft and ecclesiastical offences committed by members of the Church.

The idea of a court of inquiry into religious offences was of very early origin. Jews found guilty of deserting their faith were sentenced to be stoned to death.[1] Through-

[1] Deut. xiii. 6–10, and xvii. 2–5.

158

out the first three centuries of the Christian Church toleration existed; many of the Early Fathers were definitely opposed to persecution, and Constantine, by the Edict of Milan, in 313, confirmed the tolerant attitude. It was not until the time of Valentinian I that laws against heretics began to appear. Heretics, in early days, were seldom visited with capital punishment,[1] their sufferings being limited to exile and confiscation or loss of office.[2] There were, however, various cases of the capital execution of heretics prior to 1000, chiefly by lay authorities; and it was not till after that date that the execution by burning or strangulation of heretics became fairly common throughout Europe, though these executions were still, more often than not, carried out by the secular arm and not by the Church. The Church Council at Rheims in 1049 decreed that excommunication alone was the punishment for heretics. This view, with slight amendments, was accepted by both the Council held at Toulouse in 1119 and the Lateran Council of 1139.

It was not until the time of Innocent III that the expiation of heretics really started under the authority of the Church. In 1198 Innocent exhorted the princes of the various kingdoms to persecute heretics, as he claimed that heresy was just as much a crime against God as high treason was against temporal rulers. Thus the suppression of heresy, though still executed by temporal rulers, became part of the administration of the Church. Gregory IX again amended this by introducing the monastic inquisition, which was the appointment of mendicant Friars, especially the Dominicans, to carry out the duties of inquisitors into the crime of heresy, and, in 1231, commissions were given to the Dominican of Friesach and to Conrad of Marburg.[3] A year later the

[1] The execution of Priscillian, a Spanish heretic, by the Emperor in 385 gave rise to keen controversy. St. John Chrysostom went so far as to say that "to put a heretic to death would be to introduce upon earth an inexplicable crime".
[2] St. Augustine admitted scourging.
[3] Whose zeal exceeded the Pope's intentions.

Dominican Alberic travelled through Lombardy with the title of *Inquisitor haereticae pravitatis*, and, in 1233, the Pope addressed a letter to certain Bishops in France announcing his intention of employing friars in future for the discovery and repression of heresy.

The Holy Inquisition may therefore be said to have started in the thirteenth century, and from that time it spread all over Europe, and it still exists in Rome to-day.

In England there were few trials for heresy before the thirteenth century. Henry II (1154-1189) condemned several heretics, called before a Council at Oxford, to be scourged, branded on the face with the mark of a key and expelled from the country. The Holy Inquisition was first felt when Clement V ordered the arrest of the Templars and Edward II (1307-1327) complied. But the papal inquisitors met with so bad a reception on their arrival in England that the Pope finally forbade them to use torture. The severer punishments for heresy continued in England until 1676, when Charles II practically brought them to an end by limiting the power of the ecclesiastical courts to punish persons found guilty of atheism, blasphemy, heresy and other religious offences by excommunication, removal from office, degradation and ecclesiastical censure. The laws against heresy continued to a later date in Scotland, a youth of eighteen being hanged at Edinburgh for heresy in 1696.

The Holy Inquisition flourished in all European countries, but its barbarities reached their height in Spain and the Spanish dominions, of which the principal was the Netherlands.

It is interesting to note, in passing, that Duke Albert of Bavaria, to further the restoration of Catholicism, provided every one of the chief towns of his kingdom with a Holy Office. One of these was Nuremberg, so the instruments heretofore described as being in use at Nuremberg may all be included in the list of instruments used by the

Holy Inquisition, despite the fact that they were also used in civil and criminal cases.

The form of trial used by the Holy Inquisition made a farce of justice. The accused were arrested in secret, and the proceedings, which were in the highest degree arbitrary, were held in secret. The object of the inquisitors was to ascertain tendencies rather than definite offences.[1] The accused were presumed to be guilty and the judge was the accuser. The accused were allowed a list of the accusations against them, but were not permitted to know the names of their denouncers or the witnesses against them; their only right was to be allowed to make a statement at their first examination of any persons who might have accused them falsely. Heretics, women, children, slaves and persons deprived of civil rights could be witnesses for the prosecution, but not for the defence. No witness could refuse to give evidence under pain of being charged with heresy. In fact, injustice went so far that, according to Langhino Ugolini, witnesses who would retract their hostile evidence were punished as false witnesses, but their evidence was retained and had its full effect against the accused. The accused was forced to swear to tell the whole truth and to denounce all who were partners in his heresy, or whom he knew or suspected to be heretics. If he complied and denounced his accomplices he was reconciled with the Church. The means originally adopted to obtain convictions were by moral subterfuges, and by weakening the physical strength of the victim, but Innocent IV, by his Bull of *Ad Extirpanda*, in 1252, permitted torture.

The sentences of the court were pronounced in a church on Sunday, and consisted of various punishments, such as burning, scourging, imprisonment, penances, humiliation, and, eventually, in fines at the inquisitors' discretion. Imprisonment was of two kinds, *murus largus* and *murus strictus*, the latter being imprisonment in the deepest

---

[1] The murderers of a Dominican named Peter, in 1252, were not charged with murder but with heresy, as being adversaries to the Holy Inquisition.

dungeons with fetters. The victims liable to capital punishment were handed over to the secular arm to be dealt with, and at the same time the inquisitors made an earnest and touching supplication to the secular authorities to be merciful. If this exhortation was taken literally the secular authorities were guilty of heresy!

The Holy Inquisition was extended to Aragon between 1237 and 1238 by Gregory IX, but it was received with great hostility by the people, and it was never wholly a success in any part of Spain until it was created a national movement by Ferdinand and Isabella in 1480. Sixtus IV resisted this innovation, but finally gave way, and the Spanish Inquisition, with which we have now to deal, was founded and continued until its suppression by Napoleon in 1808. It was, however, restored by Ferdinand VII in 1814. It was again suppressed in 1820, restored in 1823, and finally disappeared in 1834. "It was not, however, till the 8th of May, 1869, that the principle of religious liberty was proclaimed in the peninsular; and even since then it has been limited by the constitution of 1876, which forbids the public celebration of dissident religions."[1]

Torture was abolished in 1816, in all offices of the Holy Inquisition.

Under the Spanish Inquisition the victim was arrested in the middle of the night by the *Familiares* or lay officers attached to the Holy Office.[2] If there was the least sign of resistance he was gagged. One form of gag used by the officers of the Spanish Inquisition was very terrible; it consisted of an instrument, pear-shaped when closed, but when pressed into the mouth it could be extended by

[1] S. Reinach.
[2] "About Nine o'clock, being a late Hour in those Counties, People knocked at my Door, I asked them what they would have? They said, they wanted to come in. I desir'd them to come next Morning, for I did not open my Doors at such an Hour. They answered, they would brake them open, which accordingly they did, being about fifteen Priests, Familiars, and a Commissioner and others belonging to the Inquisition, in Arms." Trial and Sufferings of Mr. Isaac Martin at Malaga in 1714.

means of a screw, keeping the jaws immovably open. The victim was then imprisoned in the Holy Office and went through several examinations, including examinations under torture, if necessary. He was then tried, the form of trial being described as follows:

. . . the inquisitors summon two priests out of every Parish church, and two regular Priests out of every Convent; all the Qualificators and Familiares that are in the city; the Sheriff and all the under officers; the secretary and the three inquisitors: all the aforesaid meet at the common hall on the day appointed for the tryal, at ten in the morning. The hall is hung in black, without any windows, or light, but what comes in through the door. At the front there is an image of our Saviour on the cross, under a black velvet canopy, and six candlesticks with six thick yellow wax candles on the Altar's table; on one side there is a pulpit with another candle where the secretary reads the crimes; three chairs for the three Inquisitors, and round about the hall seats and chairs for the summoned Priests, Fryers, Familiares, and other officers.

When the Inquisitors are to come in, an under officer crieth out, "Silence, Silence, Silence; the Holy Fathers are coming", and from that very time, till all is over, no body speaks, nay, nor spits, and the thought of the place puts everybody under respect, fear, and attention. The Holy Fathers, with their hats on their heads, and serious countenances, go, and kneeling down before the Altar, the first Inquisitor begins to give out: "Veni Creator, Spiritus, Mentestuorum visita, etc." And the congregation sing the rest, and the collect being said by him also, everybody sits down. The secretary then goes up to the pulpit and the Holy Father rings a small silver bell, which is the signal for bringing in the criminal."[1]

The injustice of these trials is obvious when one considers the disparity of the sentences awarded between lay and ecclesiastical offenders. The difference between the sentences for the priest and the heretic is extraordinary.

The following few trials are given as examples of this

[1] John Marchant's *History of the Inquisition*, Perth, 1770.

and show how justice was executed by the Spanish Inquisition:

All the summoned persons being together in the hall, the prisoner and a young boy were brought out, and after the first Inquisitor had finished his bitter correction, the secretary read the examinations and sentence as followeth:

"Whereas informations were made, and by evidences proved, that Fryer Joseph Peralta[1] has committed the crime of sodomy with the present John Romeo his disciple, which the said Romeo himself owned upon interrogatories of the Holy Inquisitors: they having an unfeigned regard for the Order of St. Jerome, do declare and condemn the said Fryer Joseph Peralta to a year's confinement in his own convent, but that he may assist at Divine Service, and celebrate Mass. Item, for the example to other sinners, the Holy Fathers declare that he, the said John is to be whipt through the public streets of the town, and receive at every corner, as it is a custom, five lashes, and that he shall wear a Coroza, i.e. a short Mitre on his head, feathered all over, as a mark of his crime. Which sentence is to be executed on Friday next without any appeal."

After the secretary had done, Don Pedro Guerreor did ask Fryer Joseph, whether he had any thing to say against the sentence or not? And he answered, "No", the prisoners were carried back to their prisons, and the company was dismissed. . . .

The boy was 14 years of age, under the power of Fryer Joseph. . . .

The poor boy was whipt according to sentence, and died the next day.[2]

A lady of good fortune was whipped, because she said in company: "I do not know whether the Pope is a man or a woman, and I hear wonderful things of him every day, and I do imagine he must be an animal very rare."

For these words she lost honour, fortune and life, for she died six days after the execution of her sentence.[3]

This criminal had been but six days in the inquisition before

---

[1] Joseph Peralta was a friar of St. Jerome, and was organist of the convent in Zaragosa (Saragossa?).   [2] John Marchant.   [3] Ibid.

he was brought to hear his sentence and everything being performed as before, the secretary read:

"Whereas Father Pueyo has committed fornication with five spiritual daughters (so the Nuns which confess to the same Confessor continually are called), which is, besides fornication, sacrilege and transgression of our commands, and he himself having owned the fact, we therefore declare that he shall keep his cell for three weeks, and lose his employment, etc."

The Inquisitor asked him whether he had anything to say against it; and Father Pueyo said:

"Holy Father, I remember, that when I was chosen Father Confessor of the Nuns of our Mother St. Monica, you had a great value for five young ladies of the monastery, and you sent for me, and begged me to take care of them; so I have done as a faithful servant, and may say unto you: *Domine quinque talenta tradidsi me, ecce alia quinque super lucratus sum.*"

The Inquisitors could not forbear laughing at this application of the Scripture; and Don Pedro Guerrero was so well pleased with this answer, that he told him:

"You said well, therefore *Peccata tua remittuntur tibi, nunc vade in pace, et noli amplius peccare.*"

This was a pleasant tryal, and Pueyo was excused from the performance of his penance by this impious jest.[1]

The secretary read the examinations, evidence and convictions, and Lizonda (who was Licentiate, or Master of Arts) himself did own the fact, which was as followeth:

"The said Lizondo, though an ingenious man and fit for the sacerdotal function, would not be ordained, giving out that he thought himself unworthy of so high dignity, as to have every day the Saviour of the world in his hands after the consecration. And by this feigned humility he began to insinuate himself into the people's opinion, and pass for a religious, godly man among them. He studied physic, and practised it only with the poor in the beginning; but being called afterwards by the rich, and especially by the Nuns, at last he was found out in his wickedness; for he used to give something to make the young ladies sleep, and this way he obtained his lascivious desires. But one of the evidences swore that he had used only incantation with

[1] John Marchant.

which he made everybody asleep; but this he absolutely denied as an imposition and falsity."

We did expect a severe sentence, but it was only that the Licentiate was to discover to the Inquisitors, on a day appointed by them, the receipt for making the people sleep, and that the punishment to be inflicted on him was to be referred to the discretion of the Holy Fathers.

We saw him afterwards every day walking in the streets, and this was all his punishment.[1]

Lawrence Castro was the most famous and wealthy Goldsmith in the City, and as he went one day to carry a piece of plate to Don Pedro Guerrero, before he paid him, he bid him go and see the House along with one of his domestic servants; which he did, and seeing nothing but doors of iron, and hearing nothing but lamentations of the people within, having returned to the Inquisitor's apartment, Don Pedro asked him:

"Lawrence, how do you like this place?"

To which Lawrence said: "I do not like it at all, for it seems to me the very Hell upon Earth."

This innocent, but true, answer was the only occasion of his misfortune; for he was immediately sent into one of the hellish prisons, and at the same time many officers went to his house to seize upon everything, and that day he appeared to the Bar, and his sentence was read, he was condemned to be whipped through the public streets, to be marked afterwards on his shoulders with a burning iron, and to be sent forever to the Gallies: but the good, honest, unfortunate man died that very day.[2]

In the diocese of Murcia was a parish priest in a village in the mountains. The people of it were almost all of them shepherds, and were obliged to be always abroad with their flocks, so the priest, being the commander of the Shepherdesses, began to preach every Friday in the afternoon, all the congregation being composed of the women of the town. His constant subject was the indispensible duty of paying tithes to him, and this not only of the fruits of the earth, but of the seventh of their sacraments too, which is matrimony, and he had such great eloquence to persuade them to secrecy as to their husbands, and a ready submission to

[1] John Marchant.　　　　　　　　　　　　　　[2] Ibid.

him, that he began to reap the fruit of his doctrine in a few days, and by this wicked example he brought into the list of the tithes all the married women of the town, and he did receive from them the tenth for six years together: but this infernal doctrine and practice was discovered by a young woman who was to be married, of whom the priest asked the tithe before-hand; but she telling it to her sweetheart, he went to discover the case to the next commissary of the Inquisition; he was found guilty of so abominable a sin, and he himself confessed it, and what was the punishment inflicted on him? Only to confine him in a Fryer's cell for six months.

The priest being confined, made a virtue of necessity, and so composed a small book, entitled "The True Penitent", which was universally approved by all sorts of people for solid doctrine and morality.

He dedicated his work to the Holy Inquisitors, who, for a reward of his pains, gave him another parish a great deal better than the first.[1]

At the same time almost they apprehended in the Inquisition at Seville, a noble lady, Joan Bohorquia, the wife of Francis Varquius, a very eminent man, and Lord of Higuera, and daughter of Peter Grasia Xeresius, a wealthy citizen of Seville.

The occasion of her imprisonment was, that her sister, Mary Bohorquia, a young lady of eminent piety, who was afterwards burnt for her pious confession, had declared in her torture that she had several times conversed with her sister concerning her own doctrine. When she was first imprisoned, she was about six months gone with child, upon which account she was not so straitly confined, nor used with that cruelty which the other prisoners were treated with, out of regard to her infant.

Eight days after her delivery they took the child from her, and on the fifteenth shut her close up, and began to manage her cause with their usual arts and rigour.

In so dreadful a calamity she had only this comfort, that a certain pious young woman, who was afterwards burnt for her religion by the Inquisitors, was allowed her for her companion.

This young creature was, on a certain day, carried out to her torture, and being returned from it into jayl, she was so shaken,

[1] John Marchant.

and had all her limbs so miserably disjointed, that when she lay upon her bed of rushes, it rather increased her misery than gave her rest, so that she could not turn herself without the most excessive pain. In this condition, as Bohorquia had it not in her power to show her any, or but little, outward kindness, she endeavoured to comfort her mind with great tenderness.

The girl scarcely began to recover from her torture, when Bohorquia was carried out to the same exercise, and was tortured with such diabolical cruelty upon the rack, that the rope pierced and cut into the very bones of her arms, thighs and legs, and in this manner she was brought back to prison, just ready to expire, the blood immediately running out of her mouth in great plenty.

Undoubtedly they had burst her bowels, insomuch that the eighth day after her torture she died.

And when after all they could not procure sufficient evidence to condemn her, though sought after and procured by all their inquisitorial arts, yet, as the accused person was born in that place, where they were obliged to give some account of the affair to the people, and indeed could not by any means dissemble it, in the first Act of Triumph appointed after her death, they commanded her sentence to be pronounced in these words:

"Because this lady died in prison, without doubt suppressing the causes of it, and was found to be innocent upon inspecting and diligently examining her cause, therefore the Holy Tribunal pronounce her free from all charges brought against her by the Fiscal, and absolves her from any further process, restores her both as to her innocence and reputation, and commands all effects which had been confiscated to be restored to those to whom they of right belonged, etc."

And thus, after they had murthered her by torture with savage cruelty, they pronounced her innocent.[1]

So far as this book is concerned we now come to the interesting part of the procedure of the Spanish Inquisition, the torture of witnesses and accused persons, chiefly to induce confessions, and occasionally as part of their punishment. Before the special tortures are detailed it is interesting to consider where these were carried out. The place of torture has been described as follows:

[1] John Marchant.

The place of torture in the Spanish Inquisition is generally an underground and very dark room, to which one enters through several doors. There is a Tribunal erected in it, in which the Inquisitor, Inspector and Secretary sit. When the candles are lighted, and the person to be tortured brought in, the Executioner, who was waiting for the other, makes an astonishing and dreadful appearance. He is covered all over with a black linen garment down to his feet, and tied close to his body. His head and face are all hid with a long black cowl, only two little holes being left in it for him to see through.

All this is intended to strike the miserable wretch with greater terror in mind and body, when he sees himself going to be tortured by the hands of one who thus looks like the very devil.[1]

The degrees of torture used by the Spanish Inquisition have been described by Julius Glarus in the following terms:

Know therefore that there are five degrees of torture, viz: First, the being threatened to be tortured. Secondly, being carried to the place of torture. Thirdly, by stripping and binding. Fourthly, the being hoisted up on the rack. Fifthly, squassation.[2]

From these degrees of torture we get the famous third degree over which there has been so much controversy in the Press recently.

The classical case of torture under the Spanish Inquisition was that of a Jew, Isaac Orobio, which is given below, and after it are given various descriptions of the tortures employed:

[1] John Marchant.

[2] "As to squassation, it is thus performed: The prisoner hath his hands bound behind his back, and weights tied to his feet, and then is drawn up on high, till his head reaches the pulley. He is kept hanging in this manner for some time, that by the greatness of the weight hanging at his feet, all his joints and limbs may be dreadfully stretched, and on a sudden he is let down with a jerk, by the slacking of the rope, but is kept from coming quite to the ground, by which terrible shake, his arms and legs are disjointed, whereby he is put to the most exquisite pain; the shock which he receives by the sudden stop of his fall, and the weight at his feet stretching his whole body more intensely and cruelly" (John Marchant).

The method of torturing, and the degree of tortures now used in the Spanish Inquisition, will be well understood from the history of Isaac Orobio, a Jew, and Doctor of Physick, who was accused in the Inquisition as a Jew, by a certain Moor his servant, who had by his order before this been whipped for thieving; and four years after this he was again accused by a certain enemy of his for another fact, which would have proved him a Jew. But Orobio obstinately denied that he was one. I will here give the account of his torture, as I had it from his own mouth. After three whole years which he had been in Jayl, and several examinations, and the discovery of the crimes of him of which he was accused, in order to his confession, and his constant denial of them, he was at length carried out of his jayl, and through several turnings brought to the place of torture. This was towards the evening. It was a large underground room, arched, and the walls covered with black hangings. The candlesticks were fastened to the wall and the whole room enlightened with candles placed in them. At one end of it there was an inclosed place like a closet, where the Inquisitor and Notary sat at a table, so that the place seemed to him as the very mansion of Death, everything appearing so terrible and awful. Here the Inquisitor again admonished him to confess the truth, before his torments began. When he answered he had told the truth, the Inquisitor gravely protested, that since he was so obstinate as to suffer the torture, the Holy Office would be innocent, if he should shed his blood, or even expire in his torments. When he had said this they put a linen garment over his body, and drew it so very close on each side as almost squeezed him to death. When he was almost dying, they slackened at once the sides of the garment, and after he began to breath again, the sudden alteration put him to the most grievous anguish and pain. When he had overcome this torture, the same admonition was repeated, that he would confess the truth in order to prevent farther torment. And as he persisted in his denial, they tied his thumbs so very tite with small cords, as made the extremities of them greatly swell, and caused the blood to spurt out from under the nails. After this he was placed with his back against a wall, and fixed upon a little bench. Into the wall were fastened little iron pulleys, through which there were ropes drawn, and tied round his body, in several places, and especially his arms and legs. The Executioner drawing these ropes with great violence, fastened his body with them to the wall, so that his hands and feet, and especially his fingers and toes being bound so straitly with them, put him to the most exquisite pain, and seemed to him just as though he had been dissolving in flames. In the midst of these torments the torturer of a sudden drew the bench from under him, so that the miserable wretch hung by the cords without anything to support him, and by the weight of his body drew the knots yet much closer. After this a new kind of torture succeeded. There was an instrument like a small ladder, made of two upright pieces of wood, and five cross ones sharpened before. This the Torturer placed over against him, and by a certain proper motion struck it with great violence against both his shins, so that he received upon each of them at once five violent strokes, which put him to such intolerable anguish that he fainted away. After he came to himself, they inflicted on him the last torture. The Torturer tied ropes about Orobio's wrists, and then put these ropes about his own back, which was covered with leather, to prevent his hurting himself. Then falling backwards, and putting his feet up against the wall, he drew them with all his might, till they cut through Orobio's flesh even to the bones; and this torture was repeated thrice, the ropes being tied about his arms about the distance of two fingers beneath from the former wound, and drawn with the same violence. But it happened that as the ropes were drawing the second time, they slid into the first wound, which caused so great an effusion of blood, that he seemed to be dying. Upon this the physician and surgeon, who are always ready, were sent for out of a neighbouring apartment, to ask their advice, whether the torture could be continued without danger of death, lest the Ecclesiastical Judges should be guilty of an irregularity if the criminal should die in his torments. They, who were far from being enemies to Orobio, answered, that he had strength enough to endure the rest of the torture, and thereby preserved him from having the tortures he had already endured repeated on him, because his sentence was, that he should suffer them all at one time, one after another. So that if at any time they are forced to leave off through fear of death, all the tortures, even those already suffered, must be successively inflicted, to satisfy the sentence. Upon this the torture was repeated the third time, and then it ended. After this he was bound up in his own cloaths, and carried back to his prison, and was scarce healed of his wounds in seventy days. And inasmuch as he made no confession under his torture, he was condemned, not as one convicted, but suspected of Judaism, to wear for two whole years the infamous habit called *Sanbenito*, after that term to perpetual banishment from the kingdom of Seville.[1]

Between the year 1740 and 1750 the Freemasons were subject to great persecutions in Portugal. A jeweller of the name of Moutou was seized and confined in the prison of the Inquisition, while it was reported he had absconded with a diamond; and a friend of his, John Coustos, a native of Switzerland, was also arrested as an accessory in the imputed robbery. The fact was that these two persons were the leading Freemasons in Lisbon, which constituted their crime. Coustos was confined in a lonely dungeon, whose horrors were heightened by the complaints, the dismal cries, and hollow groans of several other prisoners in the adjoining cells. He was frequently brought before the Inquisitors, who were anxious to extort from him the secrets of masonry; but, refusing to give any information, he was confined in a still deeper and more horrible dungeon. Finding threats, entreaties, and remonstrances in vain, Coustos was condemned to the tortures of the holy office.

"I was thereupon", says Coustos in his narrative, "conveyed to the torture room, built in form of a square tower, where no light appeared but what two candles gave; and to prevent the dreadful cries and shocking groans of the unhappy victims from reaching the ears of the other prisoners the doors were lined with a sort of quilt. The reader will naturally suppose that I must be seized with horror, when at my entering this infernal place I saw myself surrounded on a sudden by six wretches, who, after preparing the tortures, stripped me naked (all to my drawers); when stretching me on my back, they began to lay hold of every part of my body. First they put round my neck an iron collar, which was fastened to the scaffold; they then fixed a ring to each foot; and, this being done, they stretched my limbs with all their might. They next tied two ropes round each arm, and two round each thigh; which ropes passed under the scaffold, through holes made for that purpose; and were all drawn tight at the same time by four men on a signal made for that purpose. These ropes, which

[1] Limborch's *History of the Inquisition.*

NICHOLAS BURTON suffering the Tortures of the Inquisition.

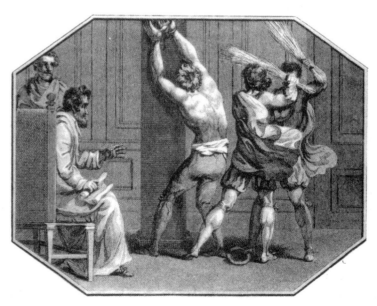

RICHARD WILMOT and THOMAS FAIRFAX terribly scourged in
the Drapers' Hall, London.

were the size of one's little finger, pierced through my flesh quite to the bone, making the blood gush out at eight different places that were so bound. At my side stood a physician and a surgeon, who often felt my temples, to judge of the danger I might be in.

"Finding that the tortures above described could not extort any discovery from me, they were so inhuman six weeks after as to expose me to another kind of torture, more grievous, if possible, than the former. They made me stretch my arms in such a manner that the palms of my hands were turned outward; when by the help of a rope that fastened them together at the wrist, which they turned by an engine, they drew them nearer to one another behind, in such a manner that the back of each hand touched, and stood exactly parallel one on the other; whereby both my shoulders were dislocated, and a quantity of blood issued from my mouth. This torture was repeated thrice; after which I was again sent to my dungeon, and put into the hands of physicians and surgeons, who, setting my bones, put me to exquisite pain.

"Two months after, being a little recovered, I was again conveyed to the torture room, and there made to undergo another kind of punishment twice. The torturers turned twice round my body a thick iron chain, which, crossing upon my stomach, terminated afterwards at my wrists. They next set my back against a thick board, at each extremity whereof was a pulley, through which there ran a rope that caught the ends of the chains at my wrists. The tormentors then, stretching these ropes by means of a roller, pressed or bruised my stomach in proportion as the ropes were drawn tighter. On this occasion my wrists and shoulders were put out of joint."

Before he had recovered he was again subjected to this torture and then remanded to his dungeon, where he continued until their *auto-da-fé*, or gaol delivery, when he was made to walk in the procession of the other victims of this tribunal. Being arrived at St. Dominic's Church, his sentence was read, which condemned him to the galley for four years, although he had suffered the torture no less than nine times.

After remaining at the galley some time, and with the utmost pain and difficulty doing the labour assigned the slaves, that of carrying water (one hundred pounds' weight) to the prisons of the city, he was, through the interest of the Duke of Newcastle, claimed as a subject of Great Britain, and released on the condition of his quitting Lisbon for ever. He sailed in a Dutch vessel for London, where he arrived safe in December 1744, after a long and dangerous voyage.[1]

Torments are sometimes inflicted upon persons condemned to death, as a punishment preceding that of death. Of this we have a remarkable instance in William Lithgow, an Englishman, who, as he tells us in his travels, was taken up as a spy in Mallagom, a city of Spain, and was exposed to the most cruel torments upon the wooden horse. But when nothing could be extorted from him he was delivered to the inquisition as an heretick because his journal abounded with blasphemies against the Pope and the Virgin Mary. When he confessed himself a Protestant before the Inquisitor, he was admonished to convert himself to the Roman Church, and was allowed eight days to deliberate on it. In the meanwhile the Inquisitor and Jesuites came to him often, sometimes wheedling him, sometimes threatening and reproaching him, and sometimes arguing with him. At length they endeavoured to overcome this constancy by kind assurances and promises. But all in vain. And therefore, as he was immovably fixed, he was condemned in the beginning of Lent to suffer the night following eleven most cruel torments, and after Easter to be carried privately to Granada, there to be burnt at midnight and his ashes to be scattered into the air: when night came on his fetters were taken off, then he was stripped naked, put upon his knees, and his hands lifted up by force; after which, opening his mouth with iron instruments, they filled his belly with water till it came out of his jaws. Then they tied a rope hard about his neck, and in this condition rolled him seven times the whole length of the room, till he was almost quite strangled. After this they tied a small cord about both his great toes, and hung him up thereby with his head towards the ground, and then cut the rope about his neck, letting him remain in this condition till all the water discharged itself out of his mouth; so that he was laid on the ground as just dead, and had his irons put on him again. But beyond all expectations he was delivered out of jayl, escaped death and fortunately sailed home to England.[2]

Allusion has been made above to the "Spanish Chair", which was a very common form of torture used in the

[1] *The Percy Anecdotes.*   [2] John Marchant.

174

Spanish Inquisition. It consisted of a heavy iron chair with arm-rests. The victim was seated and his neck and arms held by iron bands. In front of the chair and attached to the bottom were a pair of iron stocks for the reception of the bare feet of the heretic. The sufferer thus being immovably fixed, a brazier of burning coal was placed near his feet, which were roasted. To prevent the feet burning too quickly and to intensify the agony, they were constantly larded with oil or fat.

The inquisitors did not always torture for the discovery of heresy. The torture was sometimes threatened or used for other, and to them more interesting, purposes, as the following case will show.

In 1706, after the battle of Almanza, a body of French troops stationed in Aragon rescued various ladies from the clutches of the inquisitors, who had condemned them to be their mistresses for committing the offence of being beautiful. One of these ladies, aged fifteen, who had been seized and dragged from her home in the middle of the night by the orders of Don Francisco Terrejon, the second Inquisitor, was sent to the Inquisition, and was threatened by being shown various instruments of torture which would be applied if she did not comply with his requests. She describes these instruments as follows:

Early in the morning Mary[1] got up, and told me that no body was yet up in the house, and that she would show me the dry pan and gradual fire, on condition that I should keep it secret for her sake and my own too; which I having promised her, she took me along with her, and showed me a dark room with a thick iron door, and within it an oven, and a large brass pan upon it, with a cover of the same, and a lock to it, the oven was burning at that time, and I asked Mary for what use the pan was there? And she, without giving me any answer, took me by the hand out of that place, and carried me into a large room, where she showed me a thick wheel covered on both sides with thick boards, and, opening a little window in the centre of it, desired me to look with a

[1] The maid allotted to her.

candle on the inside of it, and I saw all the circumference of the wheel set with sharp razors: After that, she showed me a pit full of serpents and toads. Then she said to me, "Now, my good Mistress, I will tell you the use of these three things. The dry pan and gradual fire are for Heretics, and those that oppose the Holy Fathers' Will and pleasure, for they are put all naked and alive into the pan, and the cover of it being locked up, the executioner begins to put in the oven a small fire, and by degrees he augmenteth it till the body is reduced into ashes. The second is designed for those that speak against the Pope and the Holy Fathers, for they are put within the wheel, and the little door being locked, the executioner turns the wheel till the person is dead. And the third is for those that condemn the images and refuse to give due respect and veneration to ecclesiastical persons, for they are thrown into the pit, and there they become the food of serpents and toads." Then Mary said to me that another day she would show me the torments for public sinners and transgressors of the five commandments of our Holy Church; so I in deep amazement desired Mary to show me no more places, for the very thoughts of those three which I had seen were enough to terrify me to the heart. So we went to my room, and she charged me again to be very obedient to all the commands Don Francisco should give me, or to be assured, if I did not, that I was to undergo the torment of the dry pan. Indeed, I conceived such an horror for the gradual fire that I was not mistress of my senses, nay, nor of my thoughts: so I told Mary that I would follow her advice, and grant Don Francisco everything he would desire of me.[1]

The Spanish Inquisition found violent heresy in the Netherlands, and attempts were made to deal with it in the time of Charles V;[2] but they were not successful, and Philip II, having failed to crush the reformed faith through his late wife in England, determined not to be foiled in his

[1] John Marchant.

[2] Charles gave the following order: "J'ordonne que ceux qui agiront contre ces défenses soient punis comme seditieux et perturbateurs du repos public, et je condamme, les femmes à être enterrés toutes vives, et les hommes à perdre la tête en cas qu'ils désistent de leurs erreurs, mais tous à être brulés, s'ils y demeurent obstinés, et à la confiscation de leurs biens quelque supplice qu'ils subissent" (Sleidan).

own dominions. During the years 1568 to 1573, 18,000 people were executed. These executions were carried out with inhuman brutality, and before execution the victims were either gagged or had their tongues burnt out, to prevent their exhorting the people at the time of their death.

The chief torture used against the heretics in the Netherlands was the famous "Wooden Horse", which is described by Ernestus Eremundus Frisius, in his *History of the Low Country Disturbances*, as follows:

There is a wooden bench, which they call the wooden horse, made hollow like a trough, so as to contain a man lying on his back at full length, about the middle of which there is a round bar laid across upon which the back of the person is placed, so that he lies upon the bar instead of being let into the bottom of the trough, with his feet much higher than his head. As he is lying in this posture, his arms, thighs and shins are tied round with small cords or strings, which, being drawn with screws at proper distances from each other, cut into the very bones, so as to be no longer discerned. Besides this, the torturer throws over his mouth and nostrels a thin cloath, so that he is scarce able to breathe thro' them, and in the mean while a small stream of water like a thread, not drop by drop, falls from on high, upon the mouth of the person lying in this miserable condition, and so easily sinks down the thin cloth to the bottom of his throat, so that there is no possibility of breathing, his mouth being stopped with water, and his nostrels with the cloth, so that the poor wretch is in the same agony as persons ready to die, and breathing out their last. When this cloth is drawn out of his throat, as it often is, that he may answer to the questions, it is all wet with water and blood, and is like pulling his bowels through his mouth. There is also another kind of torture peculiar to this tribunal, which they call the fire. They order a large iron chafindish full of lighted char-coal to be brought in, and held close to the soles of the tortured person's feet, greased over with lard, so that the heat of the fire may more quickly pierce thro' them.

Other tortures commonly used by the Spanish Inquisition in the Low Countries were the cauldron, drowning, burial alive and suspending the victims by their thumbs with weights attached to their feet.

The torture of the cauldron was inflicted by turning a large dish or cauldron upside-down, with a number of mice underneath, on the naked stomach of the victim, who was bound to a bench. A fire was then lighted on top of the cauldron and the mice, in terror and pain, burrowed through the stomach into the entrails.[1]

One of the last victims of the Spaniards before they were finally expelled from the Netherlands was Anne Vandehoor, a woman of Malines, who was buried alive, being covered with earth, all except her head. As she still refused to abjure her faith, the executioner threw earth on her face, stamped on it and covered her entirely.

The famous torture known as the "Iron Virgin" was used at Toledo and was similar to the image of Apega erected by Nabis of Sparta. It is described in *The Percy Anecdotes* as follows:

On the entry of the French into Toledo, during the Peninsular War, General Lasalle visited the palace of the Inquisition. The great number of the instruments of torture, especially the instrument to stretch the limbs, the drop baths, which caused a lingering death, excited horror even in the minds of soldiers hardened in the field of battle. One of these instruments, singular in its kind for refined torture, and disgraceful to reason and religion in the choice of its object, deserved a particular description.

In a subterraneous vault, adjoining the secret audience chamber, stood in a recess in the wall a wooden statue made by the hands of monks, representing the Virgin Mary. A gilded glory beamed round her head, and she held a standard in her right hand. It immediately struck the spectator, notwithstanding the ample folds of the silk garment which fell from the shoulders on both sides, that she wore a breastplate. Upon a closer examination it appeared that the whole front of the body was covered

[1] A torture similar to the cauldron is said to have been, and probably still is, in use amongst the natives of Central Africa. The victim is stripped, tied to the ground and left with a tin box containing ants firmly fixed to his stomach. The ants in due course drive a tunnel through his flesh to escape.

with extremely sharp nails, and small daggers or blades of knives with the points projecting outwards. The arms and hands had joints, and their motions were directed by machinery placed behind the partition. One of the servants of the Inquisition who was present was ordered by the general to make the machine *manœuvre*, as he expressed it. As the statue extended its arms and gradually drew them back, as if she would affectionately embrace and press someone to her heart, the well-filled knapsack of a Polish grenadier supplied for this time the place of the poor victim. The statue pressed it closer and closer; and when, at the command of the general, the director of the machinery made it open its arms and return to its first position, the knapsack was pierced two or three inches deep, and remained hanging upon the nails and daggers of the murderous instrument.

After the trial in the Spanish Inquisition was complete the last act in the drama took place. This was the *auto-da-fé* or the sentencing and handing over of the victims to the secular authority for execution.

The following description of the Spanish Inquisition (which also extended to Portugal) gives a very fair description of the *auto-da-fé*.

This most hateful of all tribunals was introduced into Spain in the year 1478, and into Portugal at the pressing solicitation of King John the Third, about the year 1536. From its first establishment, until the recent revolution in those countries, its power had been unchecked, and the details of its proceedings, even such as have transpired, chill us with horror. In Spain alone, from the year 1481 to 1808, not fewer than 32,382 persons were burnt alive; 17,690 burnt in effigy; and 291,450 imprisoned for various periods, with the confiscation of the whole of their property. The number of victims sacrificed by this infernal tribunal diminished in proportion to the increase of knowledge. Thus Torquemada, the first Grand Inquisitor, in the course of seventeen years, had upwards of 10,000 persons burnt alive; and nearly 100,000 imprisoned, with confiscation of property; while during the first twenty years of the reign of the late King of Spain not a single person was burnt alive, only one burnt in effigy and forty-two imprisoned.

To notice the various means by which the victims of the Inquisition were murdered, with all the tortures that malice could prompt or human ingenuity invent, would but be to record crimes at which humanity would shrink with horror. For, independent of its secret tortures and murders, it made a sort of carnival of destruction.

The last act of the inquisitorial tragedy was the *auto-da-fé*, which in the Romish Church was a sort of gaol delivery, appointed for the punishment of heretics, and the absolution of the innocently accused, as often as a competent number of persons were convicted of heresy, either by their own extorted confession or on the evidence of witnesses.

The *auto-da-fé*, to describe it in the words of an eye-witness, is generally held on some great festival, that the execution may pass with the more awe; at least it is always on a Sunday. When one of these dreadful scenes is about to take place, there is a procession led by Dominican Friars; after which come the penitents, all in black coats without sleeves, bare-footed, and bearing a wax candle in their hands. These are followed by the penitents, who have narrowly escaped being burnt, who over their black coats have flames painted in an inverted fashion. Next come the negative and relapsed, who are to be burnt, having flames on their habits pointing upwards. These are followed by such as profess doctrines contrary to the faith of Rome, who in addition to habits like the last have their portraits painted on their breasts, with dogs, serpents, and devils, all open-mouthed, around it.

Each prisoner is attended by a familiar of the Inquisition, and those to be burnt have also a Jesuit on each hand, who continually urges them to abjure. The prisoners are followed by familiars on horseback, inquisitors on mules and, last of all, the Inquisitor General, on a white horse, led by two men with black hats and green hat-bands.

A scaffold is erected large enough for two or three thousand people—at one end of which are the Inquisitors, at the other the prisoners. After a sermon in praise of the Inquisition, a priest ascends the scaffold, recites the final sentence of those who are to be put to death and delivers them to the secular arm, earnestly beseeching at the same time the secular power not to touch their blood or put their lives in danger. The prisoners, being thus in the hands of the civil magistrate, are loaded with chains, then carried to the secular gaol and in an hour or two brought before the civil judge; who, after asking in what religion they intend to die, pronounces sentence on such as declare they die in the Communion of the Church of Rome, that they shall first be strangled and then burnt to ashes; those that die in any other faith are doomed to be burnt alive.

The condemned are then immediately carried to the Riberia, the place of execution, where there are as many stakes set up as there are prisoners to be burnt. The negative and relapsed being first strangled and then burnt; the professed mount their stakes by a ladder, and the Jesuits, after several repeated exhortations to be reconciled to the church, consign them to eternal destruction, and then leave them to the fiend, who they tell them stands at their elbow to carry them into torments. On this a great shout is raised, and the cry is, "Let the dogs' *beards be made*"; which is done by thrusting flaming bunches of furze, fastened to long poles, against their beards, till their faces are burnt black, the surrounding populace rending the air with the loudest acclamations of joy. At last fire is set to the furze at the bottom of the stake, over which the victims are chained, so high that the flame seldom reaches higher than the seat they sit on, and thus they are rather roasted than burnt. Although there cannot be a more lamentable spectacle and the sufferers continually cry out as long as they are able, "Pity for the love of God!" yet it is beheld by persons of all ages and both sexes with transports of joy and satisfaction.

When we reflect on the havoc made on the human species by the Inquisition, how must we rejoice that it is abolished in the two countries where it held a sway almost unlimited.

The Cortes of Lisbon, in one of their sittings, in October 1821, decreed the abolition of the Inquisition; and one of the members proposed that the following inscription should be fixed on every place it had occupied: "May eternal malediction follow every Portuguese who does not hold for ever in abhorrence an invention so infernal!"

By a decree of the Cortes the dungeons of the Inquisition were thrown open to the public; and an Englishman, then in Lisbon, gives the following account of this horrible place:

"On the 8th of October the Inquisition of Lisbon was thrown open for public inspection, and for the first four days the concourse of people of all descriptions that crowded to view it was so great that the pressure made it an enterprise of some risk.

"The building is a large oblong, with a garden in the centre; there are three floors, with a number of vaulted passages, along the sides of which are cells of different sizes, from six by seven feet to eight by nine feet. Each cell has two doors, the inner one of iron, the outer of oak, very strong. As there are no windows in the cells on the ground and middle floors, no light is admitted when the doors are shut. The cells on the upper floor are larger than the others, and each has an aperture like a chimney, through which the sky is visible. These were appropriated to the use of those who it was supposed might be liberated. In the roof of each cell (for they are all vaulted) is a small aperture of about an inch in diameter, and a private passage runs over each range; so that the persons employed by the holy office could at any time observe the conduct of the prisoners unseen; and if two persons were confined in one cell, hear their conversation. There are seats in these private passages so contrived that a person sitting might inspect two of the cells at the same time, as by a turn of the head he could fix his eye upon the hole over either cell at pleasure, or he could hear what was said in either. The persons appointed to listen to the discourse of the prisoners wore cloth shoes so that their footsteps could not be heard.

"Frequently a familiar of the holy office was put into the cell of a prisoner, as a person arrested, in order to entrap the unfortunate inmate of this horrible place into admissions that might afterwards be used against him. I saw, in several of the cells, human skulls and bones; most of them appeared to have lain there for many years, as I broke some of them easily with my fingers, others were hard and fresh. In a number of the cells the names of the unhappy inmates were written on the walls: some had strokes, apparently marking the number of days or weeks the victims of this horrid tyranny had been confined. On the wall of one cell I counted upwards of five hundred of these marks. On the wall of another cell was written, 'Francisco Joze Carvalho, entered here the last day of March 1809, and remained as many days as there are strokes in the wall.' On the wall of another cell was written, 'John Laycock'; the name had been covered with whitewash, which had scaled off. There were a number of strokes under the name, and the figures '18' were easily made out, the others were obliterated. Some of the cells, which had not been used for several years, were locked up, but the visitants soon broke them open. Human bones were found in many of these. In one was found part of a friar's habit, with a waist-girdle of rope, and some bones. The apertures, like chimneys, in some of the cells were closed; and I have been informed that it was a common mode of putting prisoners to death, to place them in these apertures, which were then walled up, and quicklime being poured in from the top, a speedy end was put to their sufferings. The furniture is very old; the chairs in the halls are covered with leather, studded all round with very large brass nails. The large tables in the halls had drawers for papers; these the visitants broke open, every one being desirous of obtaining some relic of the once terrible Inquisition. In several of the cells there were mattresses, some of them old, others nearly new, which proves that the Inquisition was not a trifle up to a very recent date. The spot on which the Inquisition stands was covered with houses in 1755, when the great earthquake happened, by which they were laid in ruins; so that the present building has not been erected more than sixty years, and all the victims that were immolated in it must have been sacrificed within that period."[1]

As will be seen, some of the victims were strangled prior to execution at the stake, but the more obstinate heretics were burnt alive in the usual manner, already described. The idea of burning the victims was to prepare them for the torments of perpetual burning which they were so soon to enjoy. As burning was the crowning act of the Holy Inquisition everywhere this chapter will be brought to its conclusion with a letter from Mr. Wilcox (afterwards Bishop of Gloucester) to Dr. Gilbert Burnet, then Bishop of Salisbury, dated the 15th of January, 1796, and sent from Lisbon.

My Lord,—In obedience to your lordship's commands of the 10th ult., I have here sent all that was printed concerning the last *auto-da-fé*. I saw the whole process, which was agreeable to

[1] *The Percy Anecdotes.*

what was published by Limborch and others upon that subject. Of the five persons condemned, there were but four burnt, Antonio Travanes, by an unusual reprieve, being saved after the procession. Heytor Dias and Maria Penteyra were burnt alive, and the other two first strangled. The execution was very cruel. The woman was alive in the flames half an hour, and the man above an hour. The present king and his brothers were seated at a window so near as to be addressed for a considerable time, in very moving terms, by the man as he was burning. But though the favour he begged was only a few more fag-gots, yet he was not able to ob-tain it. The fire was recruited as it wasted, to keep him just in the same degree of heat. All his entreaties could not procure him a larger allowance of wood to shorten and despatch him. . .

Christians hung up by the heeles and Chockaked with smoake

CHAPTER X

COLLECTIVE TORTURES

Man's inhumanity to man makes countless thousands mourn.—BURNS

Som had all their flesh torne with the Clawes of wild Beasts

THERE have been many cases, some have already been described, where the torture inflicted depended for its severity upon the number of the different instruments used and the times they were employed.

The case of Robert Francis Damien is an example of this. Damien attempted to kill Louis XV of France by stabbing him in the right side on the 5th of January, 1757. He was arrested and tortured.[1] His sentence of death was a series of tortures not dissimilar to those inflicted upon Ravaillac.

The incisions that he had received during his tortures began at length to mortify; and it being thought, by the surgeons that attended him, that he could not exist much longer, he was carried forth to be executed according to his sentence, which was, that he should be dragged in a tumbril to the gate of the principal church, with a lighted torch in his hand, and there to declare he had committed a most abominable crime: from thence that he should be dragged to the place of execution, and on a scaffold have his flesh torn off with red-hot pincers from his breast, arms, legs and thighs; then that melted lead, boiling oil, and scalding pitch should be poured on him; his hand, wherewith he attempted to

[1] "Damien appears very resolute; his feet have been scorched, and the calf of his leg pinched with red-hot irons. He shrieked indeed but confessed nothing.— In a fit of despair, it is said, he has endeavoured to bite off the end of his tongue, and that his teeth have been pulled out to prevent a repetition of that attempt" (Thomas Jones's *Particular and Authentic Narrative of the Life, Examination, Torture and Execution of Robert Francis Damien*).

do the murder, to be first burnt with flaming brimstone: after this
to be torn in pieces by four horses, his limbs and body burnt to
ashes and dispersed in the air.[1]

The tortures inflicted on Guy Fawkes are not recorded,
though it is suspected that he suffered the gauntlets and,
certainly, the rack. There seems to be no doubt that he
was tortured and the Warrant from James I to apply the
torture is authentic. Ainsworth, in his *Guy Fawkes*, allowed
his imagination to fill the blank which history has left,
but, as his description contains an excellent account of
the infliction of the Scavenger's Daughter, as well as
being a good example of collective tortures, it is set out
below:

. . . Two hours afterwards the messenger returned with the
warrant. It was in the handwriting of the King, and contained
a list of interrogations to be put to the prisoner, conclud-
ing by directing him "to use the gentler torture first, *et sic per
gradus ad ima tenditur*. And so God speed you in your good
work!"

Thus armed, and fearless of the consequences, the lieutenant
summoned Jasper Ipgreve.

"We have a very refractory prisoner to deal with," he said, as
the jailer appeared. "But I have just received the royal authority
to put him through all the degrees of torture if he continues
obstinate. How shall we begin?"

"With the Scavenger's Daughter and the Little Ease, if it
please you, honourable sir," replied Ipgreve. "If these fail, we can
try the gauntlets and the rack; and lastly, the dungeon among the
rats, and the hot stone."

"A good progression," said the Lieutenant, smiling. "I will now
repair to the torture-chamber. Let the prisoner be brought there
without delay." . . .

. . . At length, Jasper Ipgreve signified to the lieutenant that all
was ready.

"The opportunity you desired of having your courage put to
the test is now arrived," said the latter to the prisoner.

[1] Thomas Jones.

"What am I to do?" was the reply.

"Remove your doublet, and prostrate yourself," subjoined Ipgreve.

Guy Fawkes obeyed, and when in this posture began audibly to recite a prayer to the Virgin.

"Be silent," cried the lieutenant, "or a gag shall be thrust into your mouth."

Kneeling upon the prisoner's shoulders, and passing the hoop under his legs, Ipgreve then succeeded, with the help of his assistants, who added their weight to his own, in fastening the hoop with an iron button. This done, they left the prisoner with his limbs and body so tightly compressed together that he was scarcely able to breathe. In this state he was allowed to remain for an hour and a half. The chirurgeon then found on examination that the blood had burst profusely from his mouth and nostrils, and in a slighter degree from the extremities of his hands and feet.

"He must be released," he observed in an undertone to the lieutenant. "Further continuance might be fatal."

Accordingly, the hoop was removed, and it was at this moment that the prisoner underwent the severest trial. Despite his efforts to control himself, a sharp convulsion passed across his frame, and the restoration of impeded circulation and respiration occasioned him the most acute agony.

The chirurgeon bathed his temples with vinegar, and his limbs being chafed by the officials, he was placed on a bench.

"My warrant directs me to begin with the 'gentler tortures', and to proceed by degrees to extremities," observed the lieutenant, significantly. "You have now had a taste of the milder sort, and may form some conjecture what the worst are like. Do you still continue contumacious?"

"I'm in the same mind as before," replies Fawkes, in a hoarse but firm voice.

"Take him to the Little Ease, and let him pass the night there," said the lieutenant. "To-morrow I will continue the investigation."

Fawkes was then led out by Ipgreve and the officials, and conveyed along a narrow passage, until arriving at a low door, in which there was an iron grating, it was opened, and disclosed a narrow cell about four feet high, one and a few inches wide, and two deep. Into this narrow receptacle, which seemed wholly inadequate to contain a tall and strongly-built man like himself, the prisoner was with some difficulty thrust, and the door locked upon him.

In this miserable plight, with his head bent upon his breast—the cell being so contrived that its wretched inmates could neither sit, nor recline at full length within it—Guy Fawkes prayed long and fervently. . . .

On the following morning Jasper Ipgreve appeared, and placed before him a loaf of the coarsest bread, and a jug of dirty water. His scanty meal ended, he left him, but returned in two hours afterwards with a party of halberdiers, and desiring him to follow him, led the way to the torture-chamber. Sir William Waad was there when he arrived, and demanding in a stern tone whether he still continued obstinate, and receiving no answer, ordered him to be placed in the gauntlets. Upon this he was suspended from a beam by his hands, and endured five hours of the most excruciating agony—his fingers being so crushed and lacerated that he could not move them.

He was taken down, and still refusing to confess, was conveyed to a horrible pit, adjoining the river, called, from the loathsome animals infesting it, "the dungeon among the rats". It was about twenty feet wide and twelve deep, and at high tide was generally more than two feet deep in water.

Into this dreadful chasm was Guy Fawkes lowered by his attendants, who, warning him of the probable fate that awaited him, left him in total darkness. At this time the pit was free from water; but he had not been there more than an hour, when a bubbling and hissing sound proclaimed that the tide was rising, while frequent splashes convinced him that the rats were at hand. Stooping down, he felt that the water was alive with them—that they were all around him—and would not, probably, delay their attack. Prepared as he was for the worst, he could not repress a shudder at the prospect of the horrible death with which he was menaced. . . .

Guy Fawkes defended himself as well as he could against his loathsome assailants. The light showed that the water was swarming with them—that they were creeping by hundreds up the sides of the pit, and preparing to make a general attack upon him.

At one time Fawkes determined not to oppose them, but to let them work their will upon him; but the contact of the noxious animals made him change his resolution, and he instinctively drove them off. They were not, however, to be easily repulsed, and returned to the charge with greater fury than before. The desire of self-preservation now got the better of every other feeling, and the dread of being devoured alive giving new vigour to his crippled limbs, he rushed to the other side of the pit. His persecutors, however, followed him in myriads, springing upon him, and making their sharp teeth meet in his flesh in a thousand places.

In this way the contest continued for some time, Guy Fawkes speeding round the pit, and his assailants never for one moment relaxing in the pursuit, until he fell from exhaustion, and his lantern being extinguished the whole host darted upon him.

Thinking all over, he could not repress a loud cry, and it was scarcely uttered, when lights appeared, and several gloomy figures bearing torches were seen at the edge of the pit. . . .

A ladder was then let down into the pit, and the jailer and two officials descended. They were just in time. Fawkes had ceased to struggle, and the rats were attacking him with such fury that his words would have been speedily verified, but for Ipgreve's timely interposition.

On being taken out of the pit, he fainted from exhaustion and loss of blood; and when he came to himself, found he was stretched upon a couch in the torture-chamber, with the chirurgeon and Jasper Ipgreve in attendance. Strong broths and other restoratives were then administered; and his strength being sufficiently restored to enable him to converse, the lieutenant again visited him, and questioning him as before, received a similar answer.[1]

In the course of that day and the next, he underwent at intervals various kinds of torture, each more excruciating than the preceding, all of which he bore with unabated fortitude. Among other applications, the rack was employed with such rigour that his joints started from their sockets, and his frame seemed torn asunder.

On the fourth day he was removed to another and yet gloomier chamber, devoted to the same dreadful object as the first. It had

[1] This torture was sometimes known by the name of "The Oubliette".

an arched stone ceiling, and at the further extremity yawned a deep recess. Within this there was a small furnace, in which fuel was placed, ready to be kindled; and over the furnace lay a large black flag, at either end of which were stout leathern straps. After being subjected to the customary interrogations of the lieutenant, Fawkes was stripped of his attire, and bound to the flag. The fire was then lighted and the stone gradually heated. The writhing frame of the miserable man ere long showed the extremity of his suffering; but as he did not even utter a groan, his tormentors were compelled to release him.

The series of tortures inflicted upon Captain Robert Jenkins, of the *Rebecca*, by the Spaniards led, not only to an amusing scene in the House of Commons, when he produced his mutilated ear from a box in which it had been carefully preserved, but to a quite unnecessary war between this country and Spain. In the deposition of Captain Jenkins, dated the 17th of June, 1731, he states:

. . . Upon this they began with this deponent, putting a rope about his and his boy's necks, hoisting them up to the foreyard; but the boy being light, slipped down, so he had only his own weight to strain him: they kept him hanging some time, and then let him swiftly down upon the deck, and asked him if he would confess where his money was, but he still answered that he had none; then he was hoisted up again and let fall with the same violence, after which he was asked the same question, and to which he made the same answer, adding that he could give them none, altho' they tortured him to death. They then threatened to burn the ship with himself and his people in her, saying they were obstinate heretics, but after consulting about half an hour, during which space the rope continued about his neck, the person who first put the rope about this deponent's neck, told him that he was going up for the last time, and searched his pockets, took his silver buckles out of his shoes, and then he was hoisted up again and kept so till he was almost strangled, when they let him fall down the forehatch upon the casks, which bruised him much, and then hawled him up by the neck from thence upon deck, where, as his people informed him, he lay as dead for near a quarter of an hour, and when he began to recover, their lieutenant came to him with pistols and a cutlash in his hands, crying, "Confess or die." That this deponent told him he had no more money than what he showed him at his first coming on board, which was four British guineas, one pistole, and four double doubloons, which he commanding him to give him, he did so, that then he took hold of his left ear and slit it down with his cutlash (and another of the gang tore it off) and ordered him to be scalped, but his head being close shaved prevented the execution of it. . . .

Another instance was the case of a Dominican friar of Naples called Campanella, who overcame in a public disputation an old professor of the same order. The vindictive old friar charged Campanella with heresy and caused him to be imprisoned and racked seven times for twenty-four hours each time. Campanella was released after twenty-seven years of confinement by Urban VIII in 1624.

There is a curious case of a servant girl of Middleburg in Holland being punished for a crime she did not commit and a heavy fine imposed upon her judges, which was given to her by way of compensation, for not having examined the case with due care. The name of the girl is not known, but her mistress accused her of theft and this was confirmed by the finding of the missing goods in her box. She was tried, condemned and sentenced to be flogged, branded and confined, with hard labour, in a rasp house. The guilt of the mistress was finally established and she was condemned to the severest scourging the law could inflict, double branding and hard labour for life. Whether the compensation, the amount of which is unknown, made up for the punishment of the girl, it is difficult to say. It may have relieved the aching back, but could not remove the mark of the brand.

The following prayer given in his answers to interrogations of the United States Commission by Jorge Garcia del Fierro, dated the 11th of September, 1900, shows that various tortures were employed until quite a recent date in the Philippine Islands.

A Filipino prayer, written by me long before I had any notice of the interrogatories to which I am replying, will answer this question[1] satisfactorily. Here is the said Filipino prayer:—

"My God and Master! Have compassion upon us, the Filipinos.; protect us from the Dominicans, Augustinians, Recoletos, and Franciscans. By instigation of these friars thousands of Filipinos have been torn from their homes, some to eat the hard and black bread, or the Pinaua of deportation, and others to shed blood in streams at executions. They were conducted to the calabooses, and there they were suspended from a beam with a pile of rocks on their shoulders, and several others hanging from their feet and their hands. Suddenly the cord by which they were suspended was loosened, and they fell in a heap on the floor, where, if they were not killed, they suffered dislocations and fractures. Later they were lashed on the soles of the feet, on the calves, on the backside, on shoulders, and on the stomach. Their fingers and toes and privates were squeezed and mangled with pincers. They were given electric shocks. They were given to drink vinegar or warm water with salt in excessive quantities, so that they might vomit whatever they had eaten, and which had not passed through the pylorus into the small intestine. Their feet were placed in the stocks, and they were compelled to lie on the ground without even a bed mat, the mosquitos, chinch-bugs, fleas and other insects sucking their blood, and the rats, at times, coming in their mad race and biting, to render worse their sorry and afflicted situation. They were given nothing to eat or drink except from one afternoon to another, the unhappy imprisoned Filipinos thus experiencing the tortures of hunger and of thirst. And after causing them to suffer other horrible tortures invented by the inquisition of ominous memory, squalid, careworn, attenuated, hardly able to stand erect, many were taken to the field, where they died by shooting, for such was the will of the friars, who every day asked for blood—Filipino blood—the blood of those who in this country

[1] The question of the Commission was: "Charges have been made against the friars that many of their number have caused the deportation of Filipinos, members of their parishes, and that in some instances they were guilty of physical cruelty. What, if anything, do you know on these subjects?"

stood out by reason of their knowledge, their uprightness, or their wealth. Thou knowest, my God, that in 1872 the Filipino fathers, Don Mariano Gomez, Don Juse Burgos and Don Jacinto Zamora, died on the scaffold because they opposed the friars usurping the curacies of the priests, as in the end they did usurp them, because the friars were almost omnipotent at that time, and there was no human power to arrest their will. Neither are we ignorant, my God, that in 1897 there were shot to death on the field of Bagumbayan the Filipino priests Don Severino Diaz, Don Gabriel Prieto and Don Inocencio Herrera, because the two first named objected to the curate of Naga, a Franciscan friar, collecting some parochial fees belonging to the said Father Diaz, as curate of the cathedral of Nueva Caceres. Thou also knowest, my God and my Lord, that notwithstanding that Dr. Don Jose Rizal, the unfortunate Macario Valentin, and innumerable other Filipinos were wholly innocent, they also succumbed on the field of Bagumbayan, shot to death. Neither is it unknown to Thee, my God, that a multitude of Filipinos have remained marked forever as the result of blows and cruel treatment they have received, among them General Lucban, who has a rib strung, and will probably carry it through life. Inspire, O Lord, the American authorities with the idea of making an examination and excavations in the Monastery of Santa Clara of Manila, for about fifteen years or more ago a nun went upon the roof of the said monastery and there loudly begged for help—a scandalous fact which many Manilaites can not but recall. Expel, Lord, expel, from the Philippines the friars, before there is powdered glass in the rice we eat and poison in the water we drink, and before Dr. Manuel Jerez Burgos, to whom an anonymous missive was addressed, saying: 'Lara died to-day; thou shalt die to-morrow', shall be assassinated. Take, Lord, take from our sight the habits of the friars, which recall to us days of mourning and affliction, days of prisons, deportations, tortures, and executions of beings who are dear to us, whose unhappy end still draws from our eyes and fills our hearts with anguish. Do more yet, my Lord and God, dissolve, annihilate, destroy throughout the world the monastic order whose by-laws constitute a woeful system which produces, and necessarily must produce, men hypocritical, perverse, covetous, and cruel oppressors of humanity, as is evidenced by history and recently by the present war in China, occasioned by abuses, arbitrariness, and excesses of the friars. We supplicate and pray Thee, my God, that Thou cast out from the Philippines forever the friars that again are attempting to take possession of the curacies of the Philippines, to treat anew our priests as though they were their servants. Amen."[1]

som had sharp reeds thrust under theyr nailes And other parts of their Body

[1] United States Senate Document 190, Church Lands in the Philippines.

CHAPTER XI

SELF-INFLICTED TORTURES

The Gods approve
The depth and not the tumult of the soul.
WORDSWORTH

ENTION has been made previously of the sect of the Flagellants and of the tortures inflicted upon themselves by the Fakirs or Holy men of India, and, although self-inflicted tortures do not come within the scope of the meaning of the word "Torture" defined in the Preface, perhaps the reader will not object to the insertion of this chapter which is of some interest in the history of torture, and, to a certain extent, shows how our ancestors were able by faith to endure the terrible sufferings inflicted on them.

The Flagellants are not important from a point of view of torture, though there is one tale relating to them which is worth retelling.

At Lent time, when religious fraternities are accustomed to inflict on themselves certain discipline, there was in a certain Italian city a confraternity of Penitents. A pastrycook in the same city had a tame bear, which ran about the streets, doing no harm to anyone. Wandering about one evening, it found its way into the chapel (the door of which stood open), coiled itself up in a corner and went to sleep. When the penitents were all assembled, the door was locked, and after a short exhortation from the altar, they spread themselves about the chapel. The light was hidden behind a pillar; the most zealous commenced by inflicting punishment on themselves; an example that was soon followed. The noise woke up the bear, who, in trying to make his way out,

195

stumbled against the penitents, who, with their breeches down, were inflicting castigations.

The bear felt with his paw to find what it was; from one behind he passed on quietly to another; and the penitents, in their fear, began to think it was the devil who had come there to disturb them in their devotions. Their suspicions became a certainty when, the bear passing by the pillar where the light was, they saw his shadow on the wall. It was who should get to the door first! And to this day nothing would convince these worthy disciplinarians that they had not received a visit from the arch-fiend in person.[1]

But quite apart from the sect of Flagellants, whipping was often self-inflicted or inflicted by others at the request of the victim, for religious zeal or to mortify the flesh. These beatings often turned into purely sexual orgies,[2] though there are many recorded cases where the whipping was earnestly inflicted as a penance.

Dominic, Hedwig, and Margaret call for special notice in the annals of flagellation. Dominic of the iron cuirass seems to have been the great patron and example of this discipline. He showed himself no mercy; and whipped, on one occasion, till his face, livid and gory, could not be recognised. This scourging was accompanied by psalm-singing. The music of the voice, and the crackling of the whip, mingled during the operation in delightful variety.

Dominic, in the use of the whip, had the honour of making several improvements, which, in magnitude and utility, may be reckoned with those of Copernicus, Flamsteed, Newton, and La

[1] *Experiences of Flagellation*, 1885.

[2] Maria Magdalena of Pazzi, a Carmelite nun of Florence, about 1580, is celebrated for her flagellations and is mentioned in the Annals. It was her greatest delight to have the prioress bind her hands behind her and have her whipped in the naked loins in the presence of the assembled sisters. While being whipped her thoughts were of love and she frequently cried out, "Enough! Fan no longer the flame that consumes me. This is not the death I long for; it comes with all too much pleasure and delight", etc.

Elizabeth of Genton, another flagellant, used to cry out under the discipline, "O love, O eternal love, O love, O you creatures! Cry out with me, love, love!" (Professor Dr. R. von Krafft-Ebing, *Psychopathia Sexualis*).

Place! He taught flagellators to lash with both hands, and, consequently, to do double execution. The skilful operator by this means could, in a given time, peel twice as much superabundant skin from his back, and discharge twice as much useless blood from his veins. He obliged the world with the invention of knotted scourges. This discovery, also, facilitated the flaying of the shoulders, and enabled a skilful hand to mangle the flesh in fine style for the good of the soul.

Hedwig and Margaret, though of the softer sex, rivalled Dominic in this noble art. Hedwig was Duchess of Silesia and Great Poland. She often walked, during the frost and cold, till she might be traced by the blood dropping from her feet on the snow. She wore next her skin a hair-cloth that mangled her flesh, which she would not allow to be washed. Her women had, by force, to remove the clotted blood which flowed from the torn veins. The Duchess invented or adopted an effectual, but rather rough, means of sanctification. She purified her soul by the tears which she shed, and her body by the blows which she inflicted with a knotted lash.

Margaret, daughter of the King of Hungary, wore a hair-cloth and an iron girdle. She underwent not only the usual number of stripes, but made the Nuns inflict on her an extraordinary quantity, which caused such an effusion of blood from her flesh as horror-struck the weeping executioners. Her devotion still augmenting during the holy week, she lacerated her whole body with the blows of a whip.[1]

Voluntary penance sometimes took on a curious guise. Henry II walked barefoot to the tomb of Becket at Canterbury, and there received on his bare back five stripes from each of the five prelates, and three stripes, with knotted cords, from each of the eighty monks. He then knelt for a day and a night on the cold stones, clad in sackcloth. Other ways of doing penance were by wearing hair-shirts or iron belts and walking with peas in the shoes or sandals.[2]

It has often been said[3] that Henry IV of France stood

[1] Samuel Edgar, *Variations of Popery*.
[2] Wise monks boiled the peas before use.
[3] Probably falsely.

barefoot at the gate of the Castle of Canossa, in the depths of winter, to obtain the forgiveness of Pope Gregory VII.

The efforts of most of these penitents were surpassed by the *Penitantes* of New Mexico, who practised up to quite a recent date. During Lent they not only fasted but subjected their bodies to the most terrible tortures. On Good Friday they went in procession from their lodge to a cross, with their skin cut into furrows, and as they marched they scourged themselves or each other over the shoulders till their bodies were completely covered with blood. Sometimes one or more would be crucified voluntarily. They could be seen in the streets with a huge wooden cross strapped to their backs, arms drawn up and fastened to the cross-bar, and a spear fastened to their bodies so that the point touched the arm, and if in walking over the road strewn with potsherds, sharp stones, and thorny plants the foot flinched or stumbled, the spear-point wounded the flesh of the arms.

Mahometans of the persuasion of Ali still mutilate their bodies with whips and knives on the anniversary of the death of their prophet.

The Indian Fakirs are a body of men who to-day practise the self-infliction of torture in various ways. Some bury themselves in the ground for several days without food or drink, and others hold their arms above their heads till their muscles atrophy, or keep their fists tightly clenched till their nails grow through their palms, or lie on beds of nails, or tie their feet and hands together and roll long distances head over heels, or drag enormous chains loaded with masses of iron, or hang themselves on hooks before a fire near enough to slowly scorch them, or mutilate themselves by cutting or stabbing.

The Baron of Scanaw, in Bohemia, when sentenced to be racked for heresy in the sixteenth century, cut out his own tongue and left the following written message:

I did this extraordinary action because I would not, by means of
198

any tortures, be brought to accuse myself, or others, as I might, through the excruciating torments of the rack, be impelled to utter falsehoods.

He was racked to death.

The honourable form of suicide in Japan, which was abolished in 1868, but still survives voluntarily, is called *Hara-kiri*, a word meaning "belly-cutting", though, in the case of females, the throat, not the stomach, is cut. This form of disembowelment is of very early origin and consists of two kinds, obligatory and voluntary. The former was employed when a noble had broken a law and received a letter from the Emperor telling him that he must die and enclosing a jewelled dagger.[1] The latter was when a man or woman for personal reasons committed *Hara-Kiri*.[2] In the former case half the goods of the victim were forfeited to the crown, but not in the latter.

The ceremony is carried out, after careful preparations for which the victim has so many days allotted to him, in his baronial hall or in a Temple. A dais is constructed a few inches from the ground upon which is laid a small mat. The victim, clad in his full robes of office and assisted by his second (or *Kaishaku*), takes his place on the mat, and, after a few prayers, the weapon is handed to him. He then strips to the waist, tucks his sleeves under his knees to prevent his falling backwards, and plunges the dagger into his stomach, first drawing it across, turns it and then draws it upwards. At the moment that the last operation commences the *Kaishaku* strikes the victim on the neck with his sword and this ends the entertainment.

One noble, scarcely out of his teens, is said to have cut his stomach thrice horizontally, twice vertically and then stabbed himself in the throat until the knife protruded on the other side with the sharp edge to the front, and finally,

[1] In China a silken cord is sent to the noble offender, with which he is expected to hang himself.
[2] E.g. The officer in command of the defeated *Kinshu Maru* committed *Hara-kiri*.

with a supreme effort, is said to have driven the knife forwards with both hands through the neck.

The following account from the *Cornhill Magazine* gives a graphic description of the suicide of Taki Zenzaburo, the officer of the *Prince of Bizen*, who gave the order to fire on the foreign settlement of Hiago.

After an interval of a few minutes of anxious suspense, Taki Zenzaburo, a stalwart man of thirty-two years of age, with a noble air, walked into the hall attired in his dress of ceremony, with the peculiar hempen cloth wings which are worn on great occasions. He was accompanied by a *Kaishaku* and three officers, who wore the *Zimbaori* or war surcoat, with gold tissue facings. The word *Kaishaku*, it should be observed, is one to which our word "executioner" is no equivalent term. The office is that of a gentleman; in many cases it is performed by a kinsman or friend of the condemned, and the relation between them is rather that of principal and second than that of victim and executioner. In this instance the *Kaishaku* was a pupil of Taki Zenzaburo, and was selected by the friends of the latter from among their own number for his skill in swordsmanship. With the *Kaishaku* on his left hand, Taki Zenzaburo advanced slowly towards the Japanese witnesses, and the two bowed before them; then drawing near to the foreigners they saluted us in the same way, perhaps even with more deference; in each case the salutation was ceremoniously returned. Slowly and with great deference the condemned man mounted on to the raised floor, prostrated himself before the high altar twice, and seated himself on the felt carpet with his back to the high altar, the *Kaishaku* crouching on his left-hand side. One of the three attendant officers then came forward bearing a stand of the kind used in temples for offerings, on which, wrapped in paper, lay the *wakizashi*, the short sword or dirk of the Japanese, nine inches and a half in length, with a point and an edge as sharp as a razor's. This he handed, prostrating himself, to the condemned man, who received it reverently, raising it to his head with both hands, and placed it in front of himself. After another profound obeisance, Taki Zenzaburo, in a voice which betrayed just so much emotion and hesitation as might be expected from a man who is making a painful confession, but with no sign of fear either in his face or manner, spoke as follows: "I, and I alone, unwarrantly gave the order to fire on the foreigners at Kobé, and again as they tried to escape. For this crime I disembowel myself, and beg you who are present to do me the honour of witnessing the act." Bowing once more, the speaker allowed his upper garments to slip down to his girdle and remained naked to the waist. Carefully, according to custom, they tucked his sleeves under his knees to prevent himself from falling backwards, for a noble Japanese gentleman should die falling forwards. Deliberately with a steady hand he took the dirk that lay before him, he looked at it wistfully, almost affectionately; for a moment he seemed to collect his thoughts for the last time; then stabbing himself deeply below the waist on the left-hand side, he drew it slowly across to the right side, and turning the dirk in the wound, gave a slight cut upwards. During this sickeningly painful operation he never moved a muscle of his face. When he drew out the dirk he leaned forward and stretched out his neck, an expression of pain for the first time crossed his face, but he uttered no sound. At that moment the *Kaishaku*, who, still crouching by his side, had been keenly watching his every move-ment, sprang to his feet, poised his sword for a second in the air; there was a flash, a heavy ugly thud, a crashing fall; with one blow the head had been severed from the body. A dead silence followed, broken only by the hideous noise of blood gushing out of the inert heap before us, which but a moment before had been a brave and chivalrous man. It was horrible! The *Kaishaku* made a low bow, wiped his sword, and retired from the raised floor, and the stained dirk was solemnly borne away, a bloody proof of the execution. The two representatives of the Mikado then left their places, and crossing over to where the foreign witnesses sat, called us to witness that the sentence of death upon Taki Zenzaburo had been faithfully carried out. The ceremony being at an end, we left the Temple.

There have been many cases of voluntary suicide taking place to avoid capture and torture, five hundred Jews burning themselves to death in the castle at York rather than deliver themselves up to the tender mercies of the Christians in 1189,[1] and there are a few cases of self-mutilation by those who regarded suicide a sin.

[1] The same thing took place at Speyer and Eslingen in 1348 and 1349, respec-tively, at the former, burning themselves in their houses, and at the latter in their synagogue.

In the year 875 the nuns of a convent at Coldingham cut off their noses and lips on the approach of the Danes and were all burnt to- gether by their enraged cap- tors. A similar fate befell the nuns of Acre, who mutilated their own faces when the town was captured by the Saracens in 1291.

Christians tossed vpon y̌ hornes of wild Bulles.

CHAPTER XII

MASSACRE

O miserable Massacre! the wail
Swells from Lucerna! Horrors fill the vale,
Vainly the poor Waldenses supplicate;
The Papal soldiers seize them, violate,
Hack them to pieces, butcher them like sheep,
Impale the helpless, fling them from the steep;
The sword is glutted! redly burns the fire!
Mothers and babes, the maiden and the sire,
One heap of slaughter,—bones, and blood and mire.

H. Grattan Guinness

Som throwne downe from Bridges into Rivers

IT is questionable whether atrocities committed during general massacres can be included under the heading of "tortures". But it would seem that when orders to massacre are given the person responsible for the order must accept responsibility for the consequences. It is interesting to note how seldom tortures have been inflicted during massacres ordered by civil powers and how frequently the most outrageous acts have been perpetrated when religion was the contending factor.

It is difficult to estimate what acts constitute a massacre. The massacre of the Innocents in which some half a dozen infants lost their lives can hardly be included in the same term as the massacre of the Muscovites, in 1611, when 100,000 defenceless women, old men, and children are said to have been massacred by the Poles, or the massacre of Nishapûr, in 1269, in which 1,747,000 people are said to have been slaughtered by Gengis Khan—twelve days were needed to count the dead.

In all cases of massacre the number of those reported killed has to be regarded with the greatest mistrust. The numbers of those massacred on St. Bartholomew's day are

203

given as between 2,000 and 10,000,[1] 50,000[2] and over 100,000.[3]

However, we have no need here to deal with the massacre of St. Bartholomew, as tortures were not inflicted on the victims prior to execution, though insults were heaped upon the dead. Many other massacres come under the same category, and, even at Glencoe, where Captain Campbell killed some thirty Scots, no intentional cruelty appears to have been used, though some of those who escaped died of starvation and exposure in the hills.

One of the first recorded massacres was that of the Benjamites,[4] and the most terrible pre-Christian one was when Alexander slew some 10,000 Tyrians in 331 B.C. He is said to have put 8,000 to the sword and crucified the remaining 2,000.

The earliest massacre in England at which outrages were perpetrated was on St. Bryce's Day, the 13th of November, 1002, when Ethelred the Redeless caused all the Danes in England to be murdered. The massacre was accompanied by shocking barbarities, and, among other torments, the Danish women, including Gunilda, the sister of King Sweyn, had their children murdered in their presence and were then buried in the ground up to their waists. Mastiff dogs were then set upon them and they were worried to death. In revenge Sweyn successfully invaded England and was crowned king in 1013.

When Edward I captured Berwick on Good Friday, 1296, he massacred about 8,000 of the inhabitants and burnt alive the Flemish traders who held out against him in the town hall. The effect of this massacre was that Berwick ceased to be the chief merchant city of the north and sank to the level of a petty seaport.

At Drogheda, on the 13th of August, 1649, Oliver

[1] J. A. Froude. Paris alone.
[2] The Rev. Dr. E. Cobham Brewer.
[3] *A Memento for English Protestants*, 1680. The author asserting that his figures were obtained from contemporary Roman Catholic sources.
[4] Judges xx.

Cromwell followed Edward's precedent and massacred some 2,000 men, women, and children.[1] Many escaped into the church, but Cromwell ordered it to be ignited and they were burnt alive. The inhabitants who escaped the sword or the flames were transported to Barbados.[2] For this massacre the name of Oliver Cromwell has always been dishonoured. No deed, with the possible exception of the treacherous massacre of Glencoe, has raised the ire of British historians to such an extent. In the horror of the massacre of Drogheda historians appear to forget the small and unimportant Irish massacre of 1642, which was the justification for Cromwell's act.

In 1641 the Catholics of Ulster, whose estates had been confiscated and who had been harshly treated under oppressive restrictions, entered into a conspiracy to extirpate the English settled in Ireland. Roger More headed the insurgents, and Cardinal Richelieu promised the aid of French troops. The plot was discovered on the eve of execution and frustrated, but O'Neale was already in arms, a general massacre followed and, Charles I being too busy with his own affairs, it continued for some years, during which time between 40,000 and 50,000 persons were slain. Cromwell's terrible conduct ended this innocent little rising, concerning which the following are a few extracts taken from a book published in 1680.

Though the *Irish* Papists did unanimously resolve to destroy all the Protestants in *Ireland*, yet when they began to execute their damnable design, they only turned Protestants out of doors, and stript them, but afterwards finding that they every where prevailed, they at last murdered Men, Women and Children, without sparing any, as you will see by what follows. Having thus seized upon their Goods and Cattle, ransack'd their houses, got their persons, stript, Man, Woman and Child naked they turn'd them

[1] Cromwell was, as Macaulay says, "able, straightforward and cruel", but he certainly kept his troops under excellent discipline.
[2] Cromwell also exported unemployed persons, both from England and Scotland, irrespective of creed, for work on the plantations.

out of doors, strictly prohibiting the *Irish* under great penalties to give them any Relief. By means hereof many miserably perish'd through Cold, Nakedness and Hunger.

In the Town of *Colerain*, of these poor people that fled thither for succour, many thousands died in two days, so that the Living could not bury the Dead, but laid their Carcasses in ranks in waste and wide holes, piling them up as if they had been Herrings.

One *Magdalen Redman* desposeth, That she and divers others Protestants, amongst whom were two and twenty Widows, were first robbed, and then stript naked, and when they had covered themselves with Straw, the bloudy *Papists* threw in burning Straw amongst them, on purpose to burn them, where many of them died with extreme Cold, and those that survived lived miserably by reason of their many Wants.

At *Casel* they put all the Protestants into a loathsom Dungeon, kept them twelve Weeks in great misery; some they barbarously mangled, and left them languishing, some they hanged up twice or thrice, others they buried alive.

In *Castle Cumber*, two Boys were wounded, and hung upon Butchers Tenters. Some hanged up and taken down to confess Money, and then murder'd.

In the County of *Armagh* they robbed, stripped and murdered abundance of Protestants, whereof some they burned, some they slew with the Sword, some they hanged, some they starved to death. A young *Scottish* Woman's Child they took by the Heels, and dash'd out its Brains against a Tree; the like they did to many other Children.

Some others they met with, hanged them up upon a Windmill, and before they were half-dead cut them in pieces with the Skeins. Many other Protestants, especially Women and Children, they pricked and stabbed with Skeins, Forks and Swords; slashing, cutting and mangling them in their Heads, Faces, Breasts, Arms and other parts; yet killed them not, but left them wallowing in their own bloud, to languish, starve and pine to death.

In some places they plucked out the Eyes and cut off the Hands of the Protestants, and turned them into the Fields, where they perished. The Women in some places stoned the *English* Women and Children to death. One man they shot through his Thighs, digged a hole in the ground, set him upon his feet, fill'd up the hole, left out only his Head, where he languished to death.

Representation of the principal scenes in the bloody Irish
Massacre in 1642 wherein 40,000 Protestants were inhumanly
sacrificed by the Papists.

They held another man's feet in the fire till he was burned to death.

At *Glasgow* a Priest with some others drew about forty *English* and *Scottish* Protestants to be reconciled to the Church of *Rome*, and then told them, *They were in good faith and for fear they should fall from it and turn Heretics*, he with his Companions presently cut out all their Throats.

In the Town of *Sligo* forty Protestants were stript and lock'd up in a Cellar, and about midnight a Butcher provided for the purpose was sent in amongst them, who with his Axe butchered them all.

In *Tirawly* thirty or forty *English*, who had yielded to go to Mass were put to their choice, *Whether they would die by the Sword, or be drowned* they chose the latter, and so being driven to the Sea-side, these barbarous Villains with their naked Swords forced them into the Sea, the Mothers with their Children in their Arms, wading to the Chin, were overcome by the Waves, where they all perished.

They brake the Back-bone of a Youth, and left him in the Fields; some days after he was found, having eaten the Grass round about him; neither then would they kill him outright, but removed him to better pasture.

Anne Kinnard testified, That fifteen Protestants being imprisoned, and their Feet in the Stocks, a Popish Boy (Being not above fourteen years old) slew them all in one night with his Skein.

Sir *Patrick Dunstan's* Wife they ravish'd before him, slew his Servants, spurned his Children till they died, so bound him with Match to a Board that his Eyes burst out, cut off his Ears and Nose, tore off both his Cheeks, after cut off his Arms and Legs, cut out his Tongue, and after run a red hot Iron into him.

Lastly, these infernal Miscreants, to express their malice against the Protestants, did not only kill all the Cattle belonging to the Protestants that they could come at, (if they could not drive them away) but did commonly take a great delight in tormenting the Beasts, for they would not dispatch those poor Animals presently, but would either cut off a piece of two of their Buttocks, or cut off one of their Legs, and so leave them roaring and bellowing, till at last they languished and died.

These particulars with many more were attested before the Commissioners appointed to receive Informations of this nature.[1]

---

[1] *A Memento for English Protestants.*

Historians tell us that Cromwell was a heartless savage—and "historians are honourable men", but one cannot forget that the same troops who considered the German "a bit of a sport" during the Battle of Mons, had slightly grimmer faces during the advance through France and Belgium.

At Amboyna, in 1623, the Governour von Speult tortored some Japanese and nine Englishmen to death on a charge of conspiracy to take the Dutch forts. This can hardly be called a massacre, and yet it is known historically as "The Massacre of Amboyna".[1]

The capture of Magdeburg during the Thirty Years' War in 1631 resulted in another terrible massacre. The town was sacked 'some 6,400 corpses were thrown into the Elbe and the inhabitants treated with the most fiendish cruelty.

The massacre of Otranto had a curious sequel. Mahomet II slew 800 ecclesiastics in 1480, and it is said that the corpses, though left unburied for thirteen months, not only showed no signs of corruption, but were never violated by bird or beast. They were finally interred at Naples. When Solyman the Magnificent threatened Otranto in 1537, the ghosts of the 800 appeared, accompanied by a host of angels. And, again, in 1644, the same ghostly army appeared to avert another Turkish assault. All those who professed that they could not see the army of martyrs were put to death for heresy!

At the castle of Sinigaglia, in 1502, Ceseare Borgia put to death by strangulation many of the great magnates of Italy who had conspired against him.

Theodora is said to have put to death by the gibbet, stake or sword, some 100,000 Christians at the Massacre of the Paulicans.

---

[1] Among the tortures inflicted, the victim was "hoisted by the hands, with a cord attached to his wrists, upon a large door, where he was made fast to two staples of iron fixed on both sides at the top of the door posts, his hands being hauled, the one from the other, as wide as they could stretch". The water torture was also employed, and incisions were made in the flesh, gunpowder inserted and ignited.

The manner in which the Protestants were dragged through bogs in Ireland, and hung on tenterhooks fastened to poles till they perished through pain and want of food.

But all these massacres can be considered child's play in comparison with the terrible massacres of the Huguenots which raged for some centuries in the South of France.[1] The worst was probably the Dragonnades in 1685,[2] or the small but important massacre of Nismes in 1703, where the whole Protestant congregation was shot or burnt alive in its place of worship except for one girl who escaped and was hanged the next day.

One of the worst torturers of these terrible massacres was the Abbé Duchayla, who had been sent as a preacher to Siam, where he was captured and tortured in 1682.

. . . Being taken before the governor of Bangkok, the noble defender of Christ, instead of denying his faith, glorified the blessed name of God, and was given over to the executioner to be

[1] These massacres commenced during the religious civil war in France in 1562. Terrible massacres occurred on both sides. "From the south the accounts were even more dreadful;" writes Froude, "both sides becoming savage there as the famished wolves of the Pyrenees. Later in the summer the Huguenot town of Orange fell into the hands of the Catholics. The inhabitants were hacked to pieces, burnt at slow fires, or were left infamously mutilated to bleed to death. Young wives and maidens, after suffering first what made death welcome to them, were hung out of windows as targets for the musketeers. Noble ladies sacrificed to the lust of the soldiers were exposed in the streets to die—either naked or pasted over in devilish mockery with the torn leaves of their Geneva Bibles—the word of a God who for His own purposes left them to endure their agony. Old men and children, women and sick, all perished—perished under cruelties unexampled even in the infernal annals of religious fanaticism. Des Adrêts, a Huguenot leader, surprised a detachment of the men who had been concerned in this business at Orange while fresh from the scene. With the cowardice of villains they durst not defend themselves in a fort which was otherwise impregnable—and Des Adrêts hurled them down over the rocks, dashed them limb from limb; burnt, tore and tortured them with a rage which tried yet failed to satisfy the cravings of justice. Still parched for blood the Calvinist chief appeared before Montbrisson. It surrendered without a blow; but a plank was run out from the battlements of the castle, and the garrison, man by man, were driven out upon it and over it—Des Adrêts sitting below watching the ghastly heap as it rose and shouting to the victims to make haste as they shivered at the hideous leap" (J. A. Froude, *The Reign of Elizabeth*).
[2] The Dragonnades were various troops of Dragoons, each led by a priest. The victims who would not submit to the priest were handed over to the tender mercies of the Dragoons. The Dragoons were not merciful, especially to female Huguenots.

tortured. The Abbé suffered resignedly everything that the human body can endure, and live, until his patience wore out their anger, and with lacerated hands, his breast a mass of wounds, and his legs almost crushed by wedges, he fainted. He was believed to be dead and was suspended by his wrists to a tree; he was cut down and resuscitated by a pariah. . . .[1]

He returned to France and was sent to Mende, with the titles of archpriest and inspector of missions in Cevennes.

There the Abbé became the persecutor, instead of persecuted, as he had recently been; insensible to the suffering of others, as he had been inflexible in his own suffering, his apprenticeship in barbarous punishments was not thrown away upon him, and being endowed with a pretty inventive genius as a torturer, he had enlarged the science of torturing by bringing from India strange machines, or inventing new ones. People spoke with bated breath of sharpened reeds which the pitiless missionary forced under the nails; of iron pincers with which he tore out the hair of the beard, eyebrows and eyelids; of tinder saturated with oil wrapped round the fingers of the victim, making of each hand, when the match was put to it, a candelabrum with five branches; of a box turning upon a pivot, wherein the unfortunate wretch who refused to be converted was placed, and made to revolve so rapidly that he eventually lost consciousness; and of fetters so ingeniously constructed that the prisoners on their way from place to place could neither sit nor stand.[2]

The cruelty displayed throughout these massacres is incredible. The wheel and the *battoir*, as has been seen, were frequently used, but other and worse tortures were in common use on both sides. A special torture used by the Huguenots was to draw a rope tightly across a room and then drag their naked victims up and down upon it until they were literally cut in half. The following extract is an example of the type of murder which was continuous in practice for many years:

The author of the *Troubles des Cevennes* has something even worse than this to relate; it is an event which took place at

[1] A. Dumas's *Celebrated Crimes*, 1895, translation by I. G. Burnham.
[2] Ibid.

DOMINICO BERTO, after having been led round the town on an ass, with his ears and nose cut off, and holes bored in his cheeks, torn to death with red hot pincers.

Montelus, February 22, 1704. In that place, he says, there were
some Protestants, but a much greater number of Catholics. The
latter, inflamed by a Capuchin from Bergerac, organised as
cadets of the cross and determined to try their 'prentice hands
as assassins upon their fellow-townsmen. They went to the house
of Jean Barnoin, and having first cut off his ears, they cut his
throat, and let him bleed to death as if they were sticking a pig.
On leaving this poor devil's house they met Jacques Clas in the
street, and fired a shot point-blank into his belly, so that the
entrails protruded and dragged on the ground; he picked them
up and returned to his house; his wife, who was near her confinement, and their two young children, horrified at the sight, were
doing their best to help him, when the murderers appeared in the
doorway. Instead of allowing their hearts to be softened by the
shrieks and tears of the wretched woman and her poor little
children, they finished the wounded man; and as his wife attempted
to defend him they blew her brains out with a pistol. They then
discovered her condition, and that her pregnancy was so far
advanced that the child was moving in her womb; thereupon they
opened her womb, took out the child, and having put a truss of
hay in its place they fed a horse, which was tied at the door, at
this bleeding manger. A neighbour named Marie Silliot, who
offered to take the children and care for them, was murdered,
but the assassins carried their vengeance no farther at that moment.
Having left the town and gone out into the fields, they met Pierre
and Jean Barnard, uncle and nephew, one forty-five and the other
ten years old. They seized them both and put a pistol in the child's
hands, forcing him to discharge it at his uncle. At this juncture
the father came up, and they tried to compel him to shoot his
son; but no threats had any effect upon him, and the performance
was getting tedious they put an end to it by simply killing them
both, one with a sword, the other with a bayonet.

One motive for hastening this last execution was furnished by
their discovering three young girls from Bagnols going towards a
forest of mulberry-trees, where they were raising silk-worms. They
followed them into the wood, and easily overtook them, as they
had no thought of danger, it was broad daylight. They violated
them, then tied their hands and fastened them to two trees with
their heads hanging and their legs apart; while they were in that
position they opened their bodies, placed their powder-horns

inside, and, touching a match to the powder, blew them limb from limb.[1]

There were a series of massacres of the Waldenses, the worst probably being that of 1655. Cannibalism of the most disgraceful type was practised by the conquerors, and a description of the tortures employed are (like most of those used in the Irish Massacre and the massacres in the South of France) quite unprintable. A short account of this massacre is given in *The Israel of the Alps*, from which the following extract will show the kind of tortures generally employed:

The length and breadth of the valley, its villages, its houses, its roads, and its rocks were occupied by the assassins in the pay of the propaganda; and now these assassins were called upon to do their work. On Saturday, 24th of April, 1655, at four o'clock in the morning, the signal for a general massacre of the Vaudois was given to the traitorous troops from the tower of the castle of La Torre. The soldiers forewarned, had risen early, fresh with the sleep they had enjoyed under the roofs of those they were about to slaughter. The men whom, under the solemn engagement of security and protection, the Vaudois had fed and housed, were now on foot throughout the valley, converted by the arts of Rome from brave soldiers into cowardly assassins.

To give an adequate idea of the horrors that ensued, one's eye must at a single glance comprehend the entire valley, take in each house, each room, view every act of death and torment, distinguish, amid the immense voice of aggregate anguish and desolation, each particular cry of destroyed honour, of parting existence. Literally, indeed, did the unhappy Vaudois suffer the things of which the apostle speaks: "They were stoned, they were sawn asunder, were tempted, were slain with the sword: they wandered about in sheep-skins and goat-skins, being destitute, afflicted, tormented (of whom the world was not worthy); they wandered in deserts and in mountains, and in dens and caves of the earth."

Young children, writes Leger,[2] were torn from their mothers'

[1] A. Dumas's *Celebrated Crimes*, 1895, translation by I. G. Burnham.
[2] Jean Leger, a Waldensian pastor, who was living at the time of the massacre and whose history of the Waldenses was written within fourteen years of the event.

A woman with her sucking infant tied together in a bag, and thrown into a river in Scotland ; and four men hung at the same time for eating a goose on a Fast Day.

arms, dashed against the rocks, and their mangled remains cast on the road. Sick persons and old people, men and women, were burned alive in their houses, or hacked in pieces, or mutilated in horrible ways, or flayed alive, or exposed bound and dying to the sun's noontide heat, or to ferocious animals; some were stripped naked, bound up in the form of a ball, the head forced down between the legs, and then rolled over precipices; some of these poor creatures, torn and mangled by the rocks, but stayed in their downward progress by the branch of a tree or other prominence, were seen, forty-eight hours after, still lingering in all the torments of pain and famine.

Women and girls, after being fearfully outraged, were impaled on spikes and so left to die, planted at angles of the road; or they were buried alive; or, impaled as above, they were roasted before a slow fire, and their burning bodies cut in slices by these soldiers of the faith, as by cannibals. After the massacre such children as survived and could be seized were carried off and cast, like lambs into a slaughter-house, into the monasteries and convents and private abodes of the propagandists. Next, after massacre and abduction, came incendiarism: monks and priests and other zealous propagandists went about with lighted torches and projectiles, burning down the houses, previously ensanguined by the soldiers with the blood of their owners and their families.

The terrible narrative given by Leger of these atrocities was prepared by him from the testimony of eye-witnesses, who gave their depositions before two notaries, who accompanied him from commune to commune for that purpose. The pen, he says, well-nigh fell from his hand as he transcribed the horrible details. Here a father had seen his children cut in pieces by the sword, or absolutely torn limb from limb by four soldiers; there the mother had seen her daughter cruelly massacred before her face, after having been as cruelly outraged; there the sister had seen her brother's mouth filled with gunpowder, and the head then blown to atoms; there the husband had seen his wife, about to become a mother, treated in a manner which it would outrage humanity to describe. Of these the eyes were torn from their head; of those the nails from the fingers; some were tied to trees, their hearts and lungs were cut from them, and they were thus left to die in anguish. The universal conflagration of the Vaudois houses succeeded in the massacre of their inhabitants. In several communes not a single cottage was left standing, so that this fair valley of Luzerna, as Leger expresses it, resembled a burning furnace, whence cries, fewer and fainter, attested that a people had lived.

Massacre went out of fashion in Western Europe many years ago and the only important massacre during the nineteenth century was the disgraceful massacre of the Ben-Ouffias by the French in 1833. In Eastern Europe the nineteenth century produced various massacres in the Balkans and the two important massacres of the Mameluke Beys in 1811 and of the Janizaries in 1826.

In fact, massacre was in danger of dying out altogether throughout the world had not the United States carried on the grand old tradition. No more treacherous and diabolical piece of work has been recorded than the Baker Massacre of the 23rd of January, 1870. A white American ruffian, named Clark, had assaulted a young Indian, and the Indian, in retaliation, had killed Clark and escaped into Canada. Without troubling to find the culprit or to make any inquiries as to which tribe he belonged, General Philip H. Sheridan ordered Brevet-Colonel E. M. Baker, stationed at Fort Shaw, to march his cavalry to the nearest Indian village, which was on Marias river and contained a tribe of peaceful and friendly Indians under Bear's Head.

The troops surrounded the sleeping village and in a low tone Colonel Baker spoke a few words to his men, telling them to keep cool, aim to kill, to spare none of the enemy; and then he gave the command to fire. A terrible scene ensued. On the day previous, many of the men of the camp had gone out towards the Sweet-grass Hills on a grand buffalo hunt; so, save for Chief Bear's Head and a few old men, none were there to return the soldiers' fire. Their first volley was aimed low down into the lodges, and many of the sleeping people were killed or wounded in their beds. The rest rushed out, men, children, women, many of the latter with babes in their arms, only to be shot down at the door-ways of their lodges. Bear's Head, frantically waving a paper which bore testimony to his good character and the friendliness

214

to the white man, ran toward the command on the buff, shouting to them to cease firing, entreating them to save the women and children; down he also went with several bullet holes in his body. Of the more than four hundred souls in camp at the time, very few escaped. And when it was all over, when the last wounded woman and child had been put out of misery, the soldiers piled the corpses on overturned lodges, firewood and household property and set fire to it all.

Several years afterwards I was on the ground. Everywhere scattered about in the long grass and bush, just where the wolves and foxes had left them, gleamed the skulls and bones of those who had been so ruthlessly slaughtered. "How could they have done it?" I asked myself, time and time again. "What manner of men were these soldiers who deliberately shot down defenceless women and innocent children?"[1] They had not even the excuse of being drunk; nor was their commanding officer intoxicated; nor were they excited or in any danger whatever. Deliberately, coolly, with steady and deadly aim they shot them down, killed the wounded, and then tried to burn the bodies of their victims. But I will say no more about it. Think it over, yourself, and try to find a fit name for men who did this.[2]

No punishment of any kind was dealt to the perpetrators of this massacre.

Another example of the all too common American massacres is given in E. T. Seton's *Book of Woodcraft*, under the heading "Wovoka, The Prophet of the Ghost Dance".

There have been many in every tribe and every time who have brought shame on their people. There have been whole tribes who forgot their race's high ideals. From time to time great prophets have arisen amongst them to stir up backsliders, and bring them back to the faith of their fathers. The last of these was Wovoka, the Pieute—the Mystic Dreamer. About 1887 he began preaching his doctrine of the coming Messiah and taught the Redmen that they must worship him by the Ghost dance. This is his own simple setting forth of the doctrine:

[1] According to G. B. Grinnell, ninety were women, fifty-five babies and the rest chiefly very old or very young men.

[2] Schultz, *My Life as an Indian*.

"When the Sun died I went up into Heaven and saw God and all the people who died a long time ago. God told me to come back and tell my people they must be good and love one another and not fight or steal or lie. He gave me this dance to give to my people." (*Ethn. Ann.* 14. p. 764.)

At Pine Ridge, S.D., in the winter of 1890, the Sioux were learning this dance with its songs and its Christ-like creed. It meant the end of war. War had been their traditional noblest pursuit. But now at the bidding of the new prophet they agreed to abjure it forever; and they prepared to take up the new religion of love.

The Indian agent, like most of his kind, was ignorant and utterly unfitted for his position. He said it was some new sort of a *war dance*. The troops were sent for and the Indian populace were gathered together at a place called Wounded Knee near Pine Ridge (Dec. 29, 1890). They had submitted and turned in their rifles. Then, maddened by the personal indignities offered them in searching for more arms, a young Indian who still had a gun fired at the soldiers. It is not stated that he hit any one, but the answer was a volley that killed half the men. A minute later a battery of four Hotchkiss machine guns was turned on the defenceless mass of virtual prisoners; 120 men and 250 helpless women and children were massacred in broad daylight, mown down, and left on the plain, while the white soldiers pursued the remnant and the cripples, to do them to death in the hills.

Almost all the dead warriors were found lying near where the "fight" began, about Bigfoot's teepee, but the bodies of the women and children were found scattered along for two miles from the scene of the encounter, showing that they had been killed while trying to escape. (*Eth. Ann.* 14, pp. 868–70.)

As the men were in a separate company from the women and children, no one pretended that it was accidental.

The women as they were fleeing with their babes were killed together, shot right through, and the women who were very heavy with child were also killed. All the Indians fled in these three directions, and after most of them had been killed, a cry was made that all those who were not killed or wounded should come forth and they would be safe. Little boys who were not wounded came out of their places of refuge, and as soon as they came in sight, a number of soldiers surrounded them and butchered them there. (*Ghost Dance Religion*, Mooney; *Ethn. Rep.* 14. 885–6).

Nothing in the way of punishment was done by the authorities to any of the assassins. When the guards of Czar Nicholas shot down some scores of peasants who, contrary to orders, marched in a body to his palace, all America rang with horror and indignation, but nothing was said about the infinitely worse massacre at Wounded Knee.

As sure as there is a God in Heaven, this thing has to be met again, and for every drop of righteous blood spilled that day and on a thousand other days of like abomination, a fearful vengeance is being stored and will certainly break on us.

As sure as Cain struck down himself when he murdered Abel; as sure as the blood of righteous Naboth cried from the ground and wrecked the house and the kingdom and the race of Ahab; so surely has the American nation to stand before the bar of an earthly power—a power invincible, overwhelming, remorseless, and pay the uttermost price.

As sure as this land was taken by fraud and held by cruelty and massacre, we have filled for ourselves a vial of wrath. It will certainly be outpoured on us to the last drop and the dregs. What the Persian did to rich and rotten Babylon, what the Goth did to rich and bloody Rome, another race will surely do to us.

If ever the aroused and reinspired Yellow man comes forth in his hidden strength, in his reorganised millions, overpowering, slaying, burning, possessing, we can only bow our heads and say, "These are the instruments of God's wrath. We brought this on ourselves. All this we did to the Redman. The fate of Babylon and of bloody Rome is ours. We wrote our own doom as they did."

Som were pistolled to death

CHAPTER XIII

MISCELLANEOUS MERRIMENTS OF MODERN TIMES

> The most civilised are as near to Barbarism as the most
> polished steel to rust. Nations, like metals, have only a
> superficial brilliancy.—RIVAROL

Christians Crucified w
theire heads downwards

Now that we have reached the dawn of the twentieth century we expect to see the dark clouds roll away. We are approaching the millennium of civilization. No more will we see heretics hunted to the stake. No more do drunkards fear "the cloak", or "scolds" the "branks". Torture, as a means to confession, has disappeared, unless we accept as fact the rumours from the United States of "Third Degree" methods.[1] It is true that whipping continues, but in England only for assault, or in juvenile cases. "First Field Punishment" was still permitted by Military Law at the beginning of the century, but the war has had a chastening effect and this, and even "Pack Drill", is no longer practised. Torture, in all its worst forms, appeared to be losing ground in 1900. What, then, of interest can these enlightened thirty years produce?

One must remember that it is more difficult to write a history of contemporary events than of those which are long since past. It is time, and time alone, which allows incidents to be viewed in their proper perspective, and for these incidents to be marshalled in due chronological

[1] Two methods claimed to be effective for obtaining a confession from an alleged criminal are bending the head back and striking the Adam's apple till the blood spurts from the mouth and strapping the victim into a chair and drilling on the nerve of a sound tooth with a rough burr. The "Awaken" and flogging are also employed (*The Third Degree*, by Emanuel Lavine, 1931).

order. One would get a very curious impression of the French Revolution if one judged it solely from the pamphlets of the time. There is another fact, however, which makes one suspicious of modern evidence, particularly that deduced during the war era, for an old "practice", as our Virgin Queen would have called it, had been revived on a colossal scale—Propaganda. How, then, can one divide the sheep from the goats? Were the Bolsheviks nice, kind, frolicsome innocents, who were shocked by the barbarities of the Whites of Denikin? Or, were the Bolsheviks ogres of inhumanity and the Whites guiltless as babes? Did the Austro-Hungarian forces torture the Serbian civilians for their own sadic amusement, or were the acts committed as reprisals and warnings to the Serbians against even more terrible atrocities to Austro-Hungarian prisoners of which the civilians were alleged to have been guilty? In fact, did Germany invade Belgium for her own military advantage,[1] or to prevent the dastardly British from carrying out their plans for a breach of Belgian neutrality?[2]

Modern questions may find an answer in the future, but they cannot be approached at the present time without the greatest diffidence and doubt.

[1] "Gentlemen, we are now in a position of necessity (energetic assent); and necessity knows no law (energetic applause). Our troops have occupied Luxemburg (energetic "Bravo!"); perhaps they have already entered Belgian territory. (Energetic applause.) Gentlemen, this is in contradiction to the rules of international law. . . . The wrong—I speak openly—the wrong that we now do we will try to make good again as soon as our military ends have been reached. When one is threatened as we are, and all is at stake, he can only think of how he can hack his way out (Long, stormy applause and clapping from all sides of the House) (Speech of Chancellor von Bethmann-Hollweg, 4th of August, 1914).

[2] "As you know, we found in the archives of the Belgian Foreign Office papers which showed that England, in 1911, was determined to throw troops into Belgium without the assent of the Belgian Government if war had then broken out" (Chancellor von Bethmann-Hollweg to neutral Press representatives).

"Now that every detail of the English-Belgian plan of war has been discovered, the policy followed by English statesmen in this affair has been branded before the tribunal of history for all time" (Speech of Chancellor von Bethmann-Hollweg, 2nd of December, 1914).

THE PLEASURES OF THE TORTURE CHAMBER

With the exception of the Balkan War, Europe enjoyed fourteen years of peace, and cruelty found no fruitful soil in which to grow; but the Great War brought the question of Torture into vogue again, and one feels fairly safe in relying on the Bryce Report, not only from the care with which the evidence was sifted, but from the history of Prussia itself.

The history of Prussia shows clearly what was to be expected. In the time of Napoleon the Prussians committed numerous atrocities during their invasions of France and the Netherlands. They were our allies then, and though our troops were held with a firmer hand, we looked upon the Prussian delinquencies with indulgence. In 1870 the Prussian frolics were repeated. This time we were neutral, and it was a matter for argument as to how many sins could be covered by the expression "War is War". In 1914 a very different state of affairs existed. Germany was our enemy, and we formed very definite opinions as to the devilments of her troops.

Many reports of the atrocities committed by the Germans were exaggerated, or, at least, were based upon unreliable evidence which was accepted as fact during the war-fever. No general orders appear to have been given for the torture of civilians of invaded territory, and the atrocities committed were individual acts of bestiality by officers or men. The most common of these was murder, or, in the case of females, dishonour previous to murder. How far Germany is to be blamed for permitting these acts is questionable, as she seems certainly to have condoned, and even encouraged, them.

In the Austro-Hungarian invasion of Serbia a different state of affairs existed, and, according to Dr. R. A. Reiss, the troops were definitely encouraged to commit atrocities upon the Serbian civilians. The religious feelings of the invading troops were played upon, a never-failing prelude to brutality.[1]

[1] E.g. Austro-Hungarian soldiers of Serb nationality were not allowed to obtain water unless it was supplied to them by their Mahommedan or Roman Catholic comrades (Dr. R. A. Reiss, D.Sc., *The Kingdom of Serbia, Report upon the Atrocities Committed by the Austro-Hungarian Army during the First Invasion of Serbia*, 1916).

The atrocities said to have been committed in Serbia have been carefully tabulated by Dr. Reiss and show little of interest, except that the Austro-Hungarians appear to have perpetrated more crimes of sheer brutality than their allies, with the possible exception of the Turks; while the Germans, in comparison, showed a more sexual sadic intelligence in their use of physical torture.

Most of the atrocities committed by the Germans, Turks, and Austro-Hungarians were merely sordid acts of beastliness, but there are one or two which show a certain originality. To hurry a nurse up in the preparation of their coffee, certain German cavalry-men adopted the ingenious method of slowly dipping the head of her infant charge into boiling water, so that when it was examined by a British doctor some days later the whole scalp was found to be one large scab.[1] The Austro-Hungarians seem to have been rather fond of either spitting their victims or roasting them alive, which would appear to be rather unprofitable forms of amusement, but they were original in tying a man, aged fifty-three, to a mill-wheel, which was then set in motion, and, whenever the wheel carried him round, they diverted themselves with prodding him with their bayonets.

In all wars atrocities have been committed in the hot blood of battle. In all armies there are certain brutes ready to take advantage of the situation. It is in acts committed on civilians when the troops, especially in the case of the Germans, were under rigid discipline in areas uninfluenced by the excitement of battle, that their crimes can be considered in the light of tortures. And yet crimes of a like nature committed by Allied soldiers occupying Germany were very few, while the crimes of enemy troops, even viewed from their own or neutral publications, would fill a considerable volume.

The atrocities of the German troops do not appear to have been done under orders and can hardly be brought under the classification of "tortures" as set out in the

[1] Bryce Report.

preface. The orders given by the Austrians, however, seem sufficient to cover the acts committed by their troops.

Let us pass on from these horrors with a hope that they were merely the result of blood-lust created by the war, a nightmare from which we have now awakened; and that, since the Declaration of Peace, the enlightened twentieth century may reveal no signs of torture.

The hope is soon shattered. For it seems that the freedom for which mankind craves can only be achieved by emblazoning the sacred name of "Liberty" on a blood-red banner. The Red troops of Lenin and the Whites of Denikin both found that the way to obtain freedom was to be as brutal as possible to their opponents.

But it was chiefly after the war that the Bolsheviks realised the value of the use of torture. Here we strike something original. The Turks, the Germans, the Austro-Hungarians, pass into the background as rather petty and ridiculous amateurs. If one-half of the reports are true, the Russians have shown an intelligence which the Central Powers seem to have lacked. Comparing the statements of Maître Aubert[1] with the official publications of war atrocities, one feels rather sorry for the troops who wished to appear such bold, bad devils, and had yet forgotten every principle which a beneficent science had given them by modern discovery. However, can one compare Maître Aubert with these ponderous documents, and, if so, how far can he be relied upon to give an accurate picture when he was, admittedly, writing to counteract the spread of Bolshevism?

The following are a few extracts from the terrible description of Russia given by Maître Aubert, but how much reliance can be put upon their accuracy, without confirming evidence, it is difficult to say. Certainly cruelties of a most fiendish nature have been inflicted, but corroborative evidence of details is lacking.

At Blagovestchensk, they thrust gramophone needles under the nails of the officers and soldiers and tore out their eyes.

[1] *Bolshevism's Terrible Record*, 1924.

At Voronej they pierced out their victims' eyes, cut off their noses and ears, dislocated their joints, and tore off their nails, carved officers' epaulettes on their shoulders, and engraved the Soviet star on their foreheads. Other victims were plunged, wholly or partly, into boiling water, in baths specially installed in the apartments of the Cheka.[1] After these baths the skin peeled off in bits from the boiled parts, and these poor dying souls were then thrown out of doors. Melted lead was forced down the throats of others. Elsewhere have been found separate hands, fingers, feet, broken bones and teeth, sliced off ears and noses, torn-off ears and human flesh.

Still at Voronej, they put their victims into barrels pieced with nails on the inside. The body of a priest was discovered crowned with a band of barbed wire.

At Kharkoff the butcher Saenko was celebrated for his skill in scalping heads and hands. In 1919 the executioners plunged the hands of the accused into boiling water, then they tore off the skin to make human gloves.

At Yekatrinoslav, in the territory of the Dnieper, the Cheka amuses itself with crushing the victims' heads by means of a block suspended by a cord, the face turned towards the sky, so the condemned watches his death approaching. In the same town they stoned, crucified and killed the people in the streets, and left their bodies on the ground.

At Odessa officers were taken on board the steamer *Sinope*, undressed, fastened to beams with chains, put in front of the oven and slowly roasted. Others were cooked in boilers, then plunged into the sea, and thrown again into the oven.

Still at Odessa, the Bolsheviks have put to death 400 officers by means of the torture of boiling steam, alternated with exposure to currents of icy air. Others were burnt alive, fastened to planks which were slowly pushed into ovens, bit by bit, a few inches

[1] "The Cheka is ostensibly the extraordinary Commission for the struggle against counter-revolution and speculation, and at the same time a surety police, an organ of counter-spying, and an extraordinary tribunal, without a public Ministry, no defence, nor judges worthy of the name. It possesses special branches in each centre, a special service of executioners, and administers the prisons. An example of the composition of the local branches of the Cheka is the heads of the Cheka at Odessa, which comprises some Israelites, a few Chinese, and a negro whose speciality is to pull out the tendons of his victims while he smiles at them with his white teeth" (Maître Aubert).

nearer each time. Elsewhere they have killed by asphyxiation, by locking up the last victim in a chest filled with the dead. Half an hour later the chest was opened, the moribund questioned, and if his replies did not satisfy them they recommenced until death ensued.

At Simforopol the Pole Achikine made his victim walk in front of him completely naked, considered her a moment, then chose a sword and cut off her ears and hands. Suffering horribly, the victim implored him to kill her. Achikine remained unmoved. Finally he bent over her and burnt or pierced her eyes out, and only later decapitated her.

In the centre of Russia they make "The Crown of Death", by means of a cord which they fastened in a noose round the prisoners' heads and tightened by a wooden stick, twisting it the necessary number of times.

The Bolsheviks also know how to utilise the cold, so terrible in Russia, and they made the condemned stand naked for hours in a line, from time to time shooting one or two.

The state of Russia can be seen from a paragraph in the Bolshevik paper, *The Voice of Truth*:

"It is time to clear the streets of human bodies, as the dogs, which have tasted human flesh, become dangerous."

As will be seen, if there is any truth in these reports, the Holy Inquisition has a dangerous rival, perhaps lacking in its ingenuity, but certainly not in its ferociousness. The chief differences between the two being that the Holy Inquisition, or, more particularly, the Spanish Inquisition, tortured in the majority of cases to procure a confession, whereas the Cheka tortured chiefly as a means of punishment. The Holy Inquisition was a male preserve, the Cheka has appreciated the equality of the sexes.[1]

We have seen, however, that the Holy Inquisition also used torture as a punishment, the Cheka, not to be outdone, has also used torture as a means to forcing a confession.

---

[1] "Rosa Schwartz, agent for the Cheka at Keiff, counts her victims by hundreds, and, while smoking, goes naked to see the prisoners in their cells, kills them with a blow from her revolver, or burns their eyes with her cigarette. Vera Grebentchikoff, of Odessa, has personally killed some 700 people" (Maître Aubert).

A nurse writing in the *Journal de Genève* relates that:

Through the closed door I heard moaning which tore my heart, blows from a horse-whip, the noise of a falling body, and a voice that was no longer human.

"Let me go," it said, "I assure you I know nothing."

"I shall end by refreshing your memory," and the blows of the horse-whip succeeded each other with greater force.

It was the judge and two other agents who were beating an old woman.

One day a nurse saw an officer standing naked in front of his grave. Three detonations resounded; the man did not fall; the soldiers had been given the order to fire above his head.

"Give us the names of your accomplices, or we will shoot your wife and child, which are hidden behind this hedge."

The man did not move. A detonation was heard in another direction. The woman was not hurt, but when they took the officer back to his cell he was mad, and the woman behind the hedge was not his wife; it was simply a trick to make him speak.

Even in 1929 torture was being practised in Afghanistan. In January, King Amanullah and his brother Inayatullah abdicated, and the throne was taken by a rebel, Bacha Sachao, who was in turn deposed and finally shot by the orders of Nadir Khan.

During the reign of the tyrant Bacha Sachao, who took the title of Amir Habibullah, terrible tortures were practised, the most common of which was by blowing victims from the mouth of a cannon, a practice which he had, no doubt, learnt from reading histories of British rule in India. He killed Ali Ahmed Jan, Amir of Jellahabad, by crucifying him to the ground and driving a nail through his ear into his brain. This was done in public in a street of Kabul. Another victim of Bacha was chained to the rear of a motor-lorry and dragged at a speed of twenty miles an hour through the streets of Kabul. His legs were terribly injured, his face and body were battered and his arms were broken in innumerable places. He was then thrown into prison, both legs amputated from the thigh and his left arm removed. He had the satisfaction, however, if it was any consolation to him, of being present at the execution of the tyrant, who was dragged from the Citadel by his hair, stirred on to his place of execution by the aid of sharpened bayonets, amid peltings from the crowds of garbage and stones. There he was hanged by the neck for five minutes and cut down alive for execution by shooting. Through the whole affair Bacha is reported to have shown a supreme indifference and courage.

This century may not have, so far, produced any Torquemadas, but it has certainly been well represented by the Cheka, if the reports on that notorious body can be accredited, and certainly the effects of exposure to the elements, especially the Russian cold, have been fully exploited. The Block of Yekatrinoslav is a new device, but, on the whole, very few new instruments have been invented despite the scientific advance of modern times. The Austro-Hungarian torture of stabbing a victim while he is rotated on a wheel is merely a crude reversing of the order of things in the more artistic "Wheel of Aragon". Rosa Schwartz was certainly original in introducing a cigarette into the catalogue of instruments of torture, but the same results have been more effectively achieved in the past by a piece of hot iron.

No, with regard to the discovery of new instruments of torture, the beginning of the twentieth century has proved disappointing. May the latter half prove more so.

Christians Gored vpon Stakes, one end fastne in ÿ ground, the other coming out of ÿ mouth

INDEX